Ireland and the Second World War

To Irish men and women
who served in the allied armed forces
during the Second World War

Ireland and the
Second World War

Politics, Society and Remembrance

Brian Girvin and Geoffrey Roberts

EDITORS

FOUR COURTS PRESS

Set in 10.5 on 12.5 Adobe Garamond for
FOUR COURTS PRESS LTD
Fumbally Lane, Dublin 8, Ireland
e-mail: info@four-courts-press.ie
and in North America by
FOUR COURTS PRESS
c/o ISBS, 5804 N.E. Hassalo Street, Portland, OR 97213.

A catalogue record for this title
is available from the British Library.

ISBN 1–85182–482–0 hbk
1–85182–497–9 pbk

Printed in Ireland
by ColourBooks Lrd, Dublin

Contents

Preface

This book has its origins in the Volunteers Project, a research programme based in the Department of History at University College Cork. The project was established in 1995 with the primary aim of examining the experience of Irish citizens who contributed to the allied war effort, either by military service or war work in Britain. The project itself was prompted by the realisation that historians had not adequately discussed an important aspect of the Irish experience in the Second World War. Substantial historical effort had been extended on the question of Irish neutrality, but much of the research focused inwardly on Ireland itself. That a large section of Irish people travelled to Britain to work between 1939 and 1945 was in itself of considerable interest, particularly as it established a pattern of emigration which was to be a central attribute of Irish society for over 40 years after the end of the war. More controversial was the evidence that tens of thousands of Irish citizens volunteered to join the British forces at a time when Ireland itself was neutral. The numbers involved remain unclear, though Richard Doherty's guestimate in this volume is a plausible one in the absence of further, harder evidence. That this important feature of the period has been largely ignored was considered regrettable by the editors and it was this which led them to promote the project in the first place.

We were especially fortunate that the President's Fund in UCC provided a generous grant to develop the project. Without that important contribution, we could not have advanced the research as quickly as happened. Funding was also forthcoming from the Department of Foreign Affairs, from Mr Peter Barry, from the Royal British Legion in Cork, and from the British Council in Dublin. We were also lucky that Ms Tina Neylon agreed to undertake the research for the project. Her sensitivity and empathy when interviewing the veterans who agreed to talk to the project were crucial to achieving the goals set. She not only circulated a questionnaire to veterans, but also contacted and taped the interviews with a large number of them. These materials will be available for consultation and further research in the archives in University College Cork.

In March 1998 the project hosted a conference at UCC on 'Irish Responses to the Second World War'. This book includes revised versions of papers presented at this conference, as well as additional ones generously provided at short notice by the authors. In this respect, special thanks are due to Brian Barton, Eunan O'Halpin and John A. Murphy.

Although the initiative for the book comes from the conference and the Volunteers Project, it is not only about those who went to work or fight for the allied side. It is also a book about Ireland and the war and the balance of chapters reflects this. We believe that this book adds to our understanding of the relationship between Ireland and the UK in the war, but also provides new insights on domestic policies in Ireland, north and south. We hope that this publication will prompt others to explore some of the issues raised here. Much remains to be uncovered, for example, about the motivation for travelling to Britain during those dangerous years. It should be emphasised that the project's oral history has focused almost exclusively on those volunteers and workers who returned to Ireland after the war. This was a small minority of the 200,000 or more who left Ireland between 1939 and 1945. More work needs to be done on the attitudes, experience and motivation of the majority who, for whatever reason, decided to remain in Britain after the war.

For a long period the volunteers were ignored by Irish society, which was often indifferent to the experience of those who fought or worked in Britain. The changing circumstances of Irish life over the past decade or so has allowed for a more open evaluation and exploration of this past. The role played by the military volunteers has been given greater formal recognition by the Irish State in recent years. In April 1995 the then Taoiseach John Bruton spoke at the Islandbridge National War Memorial on the eve of the 50th anniversary of VE Day. He paid tribute to those Irish people, North and South, who 'volunteered to fight against Nazi tyranny in Europe, at least 10,000 of whom were killed while serving in British uniforms'. He further stated that 'in recalling their bravery we are recalling a shared experience of Irish and British people … we remember a British part of the inheritance of all who live in Ireland.'

Ironically, there has been less recognition for those who worked in the war industries, remained in Britain after the war and contributed to the sizeable Irish community there today. Given the new political circumstances, this may be the opportune time to explore further this huge movement of people from Ireland to Britain.

Brian Girvin
Geoffrey Roberts

Irish neutrality in historical perspective

John A. Murphy

Neutrality, as the policy of various European states in the twentieth century, has been expressed in a wide variety of ways. It has not conformed to any one model, and few states, least of all Ireland, have rigidly adhered to the Hague Convention of 1907 which lays down 'the rights and duties of neutral powers and persons in case of war on land'. Irish neutrality post-1945 has been an area of considerable ambiguity and would seem to fit into the cynical definition of neutrality as 'the policy conducted by countries who claim to conduct such a policy'. For example, one of the classical imperatives of neutrality – that a state should have sufficient military strength to deter aggression – was never taken seriously in Ireland.

From the 1960s, there has been an intermittent debate on the nature of the contribution Ireland might make to an emerging European defence policy. The protagonists in this debate frequently hark back to the rights and wrongs of wartime neutrality, 1939-45. The argument about the morality or otherwise of *that* neutrality is often a stalking-horse for the contemporary debate, and vice versa. Today's critics of wartime neutrality profess to feel a kind of retrospective shame about it. Moreover, a fashionable anti-Eamon de Valera revisionism regards Irish neutrality in World War II as one of his many perceived failings.

The protagonists also differ about the historical perspective of neutrality. The anti-neutrality side pooh-poohs an alleged *tradition* of neutrality and is at pains to emphasise its *ad hoc* nature. Defenders of neutrality, on the other hand, seize on various items of evidence to support their case that neutrality has been very much part of the Irish experience. Both sides strain their arguments but we can safely say that Irish neutrality was never a dogma or an ideological principle but rather a political orthodoxy and a formative feature of the developing personality of the State from the 1940s to the 1960s.

Slogans such as 'Neither King nor Kaiser but Ireland' and organisations like the Irish Neutrality League (1914) seem to indicate a neutrality lineage in the early revolutionary period. Neutrality enthusiasts also point to Sir Roger Casement's proposal (1913) for the neutralisation of an independent Ireland. Implicit in the whole nationalist aspiration was the idea that a free Ireland would control its own international policy, and there was a general nationalist feeling that Ireland must no longer be involved in 'England's wars' (cf. the great anti-conscription campaign of 1918) and even be free to participate on the other side (cf. the Boer War). In short, it is misleading to attach the label of neutrality in this period to fervent nationalist feeling.

In all this discussion, Eamon de Valera's views are of the greatest importance, since he was to become the architect of Irish wartime neutrality. But he also played variations on the theme during his career, being prepared to consider, at different times, a British-Irish defence pact and participation in sanctions under the apparent collective security of the League of Nations. During his US tour of 1919-20, he put forward the so-called Cuban analogy, much to the annoyance of the anglophobic Irish-American old guard. Anxious to maximise support for Irish independence by stressing the reasonableness of the cause and also genuinely appreciative of English security fears over the centuries, de Valera asserted that an independent Ireland would not be used as a base for attacks against her neighbour. The model here was Cuba's relationship with *its* large neighbour, the United States, as laid out in their 1903 treaty.

The Cuban analogy was an academic point at the time, but in the real world of the Anglo-Irish treaty negotiations in the last months of 1921, the idea of 'guaranteed neutrality' was put forward in Draft Treaty A, the Irish delegation's initial negotiating position. In the words of Erskine Childers (who was, understandably in the light of his career and writings heretofore, the constitutional and strategic expert on the Irish side) an independent Ireland would 'stand alone, like the vast majority of small nations, with complete independent control of our territory, waters and forces, neutral in all wars and devoted to peaceful development'. Neutrality would be guaranteed by the United States, the League of Nations and Britain itself or the Commonwealth, but a British-Irish defence pact might, in certain conditions, be an alternative possibility.

In the event, all this turned out to be aspirational and fanciful, and totally inadequate to meet Britain's imperial imperatives and strategic needs. Under the Anglo-Irish Treaty as signed, not only was a partitioned Ireland and a constitutionally subordinate Irish Free State unable to exercise an independent foreign policy, but the British retention of Irish naval bases (the so-called Treaty ports) and control over further facilities in time of war, relegated Irish neutrality to the realm of the impracticably remote. While the acrimonious exchanges in the Treaty debate largely turned on the important but somewhat abstruse topics of Oath and Crown and Republic, it was Erskine Childers who pointed out that British possession of the ports made a mockery of Irish claims to real independence.

Credible neutrality, then, was out of the question as long as the shackles imposed by the Treaty remained, though these were being steadily removed through Commonwealth evolution and Irish initiatives in the 1920s and 1930s. Membership of the League of Nations from 1923 committed the State to hypothetical obligations which would be at odds with neutrality. However, with the collapse of the principle of collective security when the League failed to impose effective sanctions on Italy after the invasion of Ethiopia in 1935, the focus was now on neutrality as the policy likely to be pursued by the State.

The neutrality option had surfaced in intermittent debate during the 1920s, though the notion of a British-Irish defence pact had not disappeared. Both ideas were contained in a significant memorandum to the Government in 1925 from the Defence Department and army chiefs. The memorandum referred to 'the necessity for taking effective steps to maintain our neutrality', a phrase which suggests the concept was widely accepted as desirable policy by the mid-1920s. A Dáil debate early in 1927 indicates that neutrality was at the least a consummation devoutly to be wished by Cumann na nGaedheal and Labour. Fianna Fáil entered the Dáil soon afterwards and in November of that year, de Valera asserted that 'the right of maintaining our neutrality is the proper policy for this country'.

De Valera 's disenchantment with the League strengthened his view that, in the anarchic world of international relations, a small nation's only course was to batten down the hatches and devote itself to survival if and when armageddon should come. A series of de Valera speeches from 1935 pointed towards neutrality. In June 1936, he affirmed that 'we want to be neutral'. The new Constitution enacted in 1937 did not, it is true, enshrine neutrality as a fundamental principle but it could be argued that it was hinted at here and there in the document, particularly perhaps in Article 29 which emphasised the State's commitment 'to the ideal of peace and friendly co-operation amongst nations' and 'to the principle of the pacific settlement of international disputes'. Meanwhile, de Valera's government's firm adherence to the principle of non-intervention in the Spanish Civil War provided a kind of rehearsal for the later drama.

In his secret talks in 1936 with Malcolm MacDonald, the British Dominions Secretary, de Valera again expressed the belief that benevolent neutrality would best serve British as well as Irish interests. When the 'ports' were handed back under the Anglo-Irish Agreement of 1938, de Valera gave his government's assurance that the State would not be used as a hostile base against Britain.

With the return of the ports, there was a turning point in the development of neutrality policy. In the words of Patrick Keatinge, the leading authority on the subject of neutrality:

> The 1938 Agreement gave the Irish government the minimal degree of credibility it needed if it was to try to pursue a policy of neutrality in the expected war in Europe. It marks the point at which neutrality became for Ireland a practical state policy as well as a political value; if later political leaders were to refer to Ireland's 'traditional' policy of neutrality it was in 1938 that this policy came to the fore.

However, it remained to be seen whether neutrality would work in a war situation. Nor was neutrality hailed as an absolute value at this stage: it was seen rather as a test of sovereignty. There was no proclamation of a *doctrine* of neutrality at this point, nor was it clear that neutrality would survive the ending of partition, if that were to happen. The tentative air surrounding the concept was to be replaced in due course by a warm commitment and attachment, so that by 1944 de Valera could assert to David Gray, the antagonistic US minister in Dublin, that 'neutrality was not for sale'. At the beginning, however, neutrality as State policy was presented in a matter-of-fact way on the outbreak of war in September 1939. The ground had been laid for its acceptance and the Taoiseach's neutrality statement in the Dáil was not an enunciation of principle but a mundane announcement of the 'emergency' measures which would now be necessary. Indeed, de Valera disclaimed the 'theoretical, abstract idea of neutrality'. For Ireland, the wartime period was commonly referred to as 'the Emergency', a curious euphemism belonging to the slightly unreal world of 'formal' neutrality, other aspects of which included a strict censorship and, most notoriously, de Valera's 'condolences' visit to the German legation in 1945 on Hitler's death.

* * *

Apart from the general movement towards neutrality, outlined above, there were other factors at work and the emphasis on any one of these varied from time to time. Partition was most frequently given as the reason why Ireland would or could not become a belligerent. In de Valera's words, 'we believe that no other position would be accepted by the majority of our people as long as the present position exists'. Irredentist sentiment, devoid of any real understanding of the Northern Ireland situation, was ardent and universal in the Southern state in the strongly nationalistic atmosphere of the 1930s. There would have been opposition to participation in 'England's wars' in any case but public opinion would certainly not countenance such involvement 'as long as England unjustly occupied our six counties', to paraphrase popular sentiment. Ironically, the availability of Northern naval bases to Britain was one of the main reasons why neutrality was not violated.

The criticism would be made again and again that the mentality informing Irish neutrality was insular and self-centred, when set against the great issues at stake in the global struggle. Indeed, it is hard to gainsay the truth of this and the decision to stay neutral was certainly not taken from the high moral ground. It may be pointed out however that awareness of the war as a crusade against the evils of nazism was not keen or widespread in Ireland at the time, nor did crusading zeal influence the stance of other countries who became reluctantly involved only when they had no other choice.

Apart from the partition factor, there was strong support for the conclusion de Valera had formed on the basis of his observation of the international order – or chaos – of the 1930s, namely, that a small state would be foolish to invite the consequences of voluntary participation in a war not of its own making. It is undeniable that there was some popular admiration for Hitler as the architect of his country's reconstruction, as well as some satisfaction at British setbacks without any real desire to see Britain defeated, but the basic line was that the country would do well to stay 'out of the war', especially a country which had experienced an independence struggle, a civil war and painful reconstruction within the previous twenty years.

Those who were to moralise huffily with hindsight about the shamefulness of Irish neutrality chose to ignore one central factor. As a matter of *realpolitik*, formal participation in the war on Britain's side even if supported by a significant section would have created serious internal dissensions, aggravated by IRA trouble-making: an overt war effort, in these circumstances, would have been counter-productive and at real risk of being sabotaged by extremists.

While the Dáil enacted, without a division, the necessary neutrality legislation, there were bound to be some reservations within Fine Gael, the main opposition party, which had stood for close association with the British Commonwealth. Nevertheless, the party as a whole backed the neutrality consensus and expelled its deputy leader, James Dillon, in 1942, for his public and morally courageous repudiation of the national policy. Otherwise, popular support for neutrality as a cause in its own right gathered momentum. A number of observers, most of them hostile, remarked on this phenomenon. They included Sir Harold Nicolson, the writer and diplomat (neutrality, he observed on a 1942 visit was 'a question of honour' and a policy of which Ireland was 'tremendously proud'); Viscount Cranborne, a member of Churchill's wartime cabinet; Elizabeth Bowen, the novelist and British intelligence gatherer; and Sir John Maffey, the British minister in Dublin. Bowen attested to the popular perception of neutrality as a positive value and one that engendered self-respect, while Maffey scotched the naïve view that neutrality was a one-man show which de Valera could replace at will: 'the creed of Ireland today is neutrality: no government could exist that departed from that principle'. Thus, it was a fallacy to think that exerting economic pressure, by restricting imports, could breed anti-de Valera resentment, and so force a change of policy. The fundamental explanation was that the people perceived neutrality as the acid test of sovereignty.

The dominance of neutrality was underlined by the Dublin government's response to Churchill's dramatic offer in June 1940: the unity of Ireland in return for Irish participation in the war – 'a nation once again'. There were a number of factors behind Dublin's refusal: suffice it to say here that neutrality had taken on such a value that it was now placed above unity; indeed, even a united Ireland, it appeared, would still be neutral.

When de Valera made his 1941 St Patrick's Day broadcast (directed, as usual, at Irish-American listeners), it is significant that partition was mentioned almost as an afterthought in the list of factors justifying neutrality, for which positive reasons of state and an international context were now advanced:

Americans who seek to understand the reasons for our attitude need only
study Washington's declaration of neutrality in 1793 and his letter to
James Monroe in 1796. Some twenty years ago, when, in the cause of
Irish freedom, I addressed many public meetings in the United States, I
pointed out that the aim of the overwhelming majority of the Irish people of the present generation was to secure for Ireland the status of an
independent sovereign state which would be recognised internationally as
such and could pursue its own life and develop its own institutions and
culture in its own peaceful way outside the hazards of imperial adventure
– if possible with its neutrality internationally guaranteed like the neutrality of Switzerland.

A small country like ours that had for centuries resisted imperial
absorption, and that still wished to preserve its separate national identity,
was bound to choose the course of neutrality in this war. No other course
could secure the necessary unity of purpose and effort among its people,
and at a time like this we heed the warning that the house divided against
itself shall not stand. The continued existence of partition, that unnatural
separation of six of our counties from the rest of Ireland, added in our
case *a further* decisive reason. [Italics mine]

Support for neutrality was merely solidified by the crass American pressure of
1944 (the 'American note' was electorally advantageous to Fianna Fáil in the general election of that year), by Churchill's vituperative strictures on Irish neutrality in his victory speech, and by what was widely perceived as de Valera's masterly
response, that of a dignified David against a blundering Goliath. This was the
high point of the vindication of a policy which had had the good fortune to succeed against the odds: of twenty states which had started out as neutrals, only
five finished the course, as it were, and Ireland was one of those.

* * *

Irish neutrality, as practised, worked on two levels – on the one hand, the legal,
the formal, the public manifestation of neutrality with strict censorship and
pedantic observation of protocol: on the other, the constant exercise of covert,
benevolent co-operation with Britain and the Allies. Berlin failed to realise that
Irish anglophobic rhetoric was both a compensation and a cover for the pro-
British tilt of neutrality. True to his promise twenty years before, de Valera not
only ensured that Ireland would not be used as a hostile base against Britain but
worked the neutrality policy so as to show 'a certain consideration for Britain', a
characteristic de Valera understatement. The actual extent of that 'consideration'
has been revealed over the years and a long list of co-operative measures was
reluctantly acknowledged at an early date by the hostile Lord Cranborne. For

example, Ireland provided valuable meteorological information and navigational facilities, extended preferential treatment to captured or stranded Allied military personnel, and even participated in joint military manoeuvres.

MI5 files released in January 1999 disclosed the close wartime co-operation between British and Irish intelligence officers regarding German activity in Ireland. Interestingly, MI5 recognised de Valera's delicate national position and, like other observers, they accepted that, as long as partition remained, his government could not have survived an attempt to bring Ireland into the war. The files also appreciate the pro-Allied slant of Irish neutrality and refer to the 'invaluable' contribution of emigrant Irish labour to the war effort in Britain, especially in the construction of airports, so desperately needed in the Battle of Britain.

Admittedly, Irish emigrants to wartime Britain – nurses, ammunition workers, skilled and unskilled labourers – were primarily interested in employment rather than in seeking to help the war effort. Yet their contribution cannot be gainsaid, neither can that of the 50,000 or so voluntary Allied servicemen and women from Southern Ireland. Whatever their motivations, their role was significant and substantial and this was reflected in the military distinctions they achieved, which included eight Victoria Crosses.

Irish neutrality in World War II was widely criticised at the time and subsequently. Louis Mac Neice's bitter indictment ('to the west, off your shores the mackerel are fat – on the flesh of your kin') was only one of several voices – the novelist Brian Moore was another – in a chorus of disapproval still echoing today. The notorious Illingworth cartoon in the *Daily Mail* showed grim interned figures representing erstwhile European neutrals warning an intransigent de Valera, mounted on a donkey labelled 'neutrality at any price' and holding aloft a placard reading 'No bases for Britain'. An American historian named Commager solemnly pronounced in the *New York Times* that the people of Ireland had 'missed out somehow on the greatest moral issue of modern history'. White House and State Department comments in the post-war period repeatedly referred to Irish neutrality as a moral cop-out and as 'missing the boat'.

These self-righteous expressions of moral outrage (not subscribed to, significantly, by specialist writers on the period) are essentially uninformed and unhistorical, and ignore the context of Ireland in 1939, as already discussed in some detail. Neutrality was the only feasible policy for the State to pursue on the outbreak of World War II. The combination of formal neutrality with considerable covert co-operation, and with various involvements (unwitting or otherwise) of masses of Irish citizens in the war effort – all this did much more for the Allied cause than a counter-productive belligerent participation would have done. And it was only the conduct of public and formal neutrality which made possible the informal and covert involvement and contribution.

One aspect of that contribution calls for particular comment. After the Great War, Irish volunteer ex-servicemen experienced a good deal of social hostility and ostracisation in the narrowly nationalist atmosphere of the new Irish Free State. (The few exceptions included those who had used their war experience to contribute to the nationalist side in the Anglo-Irish War, 1919-21.) Interestingly, no such antagonism was displayed towards Irish citizens who volunteered to fight in the British armed forces during World War II and who, incidentally, were not prohibited from doing so by a neutral Irish government. How can such contrasting attitudes (within such a short historical span) be explained? Great War servicemen were regarded as having helped the enemy in Ireland's hour of need. They were regarded as little better than traitors to a nationalist orthodoxy in an infant state.

In contrast, the Ireland of 1939 had survived a civil war, reached some kind of consensus, and attained a level of maturity. The neutrality experience was an expression of sovereignty and paradoxically sublimated anti-British feeling rather than aggravating it. The community could afford to accept the option exercised by individuals to serve in the British forces: they were, after all, only variants of the numerous Irish emigrant workers in British hospitals and ammunition factories. Irish servicemen in World War II were part of the informal world of co-operation and involvement: they did not contradict, nor were they a threat to, the consensus on public neutrality.

For their part, Irish servicemen saw no inconsistency in their role: while serving with the British, for whatever reason, they upheld their own State's right to remain neutral. Thus there is a very serious point to the well-known story of the two Irishmen arguing about the political importance of Eamon de Valera while they shelter from the blitz in a London underground station, or while they dodge anti-aircraft flak in an RAF plane high over Germany. The story's location varies but the triumphant clinching point for the de Valera follower is 'didn't he keep us out of the war!'

The historian F.S.L. Lyons, in a frequently-quoted passage, uses the image of Plato's cave to suggest that neutral Ireland was a shadowy, peripheral and negative place, pathetically cut off from the historic drama of the world at war. Lyons's metaphor is mistaken and misleading. 'Emergency' Ireland bustled with action and commitment in mobilising military and economic resources in a determined bid to make neutrality work and overcome shortages and threats to supplies. A sense of national purpose transcended party political differences, and civil war wounds were healed as former antagonists shared seats on an all-party defence council and on recruiting platforms.

The prevailing solidarity accentuated the growing twenty-six county sense of separate identity. It is hardly an exaggeration to say that the Emergency created a twenty-six county nationalism, which remained the dominant reality behind the sentimentality of the aspiration to all-Ireland unity. Wartime neutrality was *the* formative experience in the history of the State. Its very success, or apparent success, ensured its continuing popularity as a national policy, though its nature was affected by changing post-war circumstances and though there would be inter-mittent argument about what it actually meant. It was to become a sacred cow to some extent and for a long time few politicians would have the temerity to query 'our traditional policy of neutrality'.

* * *

More immediately, Ireland's neutrality meant continuing isolation in post-war international affairs. The price to be paid included difficult relations with the former Allies, particularly the anglophile United States with whose official and diplomatic representatives the Irish government had been at odds for much of the war years. Ireland was cold-shouldered by the US government for 'missing the boat' (and for not jumping on the anti-Axis bandwagon in the concluding months of the war) and there was little American support for Ireland's applica-tion for United Nations membership which in any case remained blocked until 1955 by a Soviet veto.

Irish-American relations came under further strain because of the Irish gov-ernment's refusal, in February 1949, to join the North Atlantic Treaty Organisation (NATO) on the grounds that it would involve military partnership with Britain, the 'occupying force' 'in the north-eastern corner of Ireland'. The Americans also gave a thumbs down to the Dublin suggestion of a bilateral US–Ireland defence pact which would obviate Ireland's objections to NATO membership. Thus, in the immediate post-war period, Irish neutrality was still linked to the partition issue, but in a vague and passive way it was also the con-tinuation of a policy in its own right.

On being admitted in 1955 to the United Nations (a move about which there were some slight neutrality-conscious reservations) Ireland defined its position in terms which were to apply throughout the Cold War and which to some observers smacked of ambiguous hand-washing if not of hypocrisy: namely, being a Christian country it would support the West politically but in keeping with its neutral tradition it would not become part of a military bloc. However, in the late 1950s, neutrality took on a more positive aspect if not indeed express-ing a new world-view. The evolution from self-centred isolationism to outward-looking international service took place under the aegis of Fianna Fáil's external (or foreign) minister Frank Aiken, veteran of the Anglo-Irish war, who envisaged something of a visionary role for Ireland in the United Nations, with the help and encouragement of talented civil servants and diplomats.

Briefly outlined, the new policy would be inspired by the country's history and position as a small Western nation which had been at the receiving end of colonialism for centuries, which had achieved independence through revolution-ary struggle but which had preserved and practised democratic values. It also had a special presence internationally because of its emigrant and missionary diaspora. At a time when the West was competing with the Communist bloc for the hearts and minds of the emerging ex-colonial nation-states in Asia and Africa, Ireland, so the new policy claimed, was uniquely fitted to play a constructive, mediating role. On the one hand, it would examine UN issues independently of power-bloc affiliation and vote accordingly, and, on the other, it would contribute to the containment of crises in various global trouble spots by providing politically acceptable peacekeeping volunteers from its own small military force.

Politically, the new policy resulted in some mild fluttering in American dovecotes when Ireland favoured discussing the merits of seating 'Red' China instead of Taiwan at the UN. (In most instances, it should be said, Ireland voted along Western lines and did not become involved in the ideologically neutralist or non-aligned movement.) In the peacekeeping area, Ireland gave remarkable service in such trouble spots as Cyprus, the Lebanon and, most controversially, in the Congo where the deaths of Irish soldiers in the Niembe ambush made a deep impact on domestic public opinion.

The exercise of this independent foreign policy in its pure form lasted only four or five years in the late 1950s and early 1960s before it was considerably modified by other factors, to be discussed shortly. But elements of the policy survived and even developed in subsequent decades. It went on to embrace the movement against nuclear proliferation, and the eventual signing of an anti-proliferation treaty owed much to Irish exertions. Again, Ireland (or perhaps more precisely, a section of Irish public opinion) identified with the perceived suffering of the Third World and its exploitation at the hands of Western capitalism.

All this 'positive' neutrality attitude received considerable if vague public support, especially from pacifists and anti-nuclear campaigners (unusually, Quakers involved themselves in the pro-neutrality movement); from some religious leaders sympathetic to radical churchmen in, say, Latin-America; and generally from nationalists, youth and the left. At one stage, for example, the Labour party wanted a clause inserted in the Constitution guaranteeing the permanent place of 'fundamental neutrality'. Another left view was that non-participation in military pacts should be changed to ideological non-alignment.

At its worst, the neutrality worldview from the 1960s smacked of smugness and delusions of grandeur. Ireland was accused of the luxury of playacting, knowing it could comfortably do so because, selfishly refusing to discharge its defence obligations, it was being given 'a free ride by NATO'. This was a criticism made by, for example, Michael Heseltine when he was defence minister in Margaret Thatcher's government. The grandiose aspirations of little Ireland's neutrality were superciliously dismissed by other observers: Henry Kissinger, for example, is supposed to have ruminated out loud that Ireland was 'the kind of friendly neutral you could bring home to mother'.

However, at its idealised best and no matter how imperfectly expressed in practice, post-1960s neutrality seemed to many Irish people to express the right kind of contribution, minor but important, the country could make to the wider world – a contribution moreover in keeping with the evolution of a distinctive Irish worldview from its own troubled history. A particularly pleasing feature of such a policy was the primacy of a peacekeeping image over a past of much violence. Rather than being a small, passive and insignificant component of one military bloc in nightmarish nuclear confrontation with the other, Ireland was attempting to give witness in a distinctive manner to the ideal of international peace and understanding. Neutrality was not isolationist ostrich-hiding in the face of a threatened nuclear holocaust but an attempt in a small way to prevent it.

* * *

But there were other views and voices, and different national considerations were at work from an early stage. From about 1960 full membership of the European Economic Community (now the European Union) became an Irish national objective which, it grew increasingly apparent, was not readily reconcilable with 'pure' neutrality and an untramelled, independent foreign policy. For example, anti-colonial attitudes and activities on the part of an aspirant EEC member would not sit well with such future partners as France and Belgium. More generally, 'traditional neutrality' was not going to be easily squared with the implied commitments of Community membership.

Frank Aiken, External Affairs minister, 1957-69, and Seán Lemass, Taoiseach, 1959-66, could be said to have represented these two conflicting UN and EEC strands, respectively. Both were Fianna Fáil founding fathers and government veterans. While both served in cabinet during the Emergency (Lemass being a key figure as Minister for Supplies) it is significant that whereas Aiken was absolutely unbending in his defence of neutrality (reflected in a notoriously acrimonious row with President Roosevelt) Lemass' pragmatic temperament had inclined him to at least lend a curious ear to Churchill's unity-for-participation offer in 1940. Now as Taoiseach he displayed the same brusque pragmatism in his approach to 'traditional' neutrality in the context of prospective EEC membership. (Incidentally, he is said to have commented that during all his time as a cabinet minister from the 1930s through the 1960s, partition as the supposed rationale for neutrality 'had never been seriously discussed'. The rationale was to become even more meaningless in subsequent decades, though it would occasionally be given ritual recognition.)

Lemass was the first of a number of Irish taoisigh to proclaim Irish support for European political values, while suggesting that in the fullness of Community development the sacred cow of neutrality itself would have to be sacrificed – but, like St Augustine and chastity, not quite yet. Lemass was more forthright, perhaps, than some of his Fianna Fáil successors since the party liked to think of itself – and does so still – as the guardian of the neutrality flame. He expressed the view that NATO protected Ireland's security together with the rest of Europe, that possible membership of the organisation would not entail Irish recognition of British sovereignty over Northern Ireland but that the question of joining NATO was irrelevant to joining the EEC. Clearly, he was prepared to jettison neutrality – an increasingly ambiguous position – to gain for Ireland the economic advantages of EEC membership. The sharpest definition of his views on the issue was to be found in an interview he gave the *New York Times*, 18 July 1962:

> We recognise that a military commitment will be an inevitable consequence of our joining the Common Market and ultimately we would be prepared to yield even the technical label of neutrality. We are prepared to go into this integrated Europe without any reservation as to how far this will take us in the field of foreign policy and defence.

Lemass's successor, Jack Lynch (Taoiseach, 1966-73, 1977-9) followed the same line, albeit somewhat more cautiously expressed: once Ireland was in the EEC, he declared in the Dáil in 1969, 'we would naturally be interested in the defence of the territories embraced by the communities. There is no question of neutrality there'.

In the great, if somewhat confused, referendum debate about EEC entry in 1972, the 'no' side argued that membership would also willy-nilly mean membership of NATO and an end to the hallowed principle of neutrality; pro-marketeers replied that while Irish neutrality was only ad hoc in nature it would not be compromised until the formation of a European defence organisation, sometime in the future. In the event, the overwhelming decision to join the EEC was grounded on purely economic considerations and on expectations of material benefits.

In the decades after membership, though there were fluctuating opinions in the Community on the possibility of a common foreign and defence policy, the general Irish position was that European defence co-operation would become a practical proposition only when economic integration was complete and political union was on the cards. That seemed to remove any threat to neutrality for the foreseeable future. In the interim, the interesting view was expressed that Irish neutrality was useful to the EC image by proving that the Community was not a military bloc: Irish neutrality was a distinctive aspect of the European presence. Neutrality was espoused as a Fianna Fáil value once again when Charles Haughey's government opposed Mrs Thatcher's Falklands adventure in 1982.

In the successive referenda – Single European Act, Maastricht and Amsterdam Treaties – on European developments in the late 1980s and into the 1990s, those in favour of a 'no' vote argued that these measures represented further erosions of Irish sovereignty and a drift towards military as well as political integration. The 'yes' camp maintained that the treaties did not commit the State to military involvement. Increasingly, however, it was being pointed out from Fianna Fáil as well as Fine Gael quarters that as 'good Europeans' Irish people should be prepared to undertake whatever security responsibilities were implied by a closer European union. These remained comfortingly vague and undefined, and there was therefore no need to address the obvious inadequacies of the Irish defence forces for whatever security tasks there might be. More generally, the contradiction between 'traditional' neutrality and European defence obligations was never really faced up to.

The collapse of the Soviet bloc and the end of the Cold War raised an important question about the *raison d'etre* of the role Irish neutrality had assumed for itself ever since the 1960s: was there still need for Ireland to give witness to the goal of international peace and understanding by purposefully standing back from the confrontation of nuclear-equipped military blocs? Neutrality enthusiasts would respond that such a witness was still called for as long as associations such as NATO existed, despite the end of the Cold War. It was argued that Ireland's UN peacekeeping contribution would be gravely compromised by any association with military groupings.

* * *

The latest phase in the long and intermittent debate on Irish neutrality has been concerned with Ireland's proposed membership of the NATO-sponsored organisation, Partnership for Peace (PFP). The ostensible purpose of PFP, begun in 1994, is to secure co-operation between European states in order to promote peacekeeping and humanitarian activities. From another angle, PFP is intended 'to enhance security in Europe by deepening ties between NATO and central and eastern European states'. Apparently, therefore, PFP membership can operate at two levels. A state can determine the extent of its contribution to the organisation in a *á la carte* way, or PFP may be used as a stage on the road to full NATO membership. In the first case, for example, Switzerland can claim that PFP membership, unlike NATO, is compatible with its historic neutrality. It sees the Partnership as a suitable mechanism to deal with such international post-Cold War problems as terrorism, the drug trade, mass migrations and environmental disasters.

Individual voices in Fine Gael had long been clamouring for Irish involvement in European defence and security, and the party in Coalition government in 1996 had mooted PFP membership in a White Paper. This was criticised at the time by Bertie Ahern, leader of Fianna Fáil, who however performed a blatant U-turn shortly thereafter when as Taoiseach, he announced his government's intention early in 1999 to join the PFP before the end of the year. Was Fianna Fáil finally relinquishing its role as keeper of the holy grail of neutrality?

The PFP proposal (supported by Fine Gael and Labour) also raised questions about the Irish army. The role of the army in peacekeeping missions since the

1960s had always been a matter of national pride. But such pride was considerably dented in the late 1990s by public cynicism about thousands of claims by soldiers for compensation for alleged deafness. There was low morale in the forces because of disenchanted public attitudes; poor and obsolete equipment; the closure of a number of army barracks; and government reports pressing for reduction of numbers and the creation of a leaner, meaner force. In these circumstances, it was not clear what useful function the Irish army might perform in the PFP, though representative associations of officers and other ranks kept advocating such involvement in the interests of modernisation and the creation of career opportunities. Over the years, some hard-nosed pragmatists had pointed to the commercial and employment opportunities of membership of a defence pact.

The usual 'traditional neutrality' groups and individuals called (in vain) for a plebiscite on the issue which, they claimed, would fatally undermine neutrality. Ireland's present position helped to preserve a valuable distinction between NATO and the European Union; joining PFP would be a further diminution of sovereignty, since it would effectively alienate control of the army to an outside body; it would involve the State in the world of escalating armaments and the sordid international arms industry, as well as making Ireland partners of nuclear powers; PFP was an Orwellian organisation, talking peace but intending war; it would shift the country's international allegiance from the UN to NATO, and membership would diminish Ireland's standing, and therefore effectiveness in Third World trouble spots.

The government responded (to uneasy backbenchers, as well as to opponents at large) by denying that neutrality was being compromised and that foreign policy was now being aligned with NATO. PFP membership, it was claimed, was desirable as a means of fulfilling obligations to European political co-operation. (Indeed an important reason for the move was to promote a more positive and unselfish image of Ireland at a time when the national stock was falling in EU eyes because of a perceived greedy, begging-bowl mentality.) The government pointed to the wide membership of PFP, with such 'neutrals' as Finland and Austria and, above all, Switzerland; moreover, the inclusion of such countries as Russia and the Ukraine gave the lie to the charge that PFP was just a new version of the old Cold War, pro-West alignment.

Overall, it was hard to understand how membership of PFP would allow Ireland keep a 'credible, viable and constructive neutrality', as was claimed by the Taoiseach, Mr Bertie Ahern. Indeed, sixty years after the adoption of neutrality in World War II, it was difficult to say what, if anything, an ambiguous and residual 'tradition' now stood for. The old cynical jibe of the 1970s and 1980s, 'Who are we neutral against?', was now taking on an even greater disenchanted resonance. The inadequacy of the Irish position was once again revealed in the crisis over NATO's attack on Serbia in March 1999, when the government's feeble, fence-sitting attitude provoked a caustic opposition comment that its foreign policy was neutered rather than neutral.

* * *

This writer recalls that, wearing an independent political hat, he first stood for (and won) a Seanad Éireann seat in 1977, in the National University of Ireland constituency. Then and thereafter, he subscribed to 'positive neutrality' (as worked out from the early 1960s and as discussed above) as a primary political value. Standing on that principle, he later took an active part (by way of newspaper articles, media debates, and 'town hall' type appearances) in the campaigns against the Single European Act and the Maastrict Treaty.

If he were to be rejuvenated and stand for election in 1999, he would be hard put to it to explain to his electors or even to himself what Irish neutrality meant any longer.

BIBLIOGRAPHICAL NOTE

While many publications deal with different aspects of Irish wartime neutrality, the wider perspective is admirably dealt with in Patrick Keatinge, *A singular stance: Irish neutrality in the 1980s* (Dublin, 1984). The background detail of some of my article is much indebted to Keatinge's book. For Irish co-operation with the Allies, see Ronan Fanning, *Independent Ireland* (Dublin, 1983), particularly pp 123-5. For Eamon de Valera's views over the years, see *Speeches and statements by Eamon de Valera 1919-73*, ed. Maurice Moynihan (Dublin and New York, 1980). The incipient debate on PFP membership can be followed in Irish newspapers (especially the *Irish Times*) in the last week of January and the first fortnight of February 1999. The following month, with NATO's bombing of Serbia, the newspapers reflected the renewed debate on Irish neutrality.

Politics in wartime:
governing, neutrality and elections

Brian Girvin

When war was declared in September 1939, the Irish State entered a period of further uncertainty at the very time that Ireland was stabilising after an extended period of change.[1] By this time Fianna Fáil had become the dominant party in the Irish political system, and its legislative initiatives (between 1932 and 1938) had altered Ireland's socio-economic environment.[2] These changes were further reinforced by de Valera's introduction of a new constitution in 1937 and the successful negotiations with the United Kingdom which led to the Anglo-Irish Agreements in 1938. This new constitution departed in a number of ways from the 1922 constitution, incorporating strong catholic and nationalist attributes into the document while also reflecting Fianna Fáil's political concerns. While the constitution was only narrowly ratified at the referendum, it went on to become a constitution for nationalist Ireland, an outcome predicted by de Valera at the time.[3] The 1938 agreements not only concluded the economic war on terms favourable to Ireland, but provided that Britain return a number of military and naval facilities to Irish sovereign control. This agreement was of considerable importance in 1939, as it guaranteed that Ireland would not inadvertently be drawn into the war because of the presence of British forces in the state.[4] Furthermore, the 1938 general election had firmly endorsed Fianna Fáil in government, providing de Valera with a comfortable majority in the Dáil. There was considerable self-confidence and pride in the achievements of the 1930s evident in the government and in the country generally at this time. Notwithstanding

1 In this chapter I have generally used Ireland (in preference to Irish Free State or Éire) to refer to the area of the island which seceded to form the Irish Free State in 1922 and Northern Ireland to refer to the region which remained in the United Kingdom. I have on occasions used southern Ireland or the south to refer to Ireland. 2 Fianna Fáil Archive: FF/46, Erskine Childers, 'Fianna Fáil four year social and economic programme', 9 April 1934, which predicted that Fianna Fáil could become the dominant force in Irish politics if it pursued an active nationalist policy. 3 Maurice Moynihan, *Speeches and statements by Eamon De Valera 1917-73* (Dublin, 1980), pp 330-40. 4 Brian Girvin, *Between two worlds: politics and economy in independent Ireland* (Dublin, 1989), pp 127-30; Deirdre McMahon, *Republicans and imperialists* (New Haven and London, 1984).

this understandable view, it disguised a number of political challenges and dangers to Fianna Fáil's self image in particular. Emigration had resumed in response to a slow down in the Irish economy after 1937. The economy itself, though now heavily protected, provided limited employment opportunities or growth, despite government claims to the contrary. As a consequence, there were serious divisions within the government on economic policy by 1939.[5] A further consequence of Fianna Fáil policy was that the successful promotion of self-sufficiency and sovereignty copper-fastened partition. This outcome can in part be attributed to developments in Northern Ireland, but it was also an unintended consequence of Fianna Fáil's irredentist policies and the catholic nature of the constitution.[6]

Fianna Fáil's political success led to a wide-ranging consensus on domestic issues in Irish politics. The difference between Fianna Fáil and Fine Gael narrowed, as the latter reluctantly accepted the dramatic changes introduced by de Valera. Fianna Fáil's electoral success not only made it the dominant party, but also forced Fine Gael to recognise this reality.[7] While political competition did not disappear, Fianna Fáil increasingly dictated the terms of political exchange. In addition the Irish political system remained in 1939 essentially nationalist in character. Both Fianna Fáil and Fine Gael were self-consciously nationalist parties, with a broad national electoral appeal. Nationalism defined the party system, as it had since the foundation of the state. What had changed were the key elements of competition. Between 1922 and 1932, Cumann na nGaedheal assured its dominance by insisting on the need to protect the state and stabilise its institutions and the economy, thereafter Fianna Fáil successfully reworked the constituent parts of the nationalist consensus in terms of a more vigorous development strategy, the expansion of state sovereignty and constitutional change. It was nationalism that defined both parties, though there continued to be disagreement over its interpretation and implementation. Indeed, class, regional or interest group politics never had the electoral appeal of nationalism, demonstrated by the Labour Party's participation in the consensus. By 1939 Fianna Fáil's vision of Irish nationalism had become the dominant one.[8] The existence of a

5 Girvin, *Between two worlds*, pp 120-30; UCDA: MacEntee Papers, P67/169, Department of Finance memorandum, 28 February 1938; P67/132, memorandum by MacEntee, 20 April 1939; MacEntee to de Valera, 30 April 1939; National Archives of Ireland: S. 10620, Per Jacobson to de Valera, 25 March, 1938.   6 John Bowman, *De Valera and the Ulster question 1917-73* (Oxford, 1982).   7 UCDA: FitzGerald Papers, P80/1117, Heads of Policy, September 1939; P80/1123, Notes for Fine Gael speakers, 1937.   8 The nature of the Irish party system at this time is a contentious one and my claim will not be elaborated in detail here. However, I have explored some aspects of this in a comparative context in Brian Girvin, 'Political independence and democratic consolidation', in Michael Holmes and Denis Holmes (eds), *Ireland and India: connections, comparisons, contrasts* (Dublin, 1997), pp 120-44; Michael Gallagher, *Electoral support for Irish political parties, 1927-1973* (London and Beverly Hills,

nationalist party system during the 1920s and 1930s, one which determines the
parameters of political competition reinforces the claim subsequently made by
John Whyte that Irish politics is without social bases.[9]

One of the consequences of this consensus was that all the political parties,
including Fine Gael, immediately accepted the policy of neutrality adopted in
1939.[10] In the circumstances, it is not surprising that Ireland adopted neutrality,
most small European states did so in 1939, but it was also the logical extension of
Fianna Fáil's diplomatic policy since 1932. It represented a further widening of
the emotional and political gap between Ireland and the Commonwealth. But
the policy also reflected the growing isolation of Ireland under Fianna Fáil. Most
policies introduced assumed a measure of self-sufficiency and this led quickly to
isolationism in both foreign and domestic policy. By 1939 Irish society and its
politics was becoming more conservative and nationalism was no longer promoting change, but reinforcing conservative policy trends. This was partly a
result of the consensus in the society and the policy convergence between the
political parties. The war reinforced these trends and in some cases exaggerated
them.

It has been argued that war can be a disruptive force, often breaking down
stable systems of authority and power and promoting radical changes in a society. Whatever about its general application, the evidence from Ireland between
1939 and 1945 suggests that this theory does not apply in this case.[11] There is little
break in continuity during the war years and those changes, which do occur, are
either a consequence or an extension of developments already in place. Neutrality fits in well with these circumstances, confirming the sovereign status of the
Irish State. It may be the case that Irish neutrality was operated in an evenhand-
ed fashion, yet it was a policy primarily aimed at Britain. Because of Fianna Fáil's
policy in respect of Northern Ireland, the historical memory of the independence generation and the proximity of Ireland to the United Kingdom, neutrality would always be tested in respect of this relationship rather than any other.[12]

At first, however, it was internal security rather than external threats which
taxed the authorities. The prospect of war encouraged republicans in the belief
that this provided another opportunity to end partition by force. The IRA was
already in alliance with Nazi Germany, for both practical and ideological rea-

1976); Richard Dunphy, *The making of Fianna Fáil power in Ireland 1923-1948* (Oxford, 1995);
Richard Sinnott, *Irish voters decide* (Manchester, 1995).   **9** J.H. Whyte, 'Ireland: politics with-
out social bases' in Richard Rose (ed.), *Electoral behaviour: a comparative handbook* (New York,
1974), pp 619-51.   **10** FitzGerald Papers, P80/1117, 'Heads of policy 1939'; Mulcahy Papers,
P7A/211, Mulcahy memorandum, 30 September 1939.   **11** Mancur Olson, *The rise and decline
of nations* (New Haven and London, 1983), pp 17-74.   **12** Brian Girvin, 'National interest,
Irish neutrality and the limits of ideology', in Rolf Steininger and Michael Gehler (eds), *Die
Neutralen und die Europäsche integration seit 1945* (Vienna, 1999), pp 87-111.

sons. In addition, an IRA bombing campaign in Britain had led to serious damage and the murder of five people in Coventry in August 1939. The IRA also remained active throughout the war in Ireland, where, on a number of occasions, republicans murdered members of the Gardaí. Perhaps the most serious threat to Ireland came in December 1939 when the IRA successfully penetrated the Magazine Fort in Phoenix Park in Dublin, removing over one million rounds of ammunition from the store. These and other actions led to draconian action north and south as well as in Britain. Members of the IRA were executed in each jurisdiction, while special legislation was introduced to curb their activities. In Ireland the Emergency Powers Act provided the means to effectively emasculate the republican movement for the duration of the war, though this in itself did not prevent limited actions on the part of the IRA and its attempts to support the Axis war effort.[13]

What is impressive about Irish government action after September 1939 was its effectiveness in containing any obvious threat from the IRA. The use of coercion against them does not appear to have been unpopular, though the government was clearly aided by the effective use of censorship to sustain its position. Moreover, opposition doubts about coercion could be calmed by appeals to the national interest. Fine Gael was clearly seduced by this appeal, though there were divisions within the party as to how much power to give to the government. However, resistance to arbitrary power was limited because most Fine Gael supporters believed that the IRA was the greater threat and the party itself had always pursued a strong law and order platform. De Valera appealed successfully to Fine Gael's belief in legal authority, urging the party leadership to recognise the real threat to Ireland's sovereignty and its democratic institutions.[14]

In effect, the Fine Gael leadership adopted Fianna Fáil's view of neutrality and security issues, but received very little in return. In most European states, some type of national government or at least a fairly inclusive type of consultation met the challenge of war. This did not prove to be the case in Ireland. Not only did de Valera refuse to consider a national government under any circumstances; consultation with the opposition was minimal and only occurred when absolutely necessary.[15] Co-operation in wartime was on terms almost entirely dictated by Fianna Fáil. Cosgrave privately complained that de Valera issued statements on government policy to the media before informing the opposition, even when this involved serious security matters. While Fine Gael was willing to support the government if consulted, this was not forthcoming. The dilemma for Fine Gael was that it could not openly challenge the government if it behaved in

13 Conor Brady, *Guardians of the peace* (Dublin, 1974); J. Bowyer Bell, *The secret army* (London, 1970), pp 201–81. **14** Mulcahy Papers, P7A/210, Notes on Defence Conference 30 September 1939; notes on meeting with Smith and Boland, 1 January 1940. **15** Mulcahy Papers, P7A/210, notes on meeting with de Valera and Seán T. O'Kelly, 24–5 May 1940.

this fashion without appearing to highlight divisions within the state over policy, especially neutrality. While Fine Gael may have fulminated privately, de Valera's gamble paid off. Fine Gael did not publicly oppose the government on the major issues of wartime, but restricted its criticism to relatively minor matters while accepting the government's notion of national interest and public order.[16] Elizabeth Bowen in one of her regular reports to Britain, noted at the same time that support for neutrality was widespread in the state, even among pro-British sections of the population.[17] In his classic study of Irish politics published in 1945, James Hogan suggested that the war, neutrality and Fine Gael's acceptance of the national interest as defined by Fianna Fáil deprived it of the means to distinguish itself from Fianna Fáil. The decline in Fine Gael support during and immediately after the war reflected this in large part.[18]

Yet Ireland was never fully neutral, nor could it be because of the existence of Northern Ireland. Irish appeals to Britain for an all-Ireland neutral zone were unrealistic and unrealisable, especially after the evacuation of France. However, Irish government interference in the internal affairs of the United Kingdom stretched the meaning of neutrality to breaking point. The most obvious cases of this were associated with conscription in Northern Ireland. MacEntee had mused on the possibility of defence co-operation between Ireland and Northern Ireland in 1937, though conceiving it as a preparatory step to unification:

> Should the need for common defence action ever arise there will be unified control over the country, to be vested in us but to be exercised necessarily in close co-operation and agreement with the other parties concerned. If we can attain this position then legislative and fiscal partition will not long remain.[19]

MacEntee recognised that if a common defence structure was accepted, it could provide the basis for changing the political conditions established in 1922.

This was not a course of action pursued by the Irish government then or subsequently, but it does provide an interesting insight into how alternative strategies might have led to different outcomes. The new constitution and the 1938 agreements copper fastened partition, while declaring neutrality reinforced this. When, in April 1939, the British government decided to introduce conscription, the Irish government objected to any Irish citizen (including Protestant unionists in Northern Ireland) being included under the legislation. In April and May, Irish diplomats in London engaged in a bitter dispute with the Prime Minister,

16 FitzGerald Papers, P80/1119c1. 'Memo from Mr Cosgrave', 15 November 1940. 17 PRO, London: FO. 800/310, Notes on Ireland, 9 November 1940. 18 James Hogan, *Election and representation* (Cork, 1945), pp 33-6. 19 MacEntee Papers: P67/118, MacEntee to de Valera, 20 January 1937.

Neville Chamberlain, over this issue. In one message delivered by the Irish High Commissioner, de Valera rejected the right of the United Kingdom government to act in Northern Ireland:

> The introduction of conscription in the Six counties by the British government for the British army can be regarded as an act of war against our nation and will provoke the bitterest hostilities to England wherever there are Irishmen throughout the world.[20]

At the same time as the IRA were engaging in a bombing campaign in the name of the Irish nation, and when Europe was poised on the brink of war, the Irish diplomatic service exercised the maximum pressure to force Britain to reverse its position on conscription. That it did so in May satisfied de Valera, but it may also have been noticed in Berlin.[21] While some allowance can be made for the Irish policy in 1939, this is less the case in May 1941 when once again the British government decided to extend conscription to Northern Ireland. The Irish High Commissioner, as before, led the attack on the decision and was actively supported by the Irish government, the Catholic church and nationalist MPs in Northern Ireland. During peacetime the grounds for such a challenge were weak in international law, despite Ireland's claim to sovereignty over Northern Ireland. But during a major war and at a time when the British state was under serious threat the action of the Irish government constituted interference in the internal affairs of another state and could only have been of benefit to the German war effort.[22] As a consequence of this obsession with Northern Ireland, Irish neutrality became an increasingly inflexible instrument in the hands of de Valera, Joseph Walsh, secretary of the Department of External Affairs, and Frank Aiken.[23] Not long after the fall of France, Walsh insisted that:

> Neutrality was not entered upon for the purpose of being used as a bargaining factor. It represented, and does represent, the fundamental attitude of the entire people. It is just as much a part of the national position as the desire to remain Irish and we can no more abandon it than we can renounce everything that constitutes our national distinctiveness.[24]

The active use of censorship to prevent an open or informed discussion on the issue lends further weight to this view.[25]

20 DFA: p. 70, 'British threat to enforce conscription in Six Counties, 1939-1941', Dulanty to Chamberlain, 26 April 1939; DT: S. 10967, 'Irish citizens in Great Britain: liability for conscription'. **21** DFA: P.70, Dulanty to Dublin, 27 April 1939; 3 May 1939. **22** DFA: P.70, 'Conscription in Northern Ireland', notes of meetings between Dulanty and Churchill, 22, 26 and 27 May 1941. **23** R. Fisk, *In time of war* for an assessment. **24** Cited in Dermot Keogh, *Ireland and Europe 1919-1989* (Cork, 1990), pp 143-4. **25** Donal O'Drisceoil, *Censorship in*

Nor was the use made of neutrality, though perhaps not the policy itself, necessarily in the national interest. The lack of flexibility evident in de Valera's operation of the policy suggests that there were no circumstances when neutrality might be modified or abandoned. If this is so, then it was never a policy, but instead reflected a set of presuppositions which Irish citizens were expected to conform to. This is most evident during the discussions between the two governments in June 1940. At the most difficult moment for Britain in the war, the United Kingdom government offered de Valera the opportunity to change the status quo on the island in significant fashion if Ireland entered the war. The British offer did not guarantee Irish unity immediately, but promised a significant change in policy on the part of the British government. Most assessments of this issue have concluded that it was a product of desperation, that even if genuine the United Kingdom could not have delivered on its promise and that in the circumstances the Irish government was correct of reject it.[26] There is considerable strength in some, though not all of these objections. June 1940 was perilous for Britain and Ireland, due to its own inadequate military preparation, could not have been easily protected if attacked by Germany. Britain was indeed desperate, but this could be evidence for the genuine nature of the offer. Indeed, the British government modified its proposals significantly to meet Irish objections, yet de Valera too rejected these.[27]

Nor would objections from Unionists in Northern Ireland have carried much weight if de Valera and Churchill had reached agreement. In fact, the Northern Irish government was in considerable disarray at this time, due to internal weaknesses and criticism of the unionist leadership. While an agreement might have further divided unionist opinion, a more likely outcome is that loyalty to the state and the empire would have provided a basis for unionists to accept a new arrangement with the south.[28] At the very least, an agreement would have allowed the Irish government a say in Northern Ireland, something which was not to be obtained until the Anglo-Irish Agreement in 1985. The likelihood is that de Valera never seriously considered the possibility of entering the war in 1940 or any other time, because he had not the political imagination to see beyond the limited nationalist framework he had established during the 1930s. That the British may have been more serious is given some credibility by a report prepared by Dulanty in 1942. He met one of his British government contacts 'Minister X'; who from the internal evidence is probably Ernest Bevin, one

Ireland 1939-1945 (Cork, 1996), pp 220-83 for a detailed examination of the way in which censorship was used to constrain debate.   **26** Fisk, *In time of war*, remains the most comprehensive treatment of the question; Lee, *Ireland*, p. 248 is dismissive of the offer, but Cornelius O'Leary, 'Professor Lee's Ireland', unpublished manuscript in the author's possession, makes a strong case for considering the offer a serious one.   **27** Fisk, *In time of war*, pp 203-4.   **28** See Brian Barton's chapter later in this book.

of the most influential members of the war cabinet. Bevin insisted during the discussion that the cabinet had been agreed on promoting Irish unity if an agreement had been reached with de Valera. He also rejected the view put forward by Dulanty that Churchill would have opposed any attempt to redefine the relationship between north and south. While it is obvious from the report that Dulanty did not accept this, there can be little doubt that Bevin did.[29] It is not necessary to conclude that Ireland should have joined in the war in June 1940 to suggest that a more flexible use of neutrality might have gained the state more than was the case. The decision not to enter the war in 1940 can be sustained by appeals to national interest, but if so and if national interest is the main calculation when making the decision, the refusal to enter the war in 1942 or 1944 cannot be justified in terms of national interest. What can be sustained is that the refusal to end neutrality in 1942 or 1944 was in Fianna Fáil's interest, but this cannot be equated with the national interest whatever de Valera might have thought. Ireland would not have been alone in taking such a decision and doing so would have enhanced Irish bargaining power in any post-war settlement. It might also have increased Ireland's influence in Washington, something patently missing then and later.[30]

If the integrity of the state was effectively defended during wartime, the same cannot be said for the well being of its citizens. The industrial economy suffered badly from the absence of raw materials, demonstrating Ireland's heavy dependence on the United Kingdom. Mass emigration to Britain was one consequence of this, as was unemployment and under-employment for many of those who stayed behind. The economy was held together by the efforts of Lemass at the Department of Supplies, who centralised decision making on most economic matters in his hands. Though unpopular because of rationing and shortages, Lemass secured for most people the minimum required to survive in difficult circumstances. Furthermore, the effective mobilisation of the rural economy complemented this by providing the food for the population and for exports to the United Kingdom.[31] If national interest could be successfully invoked in respect of neutrality, this was not as easily achieved when the economy was seriously dislocated. At the beginning of 1940 a trade union delegation met Seán MacEntee, now the Minister for Industry and Commerce, and estimated that there were about 100, 000 unemployed in the state. After September 1939 many Irish workers in Britain returned to Ireland to avoid conscription, but under pressure from the Irish government the British introduced favourable rules for Irish citizens who wished to work in the United Kingdom.[32] Once work became

29 DFA: P.70. Dulanty to DEA, Dublin, 12 August 1942. **30** Arieh J. Kochavi, 'Britain, the United States and Irish neutrality, 1944-5', *European History Quarterly*, 25, 2 (1995), pp 93-115. **31** Girvin, *Between two worlds*, pp 131-40. **32** NADT: S. 10967, 'Irish citizens in Great Britain, liability for conscription' for policy and correspondence between November 1938 and

scarce in Ireland, the movement back to Britain accelerated. In January 1940 the government decided that employment exchanges should not be used to recruit Irish workers for the British war industries. In March 1940 the cabinet agreed that it would be appropriate for the Department of Industry and Commerce to assure those workers who intended to work temporarily in Britain that they would not be liable for conscription.[33] This situation was further aggravated after the fall of France when the economy and its workforce quickly suffered from the absence of raw materials and essential components.[34] By June 1942, Lemass concluded that there had been a significant decline in most areas of industry, which had led to 'temporary emigration' for a large number of industrial workers. For those who remained in Ireland, part-time work was becoming the norm allied with a consequent reduction in income. Although the agrarian economy was employing more workers than previously, this type of work was not considered appropriate for urban workers and Lemass believed that the problem of urban unemployment would remain.[35] The Irish government responded by encouraging the unemployed to emigrate, a policy that was never publicly endorsed due to the sensitivities involved. The reality was that the Irish government co-operated with the United Kingdom to assure that Irish emigration to Britain would be safely controlled and would not have an adverse impact on Fianna Fáil.

The Irish government was anxious not to be seen to be promoting emigration, as Fianna Fáil had boasted throughout the 1930s that its policies would guarantee all Irish citizens the prospect of working in the state. Although there was no clear policy during 1940, close co-operation on labour transfer had been established between the Ministry of Labour in Britain and the Department of Industry and Commerce. By early 1941 it became clear that guidelines had to be established for the transfer of workers from Ireland to Britain. By March a large number of applications to work in Britain had been registered at the Dublin Employment Exchange by men who claimed to be available for work in the British war industries. As a consequence Industry and Commerce withdrew the facility to register until the government had decided on its response. Departmental officials highlighted the rising unemployment in the state, which it attributed to the impact of the war, but concluded that such emigration would be of a temporary nature:

> It seems a reasonable view that if they cannot secure normal employment here during the present emergency conditions, which will probably grow worse, the Department should not refuse them the facilities and assistance when they seek to earn their livelihood elsewhere.

September 1939. **33** S. 11582A, 'Irish Labour' cabinet decision, 18 January 1940 and 28 March 1940. **34** S. 11644A, 'Unemployment', Meeting of Minister for Industry and Commerce with Trade Union delegation, 31 January 1940; *Irish Press*, 29 November 1940 which reports on rising unemployment. **35** S. 12886, 'Labour policy' memorandum, by Lemass June 1942.

There was also concern that the rising unemployment would be used to generate unrest and officials reported that at one meeting organised by the Dublin Unemployed Workers Movement the speaker urged his listeners to 'stay at home and seek justice for themselves and their starving children'. It was also the considered view of departmental officials that organised labour was not in principle opposed to workers travelling to Britain to obtain employment.[36] Fears of social upheaval, if exaggerated, were not entirely alarmist. The Wages Standstill Order (1941) and the Trade Union Act (1941) caused considerable unrest and division within the trade union movement.[37]

The problem was resolved when Irish officials agreed to British proposals on procedures to regularise the transfer of workers to Britain. The agreement confirmed that all those travelling to Britain would be volunteers, as heretofore, but that Irish employment exchanges would not be used as a vehicle to recruit Irish labour for Britain. However selection would take place in Ireland through the employment exchanges and Irish officials would decide on who travelled. Irish officials would regulate the system, and each worker would only receive travel documentation when all conditions were met. MacEntee believed that the proposed system was the best that could be achieved in the circumstances of war. It gave the Irish and British governments control over the arrangements and was preferable to Irish labour travelling to work on an ad hoc or privately organised basis. It explicitly stated that this also provided an opportunity to avoid unrest, 'the placing of Irish unemployed workers in employment in Great Britain would provide a very welcome mitigation of the difficulties at home'.[38]

Despite misgivings expressed by Winston Churchill, the British government recognised late in 1940 that its war effort could benefit significantly from the availability of Irish labour in its factories. It was estimated by early 1941 that about 30,000 Irish workers were ready to travel to Britain if the opportunity was provided. A British Liaison Officer was appointed to Dublin with the authority to oversee all the procedures. What is clear is that a close relationship developed between Irish and British officials on how best to transfer Irish labour to Britain and this was reflected in the terms of the agreement. One British official noted in 1941 that his Irish counterparts were prepared to co-operate on transferring labour to Britain, as long as this did not expose the Irish government to criticism at home.[39] This concern was not unwarranted. A meeting of the Fianna Fáil national executive in March 1941 discussed, with concern, the provision of fares

---

36 S. 11582A, Industry and Commerce memorandum 'Employment of Irish Workers in G. B.' 13 March 1941.   **37** Kieran Allen, *Fianna Fáil and Irish labour* (London, 1997), pp 69-78; Dunphy, *The making of Fianna Fáil power in Ireland,* pp 261-67.   **38** S. 11582A, Industry and Commerce memorandum 'Employment of Irish Workers in G.B.' 13 March 1941.   **39** PRO, London: Labour Party. 8/512/EM/7084, which contains a report of the discussions between Irish and British officials in July 1941.

for unemployed workers to leave the state 'to get employment elsewhere'. Later in the year, Lemass reported to Fianna Fáil deputies that there had been a fall in the number of those emigrating, but Seán Brady TD criticised the methods used by the British to attract workers. Brady claimed that employed workers were leaving the country as a result of the incentives offered by British employers. He also asserted that the Liaison Office in Dublin was attempting to recruit for the British forces and 'there was he thought a great deal of undesirable things happening in regard to this whole problem and he urged the government to take action to have the matter straightened out.'[40]

There was also considerable criticism of the government's handing of the emigration issue in the Dáil, especially from the Labour Party. In response to some of these criticisms, the Department of External Affairs advised de Valera that the arrangements with Britain involved a 'disposition to facilitate' emigration rather than a commitment to 'discourage' such a course of action.[41] While the public position of the Irish government throughout the war was one of pained passivity in the face of insurmountable difficulties, the evidence suggests that the government was more instrumental (perhaps even cynical) in its involvement. There is also some evidence that officials in the employment exchanges were not averse to encouraging the unemployed to identify employment opportunities in Britain and in some cases co-operated with British officials to this end.[42] Notwithstanding this, the agreed procedures were in place by May 1942, remaining at the centre of the vast movement of people between Ireland and Britain until the end of the war. In effect, the Irish government exercised control over virtually every aspect of the process until the individual worker left the state, though this was not an impression that the government publicised. The strict censorship allowed the government to evade any serious political discussion on the issue for the duration of the 'emergency'.

It is possible that as many as 200,000 men and women travelled to Britain during the war. The majority of them probably went to work because of the absence of employment in Ireland, though the remainder joined the armed forces, a feature discussed in more detail in other chapters in this book. Mass urban emigration weakened the possibility of serious political unrest if employment was not available, though the government is reported to have been concerned that the 'generous' conditions in Britain would 'spoil' Irish workers when

---

40 FF/342 National Executive Minutes, 24 March 1941; FF/440, Parliamentary Party minute books, 20 November 1941; 18 December 1941. Lemass had been re-appointed to the Department of Industry and Commerce in August 1941 a post he held in addition to his position as Minister for Supplies. **41** S. 11582A, Boland to de Valera, 14 July 1941. **42** For a discussion of the many issues associated with Irish labour in Britain during the second world war, see Maureen Elizabeth Hartigan, 'Irish emigration 1931-1961' MA thesis, University College, Cork, 1990.

they returned to the state. De Valera also worried that 'up to a quarter of a million' Irish citizens might return after the war, with unimaginable consequences.[43] Others feared that Irish workers would be contaminated by British socialism and that this would have a destabilising impact on Ireland. Despite this, the strategy paid off in the short term. There was very little unrest during the war in Ireland, and what there was emerged at the 1942 local government elections and the 1943 general election not in extra-parliamentary form. Furthermore, it was estimated that at least £100,000 per week was transferred to Ireland from Britain by 1942, a calculation which may have been on the low side.[44] Nor did the government have to pay welfare benefits to those who were working in Britain, but they in turn contributed to maintaining the welfare of those who remained in Ireland through their remittances. The government could also claim that emigration was not a result of its policies, but the unintended consequence of wartime.

The Irish government was not prepared to take responsibility for Irish workers once they left the state, in large part because of the difficulties this would cause for Fianna Fáil's nationalism. In Britain, what facilities were available to Irish workers were provided by the Catholic church, by the Irish community itself or by individual employers. Emigration was a most delicate matter, especially when the Labour party was criticising the government's policy in this respect. However, there was also some unease within the Fianna Fáil party itself and these pressures reinforced the government's commitment to maintain the fiction that most of the emigrants were volunteers. While strictly true, the government played a more active role in promoting emigration and co-operating with British officials to assure the continued flow of labour.[45] Yet Fianna Fáil was not averse to using its wartime power to exercise direct control over the labour force in Ireland itself. The most obvious example of this was the regulation of labour in the rural economy. In effect, those involved in agricultural employment were prohibited from leaving the state or from moving out of rural areas. While not entirely successful, these regulations did maintain an essential part of the economy in place throughout the war. Likewise, the Wages Standstill Order exercised close control over wages and salaries. The success of the former was reflected in increased agricultural output, while the impact of the latter can be measured by the real decline in income for most sectors of the population by 1945. An analysis in 1944 reported that while farmers had increased their real income by over a third since the beginning of the war, real income for most

---

43 PRO, London: Lab. 8/512/EM/7084, notes on negotiations with Irish government July 1941; S. 12882A, 'Planning for post war situation', de Valera to O'Kelly, 4 July 1942. 44 S. 11582A, estimate provided in Industry and Commerce memorandum 13 May 1942. 45 NADT: S. 11582B. Department External Affairs, 'New proposals regarding restrictions on travel permit issues to workers', 9 May 1944; this file contains correspondence from Industry and Commerce on the need to supply further labour to Britain.

employees (rural and urban) had declined by over twenty per cent on average. Whether such an outcome can be considered a 'success' for policy is a moot point, but the reality is that a substantial section of the population suffered a real decrease in disposable income. Emigration and remittances probably offset the worst of this, but nevertheless it reinforced much of the criticism of the government by the Labour Party at this time.[46]

Fianna Fáil, however, did not restrict itself to these forms of control and used the opportunity provided by the war to intervene actively in the operation of the trade union movement. Though Fianna Fáil had significant working class and trade union support, the government was uneasy about the size and influence of trade unions operating in the state but with headquarters in Britain. There had been considerable disruption in industry as a consequence of demarcation disputes among unions, a problem exacerbated by hostility between British and Irish based unions seeking to organise the same sectors. Once the war began, Fianna Fáil alleged that the presence of British unions in Ireland endangered Irish neutrality. A further concern for nationalists was that the governing body of Irish trade unionism the Irish Trade Union Congress (ITUC) included an active minority who were officials in the British based unions. Nationalists within the Irish trade union movement, especially William O'Brien of the Irish Transport and General Workers' Union (ITGWU), were committed to limiting if not excluding these unions from independent Ireland, an objective that had not been achieved by 1939. One further complication in this complex situation was the long-term rivalry between O'Brien and James Larkin, whose Workers Union of Ireland (WUI) challenged the dominance of the ITGWU.[47]

The war provided the opportunity to secure a solution to the trade union situation on terms favourable to Fianna Fáil and to nationalists within the trade union movement. Pressure quickly built up within Fianna Fáil for change and at a party meeting in April 1940 MacEntee assured his colleagues that legislation was already in preparation.[48] The original legislation was draconian, prompting one official in the department to conclude that it would 'in effect, remove the right to strike from workers employed in any of these essential services'. The legislation was consciously drawn to emphasise the 'welfare of the community' and was contrasted to the 'irresponsible' behaviour of the trade unions. The justification for constraining the actions of trade unionists was explicit:

---

46 S. 13965A, 'Cost of living' data contained in Department of Agriculture memorandum, 6 January 1947.   **47** National Library of Ireland: O'Brien Papers, Ms. 13,971. 'Papers of the Commission of Enquiry into ITUC, 1936-39'.   **48** FF/440, Parliamentary Party minutes, 8 April 1940; this was not the first time that this issue had been brought before the party. In 1938 Lemass had asked the party to defer a discussion on compulsory arbitration on the grounds that the issue was a complex one which required careful attention before action, FF/39, Parliamentary Party minutes, 3 November 1938.

Account must be taken of the protective and social services which the community at great cost has provided for industrial and commercial workers. The country is, therefore, entitled to take steps to prevent the loss and inconvenience inflicted upon the community by a major strike in any essential industry which is often greater than is sustained by either of the parties directly concerned in the dispute.

The argument here, as elsewhere in the debate, rested on the notion of the community as more than the sum of either the individuals or the groups, which composed it. This conception was hierarchical and corporatist, but essentially nationalist. The community is used throughout the legislation as a synonym for the national interest, which is considered to be superior to any individual or group rights.[49]

The original intention of the legislation proved to be too radical for the cabinet, mainly because it risked alienating O'Brien and the ITGWU. Before the war, O'Brien's proposals to rationalise the trade union movement had been defeated, an outcome he blamed on the British based unions and the WUI. O'Brien had refused to accept the verdict insisting that:

> The desire on the part of Irish workers to be in Irish unions would survive, no matter what was the majority against it. The workers of Ireland wished to take up the same independent, self-reliant position as the workers in every other country. We believe we know what the labour movement stands for in this country.[50]

In effect O'Brien invited the government to intervene in the affairs of the movement. Once it was decided to revise the proposals, the new legislation reflected O'Brien's proposals to a large extent. MacEntee not only drew on O'Brien's proposals but departmental officials met him and other members of the ITGWU executive 'for the purpose of eliciting from these gentlemen the precise intention at the back of the proposals contained in the report'.[51] By this stage the government was effectively conceding to one union considerable influence over legislation which that union would directly benefit from. More importantly the nature of the legislation changed. The primary objective was now to provide direct state control over the movement by introducing a system of negotiating licences and

49 TIW. 766: Industry and Commerce memorandum, 14 March 1940; R.C. Ferguson, memorandum on trade union bill, 2 April 1940.   **50** Irish Trade Union Congress, *45th Annual Report* (Dublin, 1939), p. 153.   **51** TIW. 766, ITGWU to Industry and commerce, 27 June 1940; minute 12 August 1940; minute reporting meetings with O'Brien and others, 23 September 1940; 7 October 1940; 11 October 1940; O'Brien insisted that no detailed record of the meeting should be kept.

the requirement that a deposit be made in the high court without which a union would not be able to operate. The implicit intention of this approach was to effectively eliminate the WUI and to force consolidation on smaller unions, thus benefiting the ITGWU. The other objective of the legislation involved establishing a tribunal to determine which union was representative of workers in specific sectors and industries. The objective here was to circumscribe the activities of the British based unions and to eventually deny them a presence in Ireland. Such was the partiality of MacEntee by late 1940 to O'Brien that the department altered the legislation in detail to accommodate objections from the ITGWU.[52] Once the legislation was passed, opposition was muted and divided as the ITGWU effectively supported the government. Within a relatively short period of time a majority of trade unions had complied with the legislation.[53]

A number of considerations help to explain this outcome. Given Fianna Fáil's view of neutrality, the government was reluctant to accept the continued presence of British based unions in the state. While disputes between British and Irish unions were considered serious in peacetime, they could and were characterised as hostile to the national interest during the war. There were even those who believed that it was in the British interest to disrupt the Irish economy.[54]

Within the trade union movement itself, there were serious divisions between those, primarily O'Brien and the ITGWU, who advocated total support for Irish neutrality on nationalist grounds, and those who, while not necessarily opposing neutrality, identified with the anti-Fascist aspect of the war especially after the Soviet Union entered the conflict. In these circumstances it was in the government's interest to assert control over trade unionism and to break, wherever possible, the institutional connection with the United Kingdom. The 1941 Trade Union Act also broke decisively with the voluntaristic aspects of the 1906 Trade Disputes Act, the cornerstone of British industrial relations, which had been applicable in Ireland as well. British trade unionism was deemed inappropriate in Ireland, in part because of the rural nature of the society but also because of the nationalist basis of economic and social policy. The continuation of British legislation in Ireland and the institutional relationship between organised labour in the two countries were anomalies for a society under Fianna Fáil control. It should also be considered that a significant proportion of the Irish

---

52 TIW. 766, draft head of Bill November 1940 for detail; see also Brian Girvin, 'Protection and economic development in independent Ireland 1922-1960', unpublished Ph.D. (National University of Ireland, 1986), pp 146-98 for a detailed discussion of this legislation; Kieran Allen, *Fianna Fáil and Irish labour*, pp 72-82.   53 S. 12279A, 'Trade Union organisation', ITUC to Taoiseach, 20 January 1942; Lemass to Taoiseach 9 February 1942.   54 Department of Justice. S. 51/39, J. J. Walsh to department 5 November 1942 claiming sabotage in his factories. It should be noted that Walsh was a leading advocate of corporatism within industry and had pro-Nazi sympathies.

Table 1 Percentage vote, number of seats and turnout at
general elections, 1938, 1943, 1944 [% vote (seats)]

	1938	*1943*	*1944*
Fianna Fáil	51.9 (77)	41.9 (67)	48.9 (76)
Fine Gael	33.3 (45)	23.1 (32)	20.5 (30)
Labour	10.0 (9)	15.7 (17)	8.8 (8)
National Labour	– –	– –	2.7 (4)
Clann na Talmhan	– –	9.8 (11)	10.1 (9)
Others	4.7 (7)	9.6 (11)	9.1 (11)
Turnout (%)	75.8	73.8	68.5
Votes Cast	1,286,667	1,331,709	1,217,349

Source: Michael Gallagher, *Irish elections 1922-1944: results and analysis* (Limerick, 1993)

working class voted for Fianna Fáil for nationalist reasons, as well as for welfare or economic benefits. The 1941 Act was promoted by Fianna Fáil and the ITGWU as the de-Anglicisation of Irish trade unionism and the extension of nationalist control over an important segment of the nation. The trade unions had successfully avoided regulation by the Irish State during the 1930s, while benefiting from Fianna Fáil legislation. As a consequence of the 1941 Act and developments during the war, its continued existence depended on the movement complying with the new regulations.

The decisive action against the trade union movement in 1941 highlights Fianna Fáil's determination to use the issue of neutrality to achieve specifically domestic objectives. In the circumstances, it might be anticipated that Fianna Fáil would benefit from its undoubted success in protecting the state's sovereignty and providing the basic necessities to survive. However, the local government elections held on 19 August 1942 were a reminder that no democratic government can guarantee an electoral outcome. Turnout was low, attributable in part to the absence of motor transport but also perhaps to voter apathy. Whatever the reasons, a great number of voters rejected both Fianna Fáil and Fine Gael at the polls. The most striking change came in Dublin where Labour doubled its first preference vote compared to the 1936 election, while increasing its representation from 2 seats to 12. This trend was confirmed in many other areas of the country; the Fianna Fáil vote declined by about 50 per cent and that for Fine Gael by about a third. Labour was also successful outside Dublin, but so too were independent farmer, Clann na Talmhan and ratepayer candidates.[55] It was remarked

55 For details of vote, which is incomplete, and analysis see *Irish Times*, 20, 21, 22, 24 August 1942.

at the time that these results did not necessarily reflect a wider trend against the government, but this proved to be ill founded and the trend apparent in 1942 was further confirmed at the 1943 general election. The most obvious feature of this election was the decline in the Fianna Fáil and Fine Gael vote as well as the consolidation of their 1942 success by the Labour Party and Clann na Talmhan. Table 1 traces the changes in party support between 1938 to 1944.

The two main parties again lost seats, Labour and Clann na Talmhan made significant inroads, while the vote for independents doubled. In 1938 Fianna Fáil and Fine Gael accounted for 85 per cent of the first preferences cast, whereas by 1943 this had fallen to 64 per cent. Turnout was only marginally down on 1938, though the number of those who voted actually increased. The only conclusion to be drawn is that Fianna Fáil and Fine Gael suffered a severe setback in 1943, confirming the trend established in 1942, though the trends were not consistent. While Fianna Fáil lost 10 seats, it held its own in the Dublin region despite Labour successes. The further west one goes the heavier the Fianna Fáil losses, attributable in large part to the strength of Clann na Talmhan. However, the pattern for Fine Gael was even worse. Not only did it have a net loss of 13 seats, but the party did especially badly in Munster (-5) and Connacht Ulster (-4). If anything, at this election Fine Gael was more prone to Clann na Talmhan than Fianna Fáil, but in fact suffered everywhere. If the three general elections between 1938 and 1944 are analysed, it is Fine Gael, which experienced a downward trend in electoral support, something the party leadership recognised in 1945 when it concluded pessimistically that the party was weak and ineffective.[56] In this context Fianna Fáil's difficulties in 1942 and 1943 can be seen as short-term, after which the party recovered. The change in Fianna Fáil fortunes can be seen in regional terms in table 2.

Table 2 Number of seats won in each region by Fianna Fáil, 1938-44

	1938	*1943*	*1944*
Dublin	12	11	14
Rest of Leinster	16	14	15
Munster	25	22	25
Connacht-Ulster	24	20	22
Ireland	77 (138)	67 (138)	76 (138)

Source: Michael Gallagher, *Irish elections 1922-44: results and analysis* (Limerick, 1993).

56 UCDA: Fine Gael Archives, General Purposes Committee, November 14 1945.

It has been suggested that the rise of Clann na Talmhan was fortuitous for Fianna Fáil, because it allowed the party to distance itself from the small farmer vote.[57] Such a suggestion is doubtful when the time and resources invested by Fianna Fáil to regain the vote in 1944 is taken into account.

One of the surprising features of the 1943 election was the failure of Fine Gael to benefit from Fianna Fáil's difficulties. It is clear that the electorate did not see much difference between the two parties, especially on the national question. Once Fine Gael and Fianna Fáil were agreed on neutrality, traditional Fine Gael supporters may have been more inclined to consider voting for other parties and for economic reasons rather than national ones. The rise of Clann na Talmhan can in part be explained by this development, though of course Fianna Fáil was not unaffected by the emergence of a Farmers' party. Seán MacEntee openly accepted that the divisions between the two parties had been seriously eroded, agreeing with Richard Mulcahy that the differences between the Fine Gael and Fianna Fáil were 'now merely a matter of personality'. MacEntee urged Fine Gael to accept the need for 'national unity' on the grounds that the Irish state remained in danger. But he also demanded that it recognise the contribution which de Valera had made, 'I am sure that in their hearts many of the Fine Gael leaders rejoiced at what under his leadership this Nation has accomplished'.[58] While Fine Gael was unlikely to go this far, it is probable that sections of the electorate accepted this and voted accordingly. One consequence of this was that the anti-government vote went to Labour, Clann na Talmhan and independents. The most obvious explanation for the outcome was that this was a warning to Fianna Fáil, generated by dissatisfaction with wartime restrictions, shortages and emigration. In Dublin and other urban centres, working class voters were protesting against the wage standstill order and the erosion of income. Clann na Talmhan success was based on rural hostility to urban industrial priorities and a rejection of the political system as corrupt. Clann na Talmhan success was in areas of high emigration and relatively small farms. The party was essentially an anti-system movement, similar to others in Europe at the time.[59]

After the election and the formation of a minority government, Fianna Fáil looked for a scapegoat and found it in Seán MacEntee. He had engaged in a vigorous and often acrimonious campaign, attacking each of the opposition parties with varying degrees of venom. His most scathing comments were reserved for the Labour Party whom he criticised for being soft on communism and for not supporting the government in the face of external threat. He was

57 Dunphy, *The making of Fianna Fáil power in Ireland*, p. 235. 58 P67/364, Speech at Harold's Cross Bridge, 7 June 1943. 59 Michael Gallagher, *Electoral support for Irish political parties, 1927-1973* (London and Beverly Hills, 1976), pp 23-4, 53-5; Richard Sinnott, *Irish Voters Decide* (Manchester, 1995), pp 131-34; Tony Varley and Peter Moser, 'Clann na Talmhan Ireland's last farmers' party' *History Ireland*, Summer 1995, pp 39-43.

particularly critical of James Larkin's candidature for the Labour Party, in effect supporting O'Brien's objections. He also identified a number of individuals in the Labour Party who he claimed had been or still were communists. He frequently took the opportunity to defend the 1941 Trade Union Act, accusing the British-based unions of divided loyalties. MacEntee fought a campaign that highlighted the national interest, while suggesting that all other parties were somewhat suspect in this respect. Moreover, he was genuinely concerned by the influence of communism in Ireland, especially after the entry of the Soviet Union into the war.[60] The Communist Party of Ireland had dissolved itself into the Labour Party in 1941, rather than continue a separate existence in opposition to neutrality. Larkin had once been a communist and there were also concerns about the growing influence of communism in Northern Ireland. Furthermore, MacEntee and others shared O'Brien's hostility to Larkin, the WUI and the left within the Labour Party. MacEntee's interventions were criticised by leading members of Fianna Fáil, including Lemass, because it threatened the party's working class base. Lemass claimed that Fianna Fáil canvassers in working class areas were reporting that the party could not expect transfers from Labour unless criticism was modified.[61] Gerry Boland also blamed MacEntee for the loss of seats outside Dublin, charges, which were endorsed at a party meeting, held on Friday 18 June 1943. MacEntee was dismayed when de Valera joined in the criticism, offering his resignation as a consequence. He claimed that this was not the first time de Valera had criticised him, but it was the first time he had done so in public:

> On this occasion, however, you chose to attack me before those with whom, hitherto, I have been sitting as an equal in the cabinet, and it is not possible for me to allow it to pass in the same way. Nor are you now dependent on others for what may be read. ...
>
> Once again you have acted on hearsay and upon the misleading presentments with which you have been furnished of my campaign. You have given your verdict upon them.[62]

MacEntee mounted a scathing attack on his detractors within the party, defending his strategy during the election. He, in turn, condemned his colleagues for not supporting government policy with equal vigour, insisting that, unlike theirs, his campaign had been a successful one.

---

60 P67/363, Speech at Sligo Fianna Fáil Convention, 29 May 1943; Speech at Ringsend, no date; P67/364, Speech at Harold's Cross Bridge 7 June 1943; Richard Dunphy, *The Making of Fianna Fáil power in Ireland*, pp 287-92; see also P67/522, 528, 548 for MacEntee's continuing interest in the communist question in Ireland. **61** P67/363, Lemass to MacEntee, 10 June 1943. **62** P67/366, MacEntee to de Valera 28 June 1943

In a detailed rebuttal of the charges, he highlighted a number of weaknesses in party organisation and individual constituencies, which accounted for the outcome. For example, Boland had asserted that MacEntee's speeches had contributed to the loss of Daniel O'Rourke's seat in Roscommon. This charge was rejected on the grounds that he had not spoken in the constituency, countering that Boland, who was elected, had not actively defended Fianna Fáil's policy on wages and trade unions which would have, he claimed, attracted more Labour voters to the party. However, a more likely explanation for Fianna Fáil's failure in Roscommon was the presence of three Clann na Talmhan candidates, two of whom were elected. A plurality of Labour transfers and a majority of Fine Gael's went to Clann na Talmhan candidates, assuring them of victory. Moreover, when Boland's own surplus was distributed, O'Rourke received less than 60 per cent while the remainder went to Clann na Talmhan. MacEntee also suggested that some losses were to be expected due to the exceptional 1938 result and that the 1937 election provided a more realistic comparison. The intervention of Clann na Talmhan and independents, as well as the weakness of Fine Gael further accounted for the results. [63]

In urban constituencies circumstances were somewhat different. MacEntee claimed that voters had been misled by Fine Gael and Labour Party propaganda on wages, the trade union act and shortages, while public sector workers had been dissatisfied with their income. However, he reserved his severest comments for his fellow Dublin-based TDs whose poor performance, he asserted, contributed to defeat. He contrasted the outcome in a number of Dublin constituencies with that in his own Dublin Townships. In Dublin Northwest there were serious divisions in the organisation and one section of the party had refused to work for the candidate. In Dublin county, Tommy Mullins, one of the sitting TDs, had decided late in the day to withdraw as a candidate, leaving little time to put a new one in place. Also, in a number of constituencies, former Fianna Fáil members stood for other parties or as independents and in some cases won. MacEntee was particularly scathing about party organisation in the election, arguing that seats were lost, 'because of the weak and feeble direction of the campaign from Headquarters', suggesting that his own success was attributable to a well-organised campaign which vigorously promoted party policy. He also believed that his position on wages or trade unions had not alienated the working class vote for him, nor had it affected the election of Frank Aiken in the neighbouring constituency. [64]

It is difficult to judge if this rejoinder had an impact on de Valera, but MacEntee did not retire from politics and was included in the government subsequently formed. Not that the government lasted long, de Valera took the first

---

63 P67/366 ibid. The best known of these independents was Oliver J. Flanagan elected in Laois–Offaly. **64** Ibid.

opportunity to dissolve the Dáil and call a new election for 30 May 1944. As can be seen from Tables 1 and 2 Fianna Fáil recovered many of the seats lost in 1943 and also increased its first preference vote. The 1944 election was fought without the complacency of 1943 and the party seems to have been better organised than previously. Fianna Fáil also benefited from Allied criticism of Ireland's refusal to expel Axis diplomats early in 1944.

The opposition parties were less well prepared and suffered as a consequence. The loss of further seats and the retirement of W.T. Cosgrave as leader compounded Fine Gael's difficulties in 1943 in 1944. The impact of Cosgrave's retirement can be seen in Cork Borough, where the party vote collapsed and a local businessman and former Fine Gael candidate was elected on the first count. Nor by this stage did the Labour Party pose a threat to Fianna Fáil. As a consequence of James Larkin's election in 1943, the ITGWU disaffiliated from the Labour Party early in 1944 and TDs associated with the union formed a breakaway party the National Labour Party (NLP) which won four seats in the election. The split was actively promoted by O'Brien, reflecting a new consensus between Fianna Fáil and a significant section of the trade union movement on issues such as neutrality, nationalism and catholic social policy. It is open to debate whether a united Labour Party would have maintained its previous success, but the pressure from O'Brien and Fianna Fáil certainly undermined that possibility. By early 1945 the trade union movement itself was also divided along similar lines.[65]

MacEntee fought a more cautious campaign in 1944, emphasising the positive and welfare aspects of Fianna Fáil policy. He obviously felt little urgency in criticising Labour with his previous vigour now that the party was split and National Labour was so close in ideology to Fianna Fáil. Despite its success in the election, the outcome also contained a warning for the party. An analysis prepared for the national executive concluded that the party could no longer depend on transfers from other parties to secure election, noting that in 1944 seats were lost because voters did not vote for all the Fianna Fáil candidates on the list. Vote management and party discipline were now considered to be the most important factors in maintaining a Fianna Fáil majority. The report noted that the pattern of transfers from Labour, 'revealed definite hostility to Fianna Fáil', but that those from National Labour were more positive. In virtually all other cases transfers were circulated among non-Fianna Fáil parties. The conclusion to this report provides an important insight into Fianna Fáil thinking at this time, asserting a view of politics that was to remain central to the party until the 1980s:

65 O'Brien Papers, Ms. 13960 for correspondence between O'Brien and P.J. O'Brien on the origins of the NLP; NLI: Johnson Papers, Ms. 17197 contains papers on the ITGWU disaffiliation from the Labour Party.

It is obvious from the above report that Fianna Fáil, in 1944, secured victory by its own strength and superior party voting. The hostility of the various opposition groups is revealed in the transfers. There is no reason to suppose that this hostility will diminish and Fianna Fáil, should therefore, concentrate, not on securing first preference votes, but in ensuring that supporters vote for the whole team ... The corollary to these suggestions is also of importance. Canvassing for any one individual is most harmful to a good party vote and every effort should be made to suppress it, where its existence becomes known.[66]

While Fianna Fáil's position at the centre of the political system was reaffirmed in 1944, the party's own analysis highlighted a crucial dilemma for it. If Fianna Fáil could not depend on transfers from other parties to achieve a majority and if it refused to entertain formal coalition arrangements, political success was heavily dependent on its own effective organisation and the intense loyalty of its voters. Between 1927 and 1944 these conditions had been meet on most occasions, yet the party leadership could not guarantee that Fianna Fáil supporters and its voters would endorse its view of Irish politics as 'Fianna Fáil versus the Rest'.[67]

There is a danger of reading back Fianna Fáil's difficulties at the 1948 election into the period 1944-46. Fianna Fáil had not been weakened by the war, though one should not underestimate the difficulties encountered. It remained well placed in 1945 to maintain its dominant position. It was the opposition that remained weak and fragmented, while no party at this stage seemed able to offer an alternative. Fianna Fáil did well in by-elections immediately after the war and it is only in 1947 that a more substantial threat in the form of Clann na Poblachta emerges.[68] If anything, the wartime experience reinforced the domestic consensus already strong in 1939. Fianna Fáil's achievements were now openly accepted by the opposition, especially neutrality, the constitution and socio-economic policy. The party moved to the centre of a political system around which the other parties orbited. It had become *the* national party as well as the largest nationalist party. Neutrality had played an important role in achieving this consensus. Virtually no one doubted the value of neutrality during or after the war and this complemented the isolationist and protectionist nature of the political culture. As a result Fine Gael gave up its last emotional links to the Commonwealth.[69]

66 FF/793, 'General Election report-1944', prepared by Seán Bonner for the Director of Elections, Seán Lemass, 27 August 1944. **67** Tom Garvin, *The evolution of Irish nationalist politics* (Dublin, 1981), pp 160-78; Peter Mair, *The changing Irish party system* (New York, 1987). **68** UCDA: P39/1/2, Fine Gael General Purposes Committee, meeting of party leadership 14 November 1945; Eithne MacDermott, *Clann na Poblachta* (Cork, 1998). **69** Hogan, *Election and representation*, pp 33-6.

Neutrality was not merely an aspect of Irish diplomacy; it also served the political needs of Fianna Fáil. During the war, the government used neutrality as a political weapon to coerce the opposition and the public into conformity. There was no debate on issues, nor were alternatives discussed in any realistic sense. Censorship was used to constrain open discussion on this topic, if not actually to prevent alternative views from appearing. Fianna Fáil may well have believed that the use of censorship was not politically biased, but this is difficult to sustain.[70] De Valera equated the national interest with that of Fianna Fáil, thus legitimising the use of censorship in the pursuit of party objectives. This is not to suggest that neutrality was unpopular, but that it was used for party political ends and censorship was used to prevent other views from appearing.

There was a danger for Fianna Fáil in this consensus. If political competition narrowed appreciably, then voters would not have a strong incentive to remain committed to a particular party. In these circumstances Fianna Fáil could find it difficult to maintain voter loyalty, a feature of the 1947 by elections. Fianna Fáil's loss of office in 1948 confirmed that 'Fianna Fáil versus the Rest' was now the main feature of elections, but it also demonstrated the extent of political consensus within the system. It is perhaps ironic that Fianna Fáil's political, ideological and policy success should provide the conditions for its replacement in government. This consensus reinforced continuity generally in Ireland after 1945.

Wartime often provides the opportunity for political cultures to change direction, as proved to be the case in Europe at this time. In Ireland, however, there is virtually no evidence of political, social or economic change during or after the war. Emigration continued its wartime pattern, demonstrating forcefully that the socio-economic arrangements established by Fianna Fáil could not provide the basis for full employment or higher living standards in independent Ireland. Policymaking remained ineffective, highlighted by Lemass's failure to secure support for his innovative developmental strategy between 1944 and 1946. Moreover, though Ireland was relatively prosperous in comparative terms in 1945, this advantage was eroded within a decade. At the end of the war, Ireland was faced with serious challenges, which were not met. Irish isolationism during the war bred a political complacency which valued continuity over change. Traditional values were favoured over innovation and the cost was the decline of the economy over the next twenty years. Consequently, the Second World War was not a point of departure for Ireland, but it was for the significant minority who were forced to leave the state to find employment and a better life elsewhere.[71]

---

70 Donal Ó Drisceoil, *Censorship in Ireland 1939-1945* (Cork, 1996), pp 220-83 for the most recent study of the application of censorship.   71 Brian Girvin, 'Political culture, political independence and economic success in Ireland', in *Irish political studies*, 12 (1997), pp 48-77.

Northern Ireland: the impact of war 1939–45

Brian Barton

The Second World War was, arguably, a turning point in Northern Ireland's history. Significant aspects of the province's political life did not, of course, change then. The distorted nature of its internal institutions and structures, the extent of its sectarian divisions and the depth of the 'gulf' in its relations with southern Ireland which have each proved enduring features, have much earlier roots. Nonetheless, in one vital area there was change: the global conflict was the crucial context for the emergence of much warmer relations between Stormont and Westminster, and this subsequently provided the basis for the North's best years, the 1950s and early 1960s. Such a development could not easily have been foreseen when the war began. On 4 September 1939, the day following Britain's entry, Lord Craigavon promised a tense and expectant Commons at Stormont that there would be 'no slackening in [Ulster's] loyalty. There is no falling off in our determination to place the whole of our resources at the command of the [imperial] government ... Anything we can do here to facilitate them ... they have only just got to let us know.'[1] In fact from the earliest stages of the conflict a stark and, for some local ministers, embarrassing, contrast rapidly emerged between the province's wartime experience and that found elsewhere in the United Kingdom. In the former, attitudes, patterns of behaviour and the overall pace of life were uniquely static and unchanging.

Of course, a measure of disruption could not entirely be avoided. Within the first six months of war rationing had forced some modification in public consumption. Travel restrictions and censorship had resulted in a progressive narrowing of cultural life, while parts of the province were already struggling to absorb the burgeoning military camps being occupied by British troops. Nevertheless, during the spring of 1940, a Belfast diarist was justified in describing Northern Ireland as 'probably the pleasantest place in Europe', adding, 'We are unbombed, we have no conscription, there is plenty to eat and life is reasonably normal'.[2] The perpetuation of 'normality' extended to other, less desirable, peacetime characteristics. The province's industrial capacity was being seriously

1 Northern Ireland Parliamentary Debates (C), vol. 23, 4 September 1939, col. 1902. 2 Tom Harrisson, Mass Observation Archive (University of Sussex), diary MO 5462, entry for 7 March 1940; also Brian Barton, *The blitz: Belfast in the war years* (Belfast, 1989), pp 43-4.

under-utilised. In December 1940, after 15 months of hostilities, not a single new factory had been constructed. The shipyards in Belfast alone had benefited from substantial war contracts and the overall level of unemployment was similar to that experienced by Great Britain in 1932, the trough of the great depression. An official report to this effect prompted Churchill to initiate an immediate, full-scale, governmental investigation.[3] In addition, informed British visitors were shocked by the entirely different atmosphere which they detected in Northern Ireland, when compared with other regions of the United Kingdom. The absence of any real sense of urgency regarding the war effort and the general slackness in public attitudes prompted one experienced observer to speculate that if anyone were to behave in London or Liverpool as they were continuing to do in Belfast, they would at once be noticeable and might even cause a riot.[4] There is no lack of evidence to corroborate these impressions, including the persistently low level of military enlistment in the province, the recurrence of disruptive labour disputes throughout its major industries, the inferior output and productivity of its largest munitions factories compared with similar firms in Great Britain and the pervasive apathy towards and consequential inadequacy of its civil defence provision. These features may be explained by such factors as Northern Ireland's relative remoteness from the theatre of conflict and Westminster, as well as its internal sectional divisions and the absence of conscription. A further vital consideration was the complacency and ineffectiveness of the Stormont government.

Shortly before the outbreak of war, Sir Wilfrid Spender, head of the Northern Ireland civil service, wrote in his diary a devastating indictment of the collective incompetence of Craigavon and his colleagues. He itemised their serious 'mistakes' and expressed deep concern at the resulting decline in popular support and respect for their leadership. He reflected on the prime minister's alarming tendency to make important decisions in a casual, hasty manner and noted with apprehension that owing to the deterioration in his health he was unable to perform more than one hour's work daily. He concluded that Sir James was too unwell to carry on, though informed medical opinion warned that any drastic or enforced change in his lifestyle might prove fatal. Sir Wilfrid also considered that at least two other senior ministers ought to retire immediately as they too were suffering from prolonged and incapacitating illness. He observed of a third that though he was the main focus of public criticism, he was nonetheless on holiday abroad at the time and that 'his decisions his officials cannot count on'. As a consequence of the cabinet's shared inadequacy, the main burden of government fell on the willing, though ageing, shoulders of the Minister of Finance, J.M.

3 Churchill to Ernest Bevin, 23 January 1941, in PRONI COM 61/440; also B. Barton, *Brookeborough: the making of a prime minister* (Belfast, 1988), pp 172-3.   4 Tom Harrisson Mass Observation Archive, op. cit., report FR 1309, dated 12 June 1942.

Andrews. Spender concluded dejectedly that if the present loose conduct of affairs continued, it would do irreparable harm to the unionist cause and would even pose a threat to the survival of democracy itself in Northern Ireland.[5]

When war began 12 months later, the composition of the Stormont cabinet was unchanged. Against his own inclination, Craigavon had been persuaded by his wife to remain in office, mainly for reasons of financial necessity and social ambition; though she was apparently unaware of the extent to which the progressive deterioration in his health had impaired his capacity for leadership. He led his colleagues in increasingly dictatorial and whimsical fashion, in the process straining the proper functioning of the cabinet system to breaking point. He habitually reached important decisions without prior discussions with the ministers most concerned; on occasion, he encouraged colleagues to act on their own responsibility or after consultation with himself; he brought his chief whip, Lord Glentoran, more into his confidence than the members of his cabinet. Craigavon's most characteristic response to the increasing gravity and volume of attacks on his government was either to make grossly extravagant claims regarding the success of its policies or attempt to silence critics through concessions only justified by political expediency. These ranged from grants and subsidies, to the creation of a new department, with responsibility for civil defence, the Ministry of Public Security. But they fell short of what was most stridently sought – a change in the composition of the cabinet itself. Edmund Warnock, one of two junior ministers to resign on this issue protested with justification: noting that 'death, old age or promotion' were the only cause of changes in cabinet membership and that no one had ever been replaced 'because of incapacity or failure'.[6]

Criticism of the government focussed mainly on its failure to reduce unemployment or make adequate provision for civil defence and on its persistent equivocation over matters such as education, electricity and transport. The marked deterioration in the strategic position of the western allies by mid-1940 and the formation of a more dynamic administration at Westminster made the fumbling ineptitude of Craig and his colleagues seem even more indefensible. These considerations and, more particularly, the entirely unsatisfactory relationship between the Home Affairs ministry and the British military authorities based in Northern Ireland, prompted Spender to predict that the imperial government would before long impose martial law. In December 1939, he had observed ruefully: 'there is one factory in which we could probably claim that we or the Free State are the largest manufacturers – namely the factory of grievances'.[7] Apart from Sir Basil Brooke's success in raising tillage output on Ulster's farms, decisive government measures

5 PRONI: D715, Spender diary, Personal memorandum, 2 August 1938. 6 Northern Ireland Parliamentary Debates (C), vol. 23, 25 September 1940, col. 2155. 7 Spender diary, op. cit., Nov. 1939–4 May 1940, p. 84, also 16 December 1940.

were restricted almost exclusively to security matters, where ministers displayed their customary zeal. The major steps taken were, of course, initiated by Westminster (from the spring of 1940) and were common to regions throughout the United Kingdom. These included the introduction of an identity card system, restrictions on travel, the censorship of mail and of trunk telephone calls, controls on the press, the imprisonment of male enemy aliens, the formation of a local home guard and Auxiliary Territorial Service and the devising of administrative arrangements in case of 'emergency' – specifically German invasion or the breakdown of communications with London.

However, not all of the actions taken in the province were a mere replication of those being implemented in Great Britain. As the official war history of the six counties states, 'The British in their extremity could ... take no risks ... [and] ... in Northern Ireland the dangers confronting them were all the greater, because of the 'open' frontier with Éire and the existence of a potential 'fifth column' in the form of the Irish Republican Army.'[8] These considerations were reinforced by the government's profound distrust of the Catholic minority. Thus on the first night of the war internment was introduced and directed against IRA suspects. Subsequently special constabulary patrols were increased and the movement of persons across the Irish border closely monitored. Such measures may be regarded as justified by the virtual absence of internal civil disorder during the conflict; the IRA had become quiescent by late 1940. Meanwhile, in May, the imperial government had permitted Stormont ministers to emulate the protection arrangements being made in Britain by raising a force of Local Defence Volunteers. But given the political divisions within Northern Ireland this was not raised on the same basis as elsewhere in the United Kingdom. Despite strong representations from opposition MPs, Craigavon insisted that the 'B' specials should form its nucleus. Soon afterwards, given Westminster's unwillingness to apply conscription and embarrassed by the province's persistently low levels of voluntary enlistment, he asked Brooke to organise a military recruiting drive. The resulting eight-week campaign held in July-August, proved to be largely ineffective; reliance throughout on the unionist party machine must have discouraged recruitment for the minority.

During the spring of 1940 such concerns had been eclipsed by another, infinitely more grave and potentially more divisive. From April onwards, Stormont ministers and officials watched the current Anglo-Irish trade talks with growing apprehension. They feared that constitutional issues would be raised, with de Valera possibly offering, or being asked, to trade Irish neutrality for an end to partition. From late May, against the background of the Dunkirk evacuation and the fall of France, Craig came under more intense pressure from Westminster than at any time since 1921. Initially he was asked to make constructive sugges-

---

8 J.W. Blake, *Northern Ireland in the Second World War* (Belfast, 1956), p. 171.

tions as to how the Taoiseach might be drawn into meaningful discussions about the defence of Ireland; later, more ominously, he was invited to attend open-ended negotiations with the southern leader in London. His response was as inflexible as it had been 20 years before, his priority remained the preservation of the six counties within the United Kingdom. He adamantly refused to partici-pate in an inter-governmental conference before the south had abandoned its neutrality and, under any circumstances, if constitutional matters were to be considered. By mid-June, however, there are indications that a split was emerg-ing inside the Stormont cabinet. Both Brooke and John MacDermott (Minister of Public Security) were apparently prepared to accept a change in Northern Ireland's constitutional status if, in response, Éire proved willing to enter the war on the allied side. In their view, loyalty to King and empire and the defeat of the axis powers transcended their commitment to the maintenance of the union. To their immense relief the crisis passed without the issue being put to the test, as de Valera flatly refused to abandon Irish neutrality, mainly due to his assumption that the allies would be defeated and also because he anticipated irreparable divi-sions in the south if he altered his policy.[9]

On 29 October 1940, Craigavon made his last, major speech in parliament – a typically, impassioned assault on an opposition motion in favour of Irish unity. Four weeks later on 24 November, he died peacefully at his home. Spender noted that he had finally 'thrown off all the weight of illness and cares that had hung so heavily upon him during the last few years of his life'.[10] Next day, after taking private soundings, the governor, Lord Abercorn, asked John Andrews to form a government. He accepted, but his agreement was contingent on his being selected leader of the Unionist party. Some informed opinion regarded this con-dition as both procedurally wrong and politically inept, as it was likely to preju-dice his authority during the initial weeks of his premiership. Andrews' succes-sion was widely regarded as inevitable and deserving on grounds of his seniority and experience. It was, nonetheless, greeted with resignation rather than enthu-siasm and, it has been suggested, that Craigavon himself might have actually preferred Brooke. Sir James, however, had resolutely refused to nominate a suc-cessor and at the time Brooke betrayed no expectation of preferment or trace of disappointment. Rather he backed the new premier 'for all he is worth' and, along with Sir Wilfrid Spender, urged upon him on several occasions the politi-cal necessity of making far-reaching cabinet changes.[11] Unwisely, Andrews reject-ed this advice. He appointed just one new minister, Lord Glentoran, the Chief Whip, became Minister of Agriculture. From the outset it seemed unlikely that a 'new' government composed of the 'old guard' would be capable of responding

---

9 See J. Bowman, *De Valera and the Ulster question* (Oxford, 1982), pp 220-38; J.T. Carroll, *Ireland in the war years 1939-45* (Newton Abbot, 1975), pp 49-59. **10** Spender diary, op. cit., entry 26 November 1940. **11** PRONI: D3004/D, Brooke diary, 27 November 1940.

adequately to the frustration and disillusionment evident amongst unionist backbenchers, junior ministers and even within the party beyond Stormont. Hitherto, 'no attempt at revolt could survive Lord Craigavon's frown'.[12]

Andrews was unfortunate to have become prime minister in almost his seventieth year, when his health had begun to fail and in the context of total war. In family background, personality and experience he was ill-equipped to provide the leadership necessary in the supreme crisis. Inevitably, his personal appeal was lessened by his long and close identification with Craigavon's increasingly unpopular administration, while in his choice of cabinet he did nothing to reduce the negative force of this inheritance. The fall of his government was arguably the most dramatic episode in Northern Ireland's early political history. But from its inception it appeared ineffective and vulnerable. In March 1941, it lost its first by-election, in Craigavon's old seat, whilst in the commons unionist members were described as 'not inclined to give any support ... whenever they can find an excuse for abstaining'.[13] Over the course of the next two years backbench criticism tended to rise and the cabinet suffered from diminishing morale and growing fractiousness. Andrews' premiership began inauspiciously, neither its confidence nor its prestige were enhanced by the German air-raids of April–May 1941. Due mainly to earlier ministerial neglect and prevarication Northern Ireland's active and passive defences were hopelessly inadequate and the public psychologically unprepared for severe aerial bombardment. In the course of four attacks on Belfast at least 1,100 people died, 56,000 houses were damaged and £20 million damage was caused to property (at current values). Fear and panic reached epidemic proportions; perhaps as many as 220,000 fled from the city. The collapse in civilian morale prompted MacDermott to predict attacks on the parliamentary buildings at Stormont by an irate and frightened populace.[14]

The blitz exacerbated the government's problems and confirmed its directionless, hesitant posture. The province's experience of the raids helped focus interest on the conscription issue. During the aftermath of the assault, MacDermott advocated its introduction as an essential means of restoring communal discipline and achieving equality of sacrifice. Others, notably Lord Abercorn, also advised it, encouraging Andrews, to 'strike when people's feelings are hot'.[15] Meanwhile, quite independently, on 12 May 1941, Ernest Bevin, sug-

---

12 PRO FO 371/29108, Comment by H. Shaw, in report to the Foreign Office, 1 January 1941. 13 Spender diary, op. cit., 1 March 1941. 14 MacDermott discussed this with Spender, ibid., 15, 31 May 1941. See also Barton, *The blitz*, op. cit., pp 233-40. A Ministry of Home Affairs report estimated that during the aftermath of the 5 May 1941 air raid, a total of 220,000 people may have evacuated from the city. In addition, thousands of others remained in Belfast but 'trekked' into the suburbs and beyond nightly, returning shortly before dawn, by which time, they believed there was little danger of a raid occurring. 15 PRONI CAB(CD/217: O.

gested to the imperial war cabinet that its application to Northern Ireland should be given further consideration in view of Britain's deteriorating strategic position.[16] During the resulting negotiations, held at Westminster on 24 May, the response of Stormont ministers was unequivocably enthusiastic. Nonetheless, three days later, on 27 May, British ministers decided against extension. This was due to accumulating evidence of opposition from Éire, the United States and Canada and, crucially, from within Northern Ireland itself. The Nationalist MPs and senators had orchestrated a province wide, anti-conscription campaign, with Catholic church support, culminating in a mass rally on Sunday, 25 May. This had impressed Andrews in particular. On his own initiative he immediately contacted the Home Office and indicated that the level of resistance would be greater than anticipated. He advised that the 'real test ... must be whether it [conscription] would be for the good of the Empire'.[17] Almost immediately the British government issued a statement which concluded that its application would be 'more trouble than it was worth'.[18] The preceding policy vacillations on the part of the Stormont administration can only have served to reduce its credibility at Westminster and to raise serious doubts as to the quality of its leadership. Within the province, the final outcome was no doubt in the best interests of public order, but the government had failed to implement its publicly stated policy and its political opponents might reasonably claim a victory.

By the autumn of 1941, Andrews was convinced that his political position had become stronger but a second by-election defeat in November dispelled this improbable assumption. Soon afterwards he expressed concern that in a general election his government would cease to have a majority; an anxiety shared by a number of his senior colleagues. Consciousness of their vulnerability reinforced their cautious instincts. Subsequently, further by-elections were delayed and more determined efforts were made to avoid contentious policies or unpopular legislation. Nonetheless, some politically hazardous issues required their attention; amongst these were the much-publicised activities of Belfast Corporation. A Home Affairs enquiry in June 1941, indicated that it had been guilty of wide-ranging corruption and abuse of patronage, and as a result many local ratepayers supported its dissolution. The cabinet's position was an extremely delicate one as the councillors were predominately Unionist and had considerable influence both within the Belfast associations and inside the broader party organisation. Dawson Bates, the Minister of Home Affairs, therefore, recommended that, as a

Henderson, the governor's secretary to R. Gransden, cabinet secretary, 13 May 1941. **16** Cabinet conclusions, 12, 19 May 1941, in PRO CAB65/49, 51. Had conscription been applied it was estimated that 48-53,000 men could have been raised, Blake *Northern Ireland in the Second World War*, op. cit., p. 196. **17** Ibid., 26 May 1941, PRO CAB65/53. **18** Ibid., 27 May 1941, PRO CAB/54

compromise measure, city administrators should be appointed who would act as an executive but be guided by the elected council. If he were to take more punitive action, he believed that the government would find it 'impossible to hold office'.[19] Even this modest proposal was adopted by some ministers with extreme reluctance. Andrews, especially, was anxious 'not to have any trouble with the Corporation' or as he explained to colleagues, to 'detract from the unity of effort ... needed to win the war'.[20] Under strong pressure both from Belfast Corporation, and the city's unionist branches, a cabinet majority therefore agreed to dilute still further the retributive element in the terms which Bates had proposed. However, one of the two amendments which they had agreed was criticised by opposition MPs with such devastating effect that it was hurriedly withdrawn. Overall, the legislation deepened divisions within the government and alienated those who had opposed the measure, whilst failing to satisfy others who had favoured firmer action.[21]

The government's handling of industrial unrest was an unavoidable aspect of its wartime responsibilities, which also provoked adverse comment and aroused serious doubts about its competence. In part, public censure was directed at the official machinery for resolving trade disputes which even John MacDermott, then Attorney General, described as clumsy and slow. A much more damaging criticism, expressed strongly by sections of local management, some senior civil servants and the Ministry of Labour and National Service in London was that the Northern Ireland cabinet was weak and complaisant in its attitude towards labour and that this had contributed to a deterioration in industrial discipline. Thus, W.P. Kemp director at Short & Harland's aircraft factory, complained in September 1942, that refractory workers knew their actions would be 'winked at by those in authority'.[22] Next month, the worst strike of Andrew's premiership originated at a Short's disposal unit. Within two weeks it had spread to affect 10,000 men in Belfast's major strategic industries prompting Churchill to state that he was shocked at what [was] happening.[23] It had arisen directly out of an

19 Cabinet conclusions, 20 April 1942, PRONI CAB4/505; also Barton, *Brookeborough*, op. cit., pp 201, 202.   20 Cabinet conclusions, 8 June 1942, PRONI CAB4/512; also Spender diary, op. cit., 18 October 1941.   21 The cabinet had agreed, though not unanimously, to support two amendments which significantly weakened the Belfast county borough administration bill by specifying the period for which city administrators would be appointed and restoring to the council some of its powers of appointment. The latter was hurriedly withdrawn; the measure finally adopted, provided for the appointment of three city administrators for a 3 1/2 year period, who would make all appointments, purchases, contracts and rates and municipal taxes', I. Budge and C. O'Leary, *Belfast: approach to crisis, a study of Belfast politics, 1603-1970* (London, 1973), pp 153, 154.   22 W.P. Kemp to Andrews, 23 September 1941, in PRONI CAB 9C/22/1; see also MacDermott to Andrews, 2 November 1942, ibid. The Spender diary, op. cit., 24 January 1942, assesses, and considers perceptions of the Northern Ireland government's handling of labour.   23 Churchill to Andrews, 15 October 1942, in PRONI CAB9C/22/1; also

attempt by management to implement a Ministry of Production instruction regarding Sunday work. Its root causes were complex but inevitably much blame attached to the role of the government. Westminster officials considered that it had shown 'deplorable weakness' during the strike whilst locally it was castigated for its general policy of drift. By November 1942, MacDermott had become extremely despondent over the government's whole approach to labour relations. Accordingly, he suggested to Andrews that the order making it an offence to strike should be repealed, as it clearly did not deter mass industrial action and consequently threatened to bring the rule of law into contempt. Once more he strongly advocated conscription. Soon afterwards Churchill likewise reopened this issue and similarly justified its introduction on the grounds of Ulster's poor output and productivity and disappointing level of voluntary recruitment.[24] Andrews again rejected this response stating that it did not fall within the realm of practical politics. Meanwhile, the government's method of dealing with labour disputes, including its judicial machinery for their resolution, remained unchanged. So too did the tensions within the cabinet and the criticism of its performance which these circumstances engendered.

There was, of course, a more positive aspect to the policies of Andrews and his cabinet. Immediately after taking office, the new premier became noticeably more enthusiastic about raising public expenditure on social services, setting aside more resources for post-war reconstruction and asserting more forcefully his government's independence of Treasury control. He expressed these opinions all the more stridently as he became more aware of the political weakness of his administration and of the changing aspirations of the Northern Ireland electorate. As elsewhere, war stimulated expectations of social improvement, a development associated with increased levels of taxation, the province's huge imperial contribution, the publication of the Beveridge report and greater popular awareness of the inadequacy of local welfare provision compared with Great Britain as well as of the extent of poverty in Belfast, so starkly revealed by the recent German air-raids. By mid 1942 influential elements within the unionist movement were urging upon the Prime Minister the need to react positively by formulating plans for the post-war years, describing this as being essential for the future of the province as well as the party. Andrews' favourable response was, however, based on conviction as well as expediency. He fully shared public concern at the extent to which housing, health, education and poor relief in he six counties lagged behind standards in Britain, was convinced that over the years

Barton, *Brookeborough*, op. cit., pp 202-4.   **24** See Churchill to F.D. Roosevelt, 11 April 1943, in cabinet conclusions, PRO CAB 66/36, where he refers to 'young fellows of the locality … [who] loaf about with their hands in their pockets' and on how this deleteriously affected 'not only recruiting but the work of … Belfast shipyards, which is less active than other British shipyards.'

the imperial government had not treated the region equably and felt increasingly frustrated by Westminster's restraints on his proposed expenditure.[25]

The tangible result of these sentiments was both meagre and contentious. On 30 July 1942, the Prime Minister made a detailed statement at Stormont on post-war policy, containing a strong commitment to improvements in a wide range of social services and referring to future plans for transport, local government and industry. It immediately prompted an angry response from Kingsley Wood, the Chancellor of the Exchequer, and from Treasury officials. They were baffled by its timing, concerned by the specific nature of its content and irritated by the total absence of any preliminary consultation, more especially because they regarded parity of services as the sheet anchor of inter-governmental financial relations. In subsequent correspondence, Wood recognised that the major responsibility for post-war planning in Northern Ireland lay with the regional government. But he also stressed that though it might legitimately exercise the right to make up 'leeway' with Britain in its social services, it could not claim preferential treatment. Andrews deduced from this that he had gained 'extended financial powers ... from before'.[26] This interpretation was not shared either by Treasury or Ministry of Finance officials. Spender presciently observed that the Chancellor's letter merely confirmed existing arrangements. In the meantime, the governmental machinery for post-war reconstruction established at Stormont by the Prime Minister had degenerated into a hopeless muddle of competing committees duplicating the tasks of planning and preparing policy recommendations. Not surprisingly when the question was eventually debated in the commons, a number of backbenchers expressed strong reservations regarding Andrews' ability to fulfil the promises made in his earlier statement. His claim that he would apply foresight, energy and courage to resolve future problems lacked credibility.

Overall, there seemed no shortage of evidence to confirm the collective incompetence of the 'old guard' wherein the lack of preparation for the blitz, the level of unemployment, the persistent industrial unrest, the failure to apply conscription or the confusion over post-war planning. There was obvious legitimacy

---

25 Cabinet conclusions, 2, 19 June 1942, PRONI CAB4/510, 513; Spender diary, 6 June 1942. Spender and Gransden were surprised by Andrews' sudden enthusiasm for greater government spending and struck by the contrast between his views as premier and those which he had earlier held as Minister of Finance. Spender dismissed the change as an attempt at 'getting credit from the electorate by the distribution of government funds'. He suspected that Andrews sought better terms for the province than were available in Britain and regarded this as unjustifiable and damaging to Northern Ireland's reputation. This view was shared by Brooke and influential junior ministers, such as Maynard Sinclair, and contributed to their overall uneasiness at the unpredictable nature of Andrews' leadership. See Barton, *Brookeborough*, op. cit., pp 204-11. **26** Spender diary, op. cit., 24 September 1942; see also Lawrence, op. cit., pp 68-73.

in MacDermott's comment that Northern Ireland appeared to be 'only half in the war'; an impression which struck informed British observers even more forcefully.[27] Though the ultimate responsibility for some of the province's unenviable features lay at Westminster, rather than at Stormont, a growing and influential sector of local opinion attributed them to the failings of Andrews and his colleagues. In Spender's view they had encouraged complacency and, unlike Carson in 1914, had failed to offer leadership and sacrifice. By January 1943, he had become convinced of the need for cabinet change. Brooke, the deputy leader, also considered that there was a great deal in what the critics were saying and that the prime minister 'must come in with a declaration that he is out to win the war and nothing else matters'.[28] Neither he nor his leader, however, appreciated just how tenuous the political position of the government had become, particularly in parliament. At the time, any revolt at Stormont which might seriously threaten the survival of Andrews' administration seemed highly improbable. Out of 38 government supporters in the House, 16 held offices of profit under the crown, whilst the total number of private members was depleted by military service. Moreover, there was a dearth of decisive leadership amongst unionist backbenchers capable of articulating their unease or mobilizing effectively their voting strength. Nonetheless, there are clear indications that dissension within their ranks was growing. Parliamentary party meetings had gradually become more tense with, on occasion, even routine business leading to acrimonious debate and resentment. As a result, ministers were more reluctant to meet members, their reticence was used by critics to justify moving private motions on the grounds that they were being denied any alternative means of ventilating grievances. There is also evidence of a deterioration in party discipline during commons divisions. Moreover the arrival at Stormont of newly elected, independent members helped sharpen debate and focus the attack more effectively on familiar targets such as the inadequacy of the war effort, unemployment, the lack of post-war planning and the incompetence of the cabinet.

The extent of parliamentary disaffection was starkly revealed on 9–10 January 1943 when unionist backbenchers held a secret meeting at which they formulated demands later forwarded to the chief whip. They called for a change of leadership and the immediate appointment of younger ministers. Their action was as much a symptom as a cause of political crisis. There was at the time a widespread recognition amongst senior party members and civil servants that the public had lost confidence in the government. A number of junior ministers already favoured not just a reshuffling of the cabinet but the removal of Andrews himself. They had come to regard him as the source of the administration's ineffectiveness and his continuation in office as a threat to the preservation of law

27 Cabinet conclusions, 15 May 1941, PRONI CAB4/473.   28 Brooke diary, op. cit., 4 December 1941.

and order, to party unity and even to the union. After hearing of the back-benchers' proposals Brooke noted privately that Andrews ought to 'retire at once', adding that it was 'difficult for any of us to remain'.[29] Somewhat surprisingly, given his government's consistently conciliatory record, Andrews' own response was to resist the malcontents and to defend himself and his ministers. However, at a party meeting held to discuss the crisis, on 19 January, eight speakers called for a 'new team' and a 'change of leadership' if electoral disaster was to be avoided. A resolution followed which was passed unanimously; it stated that the 'subject requires careful … consideration' and that the premier would make a further statement at a future meeting convened for the purpose.[30]

Though it was now generally assumed that Andrews would at least make changes in his cabinet, informed sources reported that his attitude was in fact stiffening. This was soon evident from his efforts to rouse support for his government through a series of speeches delivered to audiences around the province and from the expansive content of the King's speech. On 23 February he instructed the parliamentary party, just returned for a new session of the commons, that no decision regarding ministerial changes would be made before Easter. This prevarication served to confirm doubts as to his suitability for leadership, which were reinforced still further by the political context – a further by-election defeat (in West Belfast), a labour dispute which paralysed the docks and large-scale IRA breakouts from prisons in Belfast and Londonderry. Newspapers meanwhile reported rumours that three ministers had resigned and that the cabinet was 'split from top to bottom'.[31] At a further party meeting held on 19 March, Andrews stated categorically that he would not tolerate interference in his selection of ministers, reaffirming his opinion that his government colleagues were the best available. A vote of confidence in the premier was then moved, challenged and reluctantly withdrawn. A second resolution requesting that the prime minister 'reconsider the question of changes in the cabinet' was passed unanimously.[32] Clearly Andrews had seriously miscalculated the mood of the MPs; and did not abandon his unyielding response. Instead, he again sought to rally support by addressing local unionist associations and preparing an appeal to the annual meeting of the Ulster Unionist Council. It seemed likely that he would proceed to purge his front bench critics (junior ministers) and probably replace them with older men. Senior civil servants privately expressed fears that this would precipitate a terminal split in the party. When the UUC met on 16

29 Ibid., 11, 12 January 1943.   **30** PRONI D 1327/10/1: Ulster Unionist Parliamentary Party, minute book of meetings, 19 January 1943.   **31** *Sunday Dispatch*, 28 February 1943. The article was written by the marquess of Donegall for whom Dawson Bates acted as solicitor. This prompted speculation that Bates was the source of her information. The matter was discussed by cabinet, cabinet conclusions, 2 March 1943, PRONI CAB4/533.   **32** Ulster Unionist Parliamentary Party, minute book, op. cit., 19 March 1943, PRONI D 1327/10/1.

April, it passed by acclamation a resolution of unabated confidence in the prime minister; who later informed Churchill that out of 750 delegates, just two or three had dissented. Possibly Andrews now believed that the crisis would pass given this success, the expressions of support received from some local associations and the assumed backing of a majority of the party at Stormont. During his statement to the council however, he had again implied that he would make no cabinet changes. As a result at least three junior ministers were 'eager to push in their resignations right away'.[33] On reflection, they decided to delay until the next party meeting, reluctantly arranged by the leadership for 28 April. Meanwhile, Brooke placed his resignation in Andrews' hands so that he would 'have an opportunity to speak'.[34]

When the 33 Unionist MPs assembled at Glengall Street, Andrews defiantly repeated his defence of his colleagues and insisted that he must be free to appoint his own ministers. Over the next three-and-a-half hours, most of those present spoke. No formal vote was taken, but it was far from certain that the Prime Minister enjoyed the support of a majority of those present. It was evident that, if he continued as leader, six junior ministers would leave the government and the party, in parliament and beyond, would be irretrievably divided. Clearly shocked and saddened he reluctantly decided to resign, and accordingly next day reported to the Governor. Andrews' unwillingness to make the cabinet changes urged upon him stemmed not only from loyalty to long-serving colleagues and the context of war but also political weakness; he refused to replace ministers whose inadequacies he recognised. His uncharacteristic obduracy also owed something to the confrontational manner in which the issue of government restructuring had been raised initially by the unionist backbenchers. In any case he regarded cabinet appointments as the prerogative of the Prime Minister. His overall response to the crisis suggests as well a considerable measure of political miscalculation, specifically his assumption that he could silence his critics by a resolute, inflexible stand and his apparent inability to appreciate the true nature of the pressures which ultimately forced his resignation.

Amidst confusion over correct procedure, Lord Abercorn took soundings from representative opinion and on 1 May asked Brooke to form a government. It is unlikely that any other member would have commanded a majority in the house. Nonetheless, it is improbable that he had been nominated by Andrews who was firmly convinced that Sir Basil had conspired against his leadership. Brooke dismissed such allegations as being without foundation. Certainly his career was not marked by over-riding personal ambition. He had entirely failed to anticipate either the timing or the scale of the party revolt in January 1943. His role during the crucial weeks which followed was a passive one. He made no

---

33 The three junior ministers were Brian Maginess, Maynard Sinclair and Dehra Parker. See Brooke diary, op. cit., 19-21 April 1943. **34** Ibid., 21 April 1943.

attempt to contact or instruct disaffected unionist backbenchers and those junior ministers who sought his advice did so of their own volition. The talent of the dissidents weakens the credibility of any claim that they were used to engineer his progress to the premiership. The final outcome was not the product of his manipulative skills or unsated appetite for power, rather the province's administration collapsed through the weight of its own incompetence.[35]

Brooke had much to offer the unionist movement, including his relative youth, a distinguished record of ministerial service, military experience, useful contacts in Britain and a genial, affable personality. As premier, he displayed more courage, energy and tact than either Andrews or Craigavon in his later years. Arguably, however, like his predecessors, he failed to rise to that higher level of leadership which does not simply pander to its own supporters but dares to chip away at their prejudices. His ministers were little known and, by Stormont standards, also young.[36] Most had proven administrative experience and probably all had been convinced for some time of the need for a change of leadership. A non-unionist, Harry Midgley, became a Minister of Public Security, in order to broaden the government's representation in Northern Ireland and to create a favourable impression at Westminster. Officials there had long been advocating that the Stormont cabinet should be composed on a more inclusive basis. Brooke appointed no deputy and he advised his colleagues not to regard their appointments as permanent. Their agreed policy priorities were to maintain the present constitution, bring greater drive to the war effort and devise plans for the post-war years.

The change of government and, more particularly, the manner in which it had occurred, caused deep and enduring tensions inside the party. There was considerable, residual sympathy felt for the 'old guard' in the influential but increasingly unrepresentative committees of the UUC and within sections of the unionist press. Most of the ex-ministers felt embittered by recent events: some undoubtedly shared the late premier's conviction that they had been manipulated from office by backstairs' intrigue. Andrews himself was also disappointed by his own exclusion from Brooke's cabinet and as a backbencher was acutely sensitive to any perceived criticism of his government. He invariably attacked, with Lord Glentoran's support, less popular aspects of Brooke's policy and, on occasion, briefed disaffected MPs on points of criticism which they might raise in

35 See Barton, *Brookeborough*, op. cit., pp 221-9.   **36** Of the new cabinet, H. Midgley, Revd W. Conkey and Revd R. Kane had never before held ministerial office. Brooke, W. Grant, J.M. Sinclair and W. Lowry had served in the previous government as Minister of Commerce, Minister of Public Security, parliamentary secretary at Finance and parliamentary secretary at Home Affairs respectively. It was overall a 'new team', D. Harkness, *Northern Ireland since 1920* (Dublin, 1983), p. 96. Spender said of it that though 'little known', it would 'be able to carry out its duties very effectively', Spender diary, op. cit., 12 May 1943.

debate. He persisted with his claim that when in office he had reached an agreement with the imperial chancellor enabling him to do almost anything he wished despite the context of war, so tending to belittle the achievements of his successor. In March 1944, his querulous behaviour attracted a strongly worded, though ineffective, public rebuke from Lord Londonderry.[37]

Amongst backbenchers, old loyalties and frustrated ambitions helped ensure that the new administration's initial control over the house was at best uncertain. During its first months in office, one measure had to be withdrawn when it became evident that it would be defeated and another was substantially amended as none of the private members present would give support.[38] Soon afterwards, a commons select committee report on parliamentary salaries was shelved because some MPs strongly criticised the continued payment of expenses to ministers. Brooke conceded that it was in essence an evasion of income tax. Such circumstances fuelled speculation regarding his prospects as prime minister. In December 1943, Spender recorded rumours then current in local business circles, that Glentoran would replace him inside three months. Four weeks later, a newspaper reported that Andrews and Glentoran could, if they wished, defeat the government on the forthcoming King's speech.[39] At the time Sir Basil stated privately that he would not continue if they remained 'part of the machine and are not supporting me'.[40]

Like Craigavon and Andrews, Brooke sought to avoid making controversial decisions in wartime when a general election was impracticable and disunity might disrupt the war effort. Nonetheless, as premier, he showed greater enterprise and activity than his predecessors. In addition, a number of divisive issues arose, some self-imposed, others inherited or related to the war, which required his immediate response. Amongst these was his decision, in February 1944, to ask his Minister of Education, Revd Professor Robert Corkey, to resign. Sir Basil was satisfied in spite of repeated warnings, that his minister had consistently neglected his duties, having attended his department in Portrush just three times during the previous six months. In a statement, however, Corkey protested that his dismissal had been precipitated by disagreements on matters of principle relating to future educational reform. Specifically, he alleged that Brooke was not committed to the compulsory provision of religious instruction in state schools. He also claimed that an anti-Presbyterian bias operated in the administration of

---

37 See minutes of annual meeting of UUC, 2 March 1944, in PRONI D1327/8/10.   38 The Local Government Officers' Bill was withdrawn, 16 June 1948, Northern Ireland Parliamentary Debates (C), vol. 26, col. 1149; its purpose was to standardise employment practices amongst local authority employees. The Planning (Interim Development) Bill was substantially amended. It was devised to extend and strengthen planning controls throughout Northern Ireland; see Spender diary, op. cit., 25 November 1943.   39 Ibid., op. cit., 23 December 1943, and 31 January 1944.   40 Brooke diary, op. cit., 19 November 1944.

his own ministry, connived in by Brooke, though attributable mainly to the influence of its permanent secretary and parliamentary secretary.

The effect of Corkey's allegations was to impose a severe additional strain on party loyalty; he received strong sectional support from the members of his own denomination, having in Spender's opinion introduced a 'sectarian' point of view.[41] Thus, when Brooke suggested that in response he would move a commons resolution of confidence in his government, even backbench sympathisers advised against, anticipating defeat. Yet the alarm generated by the controversy regarding future educational policy would appear to have been without foundation. When the cabinet first discussed the question fully three months later, the principle of compulsory religious instruction was unanimously and unhesitatingly endorsed. Instead, debate centred on whether Stormont would require enabling powers from Westminster in order to proceed, and consideration of the means whereby teachers' freedom of conscience might be protected. The far-reaching nature of the proposed legislation did, of course, raise a number of sensitive and complex issues – that these required three more years to resolve was due in part to the bitterness aroused by Corkey's dismissal.

From its inception, the government was obliged to focus attention on another, similarly delicate matter which was for several years a source of tension within the unionist movement. Its members experienced persistent pressure from councillors, high ranking party officials and a number of local associations to restore to the formerly discredited Belfast Corporation those powers transferred to administrators in 1942. They were sympathetic in their response anxious to remove a long-standing source of contention and of grievance, but also concerned to prevent a recurrence of the corruption and nepotism which had previously disfigured the administration of the borough. In 1943, they agreed to a measure which whilst returning some functions to the council restricted its powers of patronage and conferred exclusive authority to place contracts on the town clerk and town solicitor. This proposal was so severely criticised by dissatisfied councillors, who in Spender's view had learnt nothing from past experience, that the cabinet decided to abandon all legislation on the question until it had passed out of controversy. Eventually, one year later, a bill which preserved the earlier conditions relating to contracts was proposed by leading party officials and sponsored by the government. Though it had received almost unanimous support at a preliminary meeting of Unionist MPs, a vociferous minority ferociously and unexpectedly attacked it during the second reading debate. Once more, Brooke decided not to proceed and, suspecting a conspiracy amongst his backbench 'revolters' (i.e., critics), he made immediate changes in the composition of the whips office. The issue was finally resolved when in the spring of 1945, the government relented and introduced legislation which in essence restored to the

41 Spender diary, op. cit., 17, 25 February 1944; Brooke diary, op. cit., 8, 11, 17 February 1944.

Corporation its original functions. It passed through the commons quickly, with little debate and without controversy. There was by then a widespread feeling that the council had been sufficiently punished for past, almost forgotten, misdeeds, whilst the restrictions prepared earlier by the cabinet had been consistently denigrated as undemocratic. Government members themselves hoped that their action would assuage internal party divisions, particularly at a time when they were conducting complex negotiations over future arrangements for electricity and transport. It was in Brooke's view: 'politically quite wrong that the representatives of one-third of the population should be antagonistic.'[42]

However, the most widespread criticism of the government's performance centred on its allegedly inadequate response to the province's acute housing shortage. By 1943, Ministers considered that this had become the major focus of contemporary public interest, surpassing unemployment, and concluded that even in wartime it was politically necessary to do something. Northern Ireland's first official housing inquiry, which was initiated by Brooke soon after becoming premier, estimated that 100,000 new houses were required to meet immediate needs. Nonetheless, the obstacles blocking an effective cabinet reposte proved insurmountable; these included the customary dilatoriness of local authorities in fulfilling their housing obligations due to conservatism, inertia, financial constraints and, in some cases, the political difficulties associated with aiding the nationalist section of the population. There was also a shortage of building materials, of appropriate sites and of labour. These problems were compounded by avoidable confusion over departmental responsibility between the Ministers of Finance and Home Affairs, Sinclair and Lowry, and the difficulty of attracting Treasury approval and funding for schemes at a time when housing construction in Britain had been virtually abandoned, in response to the priorities of war.

Nonetheless, in late 1943, representations were made to London appealing for financial support for a local housing programme. When Westminster agreed to the immediate construction of 250 houses with generous subsidies, Lowry greeted the offer with derision, stating: 'people would reply that they had asked for bread and been offered a stone'.[43] Belfast Corporation responded by claiming that no suitable sites for their construction were available within the city boundary, while later, in November 1944, it indicated that it would take no action until building costs had fallen. In order to expedite progress in the city and elsewhere the cabinet decided in July 1944 to establish a Housing Trust, a corporate body,

---

42 Ibid., 19 April 1945; also 3 October 1944. See minutes of meetings of the Parliamentary Unionist Party, 19 September, 10 October 1944, and 2 May 1945 in Ulster Unionist Council papers PRONI D1327/22; cabinet conclusions, 15 September 1944, 19 April 1945, in PRONI CAB4/597, 622.   **43** Quoted in Spender diary, op. cit., 27 September 1943; cabinet conclusions, 27 September 1943, PRONI CAB4/556. W. Grant stated that there were 43,010 'totally unfit houses' in Ulster, 10 August 1944, in ibid., CAB4/595.

empowered to secure in co-ordination with local authorities the provision of housing accommodation for workers. The associated legislation elicited a predictably hostile response from unionist backbenchers who claimed that such centralisation was unprecedented and unwarranted and expressed concern regarding the respective roles of private enterprise and of local government in meeting future housing needs.[44]

During late 1944, Brooke's considerable political difficulties were accompanied by a succession of domestic tribulations. On 2 October, Henry, the older of his surviving sons, was wounded by schrapnel when serving with the 10th Hussars in North Africa. On 13 October, his wife, Cynthia, was diagnosed as suffering from a serious spinal disorder, which severely incapacitated her for the next two years. One week later, he himself was forced by a duodinal ulcer to relinquish his prime ministerial duties until late January 1945, evidence perhaps of the accumulating demands of his public and private life. Brooke responded to these political and personal strains with ability and confidence. He had anticipated strong initial opposition to his cabinet; throughout his premiership he was constantly aware of and sensitive to the fissiparous tendencies within the Unionist movement. He always regarded unity as, at best, tenuous and ultimately dependent on the 'border question', without which he believed, 'various opinions would make themselves felt'.[45] He fully recognised the initial necessity of boosting party morale. Hence, he was concerned to ensure that his government won its first by-election and, from the outset, invited a succession of leading British politicians to address public meetings in the province. Unlike Andrews, he regarded publicity as a priority. Soon after becoming prime minister he set up a cabinet publicity committee and appointed both a public relations officer in London and a government publicity officer in Belfast. He himself consistently briefed and sought advice from journalists and at his first cabinet exhorted his colleagues to do likewise.[46]

Shortly before Andrews' government collapsed, Sir Basil had strongly advised him that the parliamentary party was 'the only thing that mattered', as prime minister he employed a variety of tactics to win over and sustain its support.[47] He sought to improve consultative procedures between ministers and backbenchers on proposed legislation. Thus meetings were held more regularly in order that cabinet policy could be explained and defended, alternative measures

---

44 See *Interim report of the planning advisory committee*, Cmd. 224 (Belfast 1944), passim; cabinet conclusions, 10 August, 19 October 1944, PRONI CAB4/595, 602; Lawrence, op. cit. pp 146-57. **45** Brooke diary, op. cit., 9, 10 October 1943. **46** Cabinet conclusions, 6 May 1943, PRONI CAB4/541. The list of British politicians to visit the province (1943-5), included Stafford Cripps (Minister of Aircraft Production), Herbert Morrison (Secretary of State for Home Affairs), Oliver Lyttleton (Minister of Production), Hugh Dalton (President of Board of Trade) and J.J. Llewellin (Minister of Food). For Brooke, however the real coup was the visit of George VI and family, 17–19 July 1945.

considered and grievances aired. Not infrequently, Sir Basil intervened to appeal for unity, urging its necessity in the interests of both the war effort and the preservation of the Union. Reflecting by implication on recent experience, he suggested that constant criticism would, in itself, induce amongst ministers a defensive hesitancy which would result in political stagnation. On occasion he indicated his own willingness to resign, but stressed that the alternative to his continued leadership was a general election. In addition, he set in motion a process of party reorganisation, mainly in response to demands from the UUC, which had originated during the final months of Andrews' premiership. The British Conservative Party provided the model, which the membership wished to emulate, and the holding of an annual Unionist conference and appointment of a paid party chairman were amongst the earliest innovations which resulted.

Meanwhile, Brooke also strove continuously to reduce the level of personal bitterness between himself and the politically active remnants of the 'old guard'. In March 1944, he proposed as a conciliatory gesture that Andrews be re-elected President of the Unionist Council, it was a post which he himself aspired to but which the incumbent showed no apparent inclination to vacate. Moreover, from July 1944, acting on a suggestion by his chief whip, Sir Basil consciously chose to bring Glentoran more into discussion and helped ensure that he was appointed both party treasurer and a trustee. These carefully calculated steps reflect Brooke's mounting confidence in his own authority; he noted privately that he was 'quite prepared' to take them now, whereas he was not 'going to appear as an appeaser before'.[48] No doubt partly in reciprocation, Andrews proposed and Glentoran seconded his nomination as party leader at a specially convened Standing Committee meeting held in March 1945. It was certainly a response which Brooke valued. He had earlier complained that he had 'no status' and had become leader merely by virtue of being prime minister.[49] Nonetheless, for the moment, the presidency remained beyond his grasp. When eventually Andrews did resign, in 1947, Glentoran succeeded him, even though Brooke had indicated his willingness to accept if he was offered the position. At the time he reflected dispondently on how residual sympathy for the 'old guard' could still influence unionist voting behaviour.

In the meantime, Sir Basil and his colleagues began to devise plans for the post-war years in response to these pressures from within the party which had earlier helped precipitate Andrews' fall. The latter had at first reacted guardedly to the Beveridge report, concerned that he might otherwise arouse unrealisable expectations. As premier, Brooke stated his firm intention to keep pace with the rest of the United Kingdom in health and social services including the Beveridge

---

47 Brooke diary, op. cit., 25 March 1943. For the internal structural changes within the Unionist party discussed here, see Ulster Unionist Council papers, op. cit., 1943-5, PRONI D1327/8, 9, passim.   **48** Brooke diary, op. cit., 19 July 1944.

scheme of social security, and he immediately initiated a series of investigations aimed at quantifying more precisely the comparative backwardness of Northern Ireland's welfare provision. The impending, substantial increase in government spending required a re-examination of the financial relationship between Stormont and Westminster. Local officials regarded the winter of 1943 as an opportune moment to initiate preliminary negotiations, aimed at ensuring that their departments had sufficient funds both to maintain parity in social services and to recover any proven leeway relative to British standards. Spender observed that there had been a general loosening in the recent budgetary policy of the imperial government, relations with Treasury officials were friendly and the Chancellor was sympathetic. He also noted with obvious gratification that the Labour members of the coalition were appreciative of Ulster's efforts.[50] By early 1944, the basis for a future reinsurance agreement had been laid which guaranteed adequate financial support from the Exchequer to meet all Ulster's reasonable expenditure. Inside the next twelve months the Northern Ireland cabinet prepared an unemployment insurance scheme and a system of family allowances, both based on the British model, and agreed to establish a Ministry of Health.

The substantial expansion of governmental responsibility envisaged in these wartime decisions and plans helped precipitate a major reallocation of functions between the Stormont departments. This issue had first been considered during the spring of 1943 when Andrews was premier. It had arisen then partly because of the foreseeable closure of the Ministry of Public Security as well as the widespread perception that the duties of the Ministry of Home Affairs were too disparate and unwieldy to be conducive with administrative efficiency. Brooke's eventual implementation of the necessary changes, in 1944-5, was complicated by the political context. His ministers were reluctant to relinquish functions which they had quite recently acquired fearing that the electorate would conclude that they were 'unable to cope with' the work done by their predecessors.[51] Also, during the consequent cabinet reshuffle, unionist backbenchers blocked the prime minister's choice of Midgley as Minister of Health considering that he might 'do harm' there at a time when major National Health Service legislation was imminent. Sir Basil was obliged to retract the appointment and eventually persuaded his reluctant minister to accept the Ministry of Labour portfolio instead. The economy represented the government's other major area of attempted post-war planning. As at Westminster, Northern Ireland ministers were committed to a policy aimed at full employment after hostilities had ended. As the flow of military contracts diminished from 1943 onwards, howev-

---

49 Ibid., 23 March 1945, also 29 July 1943.   **50** Spender diary, op. cit., 17 August, 2 December 1943 and 28 April 1944; Lawrence, op. cit., pp 71-3; J. Ditch, *Social policy in Northern Ireland between 1939-50* (Aldershot, 1988), pp 86-8.   **51** This is discussed in Spender to E. Clark, 4 August 1943, included in Spender diary, op. cit.

er, they shared a deepening apprehension at the approaching spectre of severe peacetime recession. When the Ministry of Labour estimated the likely cost of applying the Beveridge report to the province it assumed an unemployment level of 12.5 per cent a figure 4 per cent above the projection for Great Britain. Maynard Sinclair expressed the conviction that no government could survive if the percentage of jobless locally remained 'substantially above' that of other regions of the United Kingdom.[52]

In response to these anxieties, a post-war reconstruction committee was established in September 1943; its purpose was to help formulate solutions for the province's anticipated post-war economic problems.' Six months later, Sir Roland Nugent (then Minister without Portfolio and soon to become Minister of Commerce) was given overall responsibility for the development and co-ordination of planning.[53] In addition, further legislation was prepared at Stormont with the objective of attracting new industry to Northern Ireland in the post-war period. Both ministers and established local firms regarded the dismantling of the pervasive wartime controls imposed by Westminster as a peacetime priority. Meanwhile, Brooke and his colleagues constantly pressed imperial departments for further orders and investment, attempting to clarify more precisely with them the respective area of inter-governmental responsibility in generating employment in the six counties. They also sought better liaison regarding post-war planning and future legislation which might affect the region and urged, in particular, that Northern Ireland be officially designated a development area by the British Board of Trade.

Both Brooke's commitment to parity of social services with Great Britain and his growing concern with regard to post-war prospects for the local economy contributed to his continuing enthusiasm for the introduction of conscription. In early 1945, he became aware of the imperial government's intention to extend compulsory service beyond the period of hostilities and he immediately requested that it be applied to the province then as well. He justified its extension partly on grounds of principle; it would be a potent affirmation of Northern Ireland's constitutional status. He anticipated Westminster's previous response that it would be 'more trouble than it was worth' by stressing that, after the war, larger numbers would be available for military service than in 1941 or 1943 and that any disruption which might result from its application would have much less grave consequences in peacetime. However, he also particularly emphasised that if conscription was not applied it would be 'difficult for Britain to help' the province either by contributing to the cost of its social services or of assisting it to achieve full employment. He noted that military service would in itself ease

52 Cabinet conclusions, 6 February 1945, PRONI CAB4/614; also Brooke diary, op. cit., 21 March, 2 May 1944.   **53** Cabinet conclusions, 16, 27 September 1943, 23 March 1944, in PRONI CAB4/555, 556, 576.

the difficulties of reinstating in civilian life whose who had been demobilised. Such was Brooke's enthusiasm for its introduction that he favoured establishing contact with the Catholic hierarchy in order to explore whether more generous grants to voluntary schools would lessen hostility to its adoption.[54]

To British ministers and officials these well-rehearsed and wide-ranging arguments amounted to 'no case at all'. British ministers dismissed these arguments. They considered that to extend conscription to Northern Ireland for economic reasons would be 'indefensible' and that to apply it after hostilities had ended would be to invite universal condemnation, whereas in 1941 military necessity had enhanced its legitimacy. Moreover, they believed that Brooke would be exposed to ridicule if he were to introduce military service at a time when it involved no risk to the conscripts. One further factor helped to determine Westminster's response, the conviction that Brooke's request was not in the best interests either of Ulster or of the Union. Some officials had clearly come to value the latter more highly, no doubt influenced by the context of war. Thus one observed: 'Nothing should be done to provoke rebellion … by a large minority who could always look for support from across the border.'[55]

Relations between Westminster and Stormont certainly became closer and warmer in wartime, irrespective of the decision regarding conscription. This was not primarily related to any outstanding commitment shown or sacrifice made by the people of the province in the course of the conflict. Their voluntary recruitment levels remained a source of disappointment, even embarrassment, to Northern Ireland ministers, and local munitions industries performed only moderately well throughout.[56] Rather it was Ulster's strategic position which

---

54 Ibid., 19 April 1945, PRONI CAB4/622. Brooke suggested that initially contact should be made with local Catholic 'leaders', presumably nationalist politicians, who he hoped could establish whether increased expenditure on voluntary schools would win the hierarchy's acceptance of conscription. He was aware of the risk that this strategy might provoke Protestant anger. No more formal lines of communication appears to have existed between the government and the Catholic community.　　**55** See minute by C. Markbreiter, 9 May 1945, also note by H. Morrison, 29 October 1946 in 'Conscription 1945-6', PRO Ho45/24213. No one was more concerned to preserve the union than Brooke. But he believed that if conscription was not applied, it would cause 'ill-feeling' in Britain. Above all, he was convinced that if Northern Ireland expected to be treated by Britain as a development area after the war (in which special measures would be applied to reduce unemployment) then it must accept the 'obligations of common citizenship', PRONI CAB4/622, op. cit.　　**56** After an initial spurt in October 1939, average monthly enlistment dropped below 1,000. The rate was influenced by a multiplicity of factors including seasonal unemployment, the growing absorption of people in war work, the needs of the services themselves and the war situation. There was a surge of volunteers after Dunkirk, and again between June–September 1943. This apart the level rarely surpassed the unimpressive monthly figure of 1,000. During the war years *c*.38,000 men and women of Northern Ireland are known to have enlisted. See J. Blake, op. cit., pp 199-200.

alone ensured that its contribution to the war effort was a crucial one. It significance derived from Germany's military domination of Western Europe combined with Éire's undeviating policy of neutrality. As VE day approached Brooke
expressed the 'hope that you [Britain] now realise that we are necessary to you'.[57]
His wish was fully vindicated; the imperial government's changing perception
was to find tangible expression after hostilities had ended in the declaratory
clause of the Ireland Act.

Meanwhile, within Northern Ireland itself there is little indication of any
comparable shift in traditional political perspectives or relationships. War did
cause some disruption of pre-war trends. In Londonderry, above all, unprecedented prosperity seems to have reduced inter-communal tensions. More generally, in war the border issue receded as a factor in politics, and 'real' social and
economic issues rose to greater prominence. This was evidenced in successive by-
election defeats for the government, and a measurable swing to the left which
alarmed prominent Unionist Party members. Also Protestants and Catholics did
share some vital aspects of wartime experience. Civil defence activities provided
increased opportunities for social integration and, as the *Irish Times* stated, the
Luftwaffe's air raids 'made no question of religious or political difference'.[58] But
even during the blitz, there were limits to the shared nature of experience. The
unclaimed dead were buried separately according to their presumed faith, and
evacuees were billeted along with those of their own religion. Even the geograph-
ical distribution of death and destruction reinforced Protestant suspicions that
there had been collusion between nationalist areas of Belfast and the enemy.

Wartime attitudes seem broadly to have split along sectarian lines. No-one
could doubt that the Unionist Party supported the war effort, even if it notably
lacked the degree of urgency about defeating Hitler found elsewhere in the
United Kingdom. In contrast, among northern nationalists there is much evidence of a deep-seated hostility to, or at least indifference, felt toward the war
effort. F.H. Boland, assistant secretary in the Department of External Affairs in
Dublin, stated categorically on 22 April 1942, that 'the vast majority of nationalists in the six-county areas were absolutely pro-German on account of their
unjust treatment by the British government and its Belfast puppet'. Even before
the war in 1938, nationalist MPs and Senators had identified closely with the
German minority in Czechoslovakia, and highlighted British government sensitivity towards its circumstances compared with its alleged indifference towards
Northern Irish Catholics. Cahir Healey, the Fermanagh nationalist MP, in
September 1938 feared Britain would try to influence the United States to join
with Britain and France, and proposed that the most influential Irish, Italian and
German people in the USA should be organised to make an Anglo-American

57 R. Fisk, *In time of war* (London, 1983), p. 470.   **58** Cited in Barton, *Northern Ireland in the Second World War*, p. 120.

'union of hearts' impossible. In 1940, he stated 'at all events, we [nationalists] have the consolation that we cannot be much worse off politically than we are'.[59] Throughout the war, he and his colleagues whole-heartedly supported neutrality and urged that Britain should apply the rights of small nations to decide their own destiny to the Irish nation. A conference of northern nationalist representatives in June 1940 passed a resolution stating, 'there is no issue which ought to take precedence of Partition'.[60] Minority leaders argued that it endangered Irish neutrality, and prevented Ireland from being defended as a strategic unit.

After the war, Brooke alleged that 'one of the Nationalist MPs ... went so far as writing to the German ambassador [Hempel] in Dublin, asking that, if Germany won the war, would they unite the two parts of Ireland'. The MP concerned was probably Healey, though others have disputed Brooke's claim. Nonetheless, when German invasion of Ireland seemed imminent, a Garda report to the Department of Justice referred to northern contacts with the legations in Dublin. In August 1940, three nationalist politicians (Senator McLaughlin from Armagh, with John Southwell and Paeder Murney from Newry) decided at a meeting in Dublin, 'to place the Catholic minority in the north under the protection of the Axis powers'. Soon afterwards an unnamed nationalist delegation from Lurgan raised the issue with the German and Italian ministers in Éire. The both 'promised support', and indicated that the matter would be raised in broadcasts by 'German and Italian controlled radio stations'.[61] For nationalists the supreme question remained partition, and sympathy for the IRA's aims was ever present. When the United Kingdom government executed two IRA men involved in the bombing campaign, nationalist leaders declared that 'if the result be to establish here a united front amongst all classes against British Imperial aggression, the lives of the two Irishmen will not have been given in vain'.[62]

There is also evidence that the two communities reacted differently to key issues raised by the war. The expectation of powerful minority opposition to conscription effectively determined Westminster's decision not to introduce it. On 22 May 1941, Cardinal MacRory indicated the grounds of the Catholic church's opposition, noting that Ireland was 'an ancient land, made one by God ... partitioned by a foreign power, against the vehement protests of its people. Conscription would now seek to compel those who writhe under this grievous wrong to fight on the side of its perpetrators'. MacRory's broad attitude to the war effort has been described as 'fervently anti-British, if not actually pro-Nazi'. Though the contrast in attitudes can be overstated, committed unionists would certainly have welcomed the introduction of conscription. Similarly, Catholics were significantly underrepresented in the various civil defence services, though

59 Ibid., pp 120-2. **60** T. Hennessey, *A history of Northern Ireland, 1920-96* (Dublin, 1997), p. 84. **61** Barton, *Northern Ireland in the Second World War*, p. 123. **62** Hennessey, *History of Northern Ireland*, p. 87.

less so in Londonderry, where the local Catholic bishop, Neil Farren, encouraged members of his congregation to join. Religious identity also helped determine local reaction to the arrival of United States troops in Northern Ireland. Tom Harrisson, in a 1942 survey, concluded that Protestants were enthusiastic in their response. They welcomed the troops for themselves, for the war effort and 'almost unconsciously, as a strengthening of the forces of order against the constant fear of Catholic trouble'. In contrast, he concluded that the minority was 'biased towards antagonism', considered the presence of the troops an insult and suspected that they were 'really there to ensure partition and possibly even to invade the south'. David Gray, the United States consul in Dublin, was particularly concerned that MacRory's condemnation of their arrival would be 'taken as an approval of … the recent IRA manifesto declaring war on the United States' and could, by fanning Irish 'resentment', contribute to the murder of American soldiers in the six counties.[63]

On 7 November 1944, comments made by Dr Griffin, archbishop of Westminster, caused outrage amongst Stormont ministers and their supporters. Whilst referring to Catholics being 'persecuted in Germany and Poland', he added 'I need hardly mention the persecution going on even at the present time in Northern Ireland'. An imperial government report which referred to the controversy this aroused accepted his conclusion.[64] Certainly, it is clear that unionist suspicion of the minority did not diminish in wartime. A recurring theme of the resolutions then being discussed by the party's standing committee was concern at Catholics 'getting in all over the province', whether purchasing houses or farms or finding employment in the civil service, post office or local industry.[65] In 1943, when he was struggling for his political survival, Andrews stated privately that the appointment of a single Catholic permanent secretary or assistant secretary would be sufficient to 'end the government'. His confidante, Spender, noted at the time that the highest echelons of the bureaucracy were exclusively Protestant.[66] The context of war could in itself be used to justify illiberal policies and practices. During its final stages, Spender received representations that houses should be erected 'in certain places on political grounds' (i.e. that houses should be built for Protestants, in areas which would enhance their electoral strength). Though he had in the past forthrightly condemned sectarian discrimination, he considered that there was now 'some justification' for it because 'Protestants have been more willing to join the forces and volunteer for work in England than Catholics and are therefore entitled to preferential treatment'. A

63 Barton, *Northern Ireland in the Second World War*, pp 123-5.   **64** Griffin's speech was discussed by cabinet, 9 November 1944, PRONI CAB4/605; minutes agreed to send a letter of protest to Herbert Morrison, at the Home Office, and pressed him to see the archbishop.   **65** Minutes of Ulster Unionist Party Standing Committee, 11 April, 10 November 1944, 9 February 1945, in PRONI D1327/7.   **66** Spender diary, op. cit., 30 March 1943.

more substantial Catholic 'contribution' was unlikely to have been encouraged by the Stormont government's endemic suspicion and insensitivity towards the minority. This was reflected, for example, in its decision to use the 'B' specials as the nucleus of the Local Defence Volunteers (Home Guard) and its use of the Unionist party organisation in military recruitment rallies. Senior officials noted that Catholics were under-represented in the local civil defence services. Sectarian differences also helped determine local attitudes towards the US troops based in Northern Ireland. Protestants were 'often enthusiastic', Catholics 'largely antagonistic'.[67] No doubt many northern Catholics regarded the outcome of the conflict with at most indifference. Unionists certainly tended to regard them as a sort of fifth column, instinctively pro-German and anti-British, and ever-willing to aid and abet the enemy; a community whose grievances were not as great as they protested.

Though aspects of Northern Ireland government policy were influenced by these narrow presumptions and prejudices, it was by no means invariably determined by them. On occasion, ministers led by example and attempted positively to counteract local discriminatory forces. Thus, for instance, the Housing Trust, from its inception in 1945, had a statutory obligation to allocate houses fairly. Its first chairman, Sir Lucius O'Brien, stated with apparent confidence that there was 'never any opportunity for undue influence to be used', mainly, he explained, because it selected tenants on the basis of an objective and undisclosed points system.[68] The Trust was exposed to powerful political pressures, nonetheless authoritative research has generally 'exonerated [it] of all conscious desire to discriminate'.[69] Similarly, when the cabinet began to consider the scale of future government grants to voluntary schools, in mid-1944, Brooke spoke strongly in favour of generous treatment, advising colleagues that the children must be the 'first consideration'. Hall-Thompson, the new Minister for Education, likewise argued that as Catholic pupils comprised about 40 per cent of the school population they 'must be dealt with on a statesmanlike basis' and be accorded 'just treatment'. Furthermore, when Stormont ministers decided to

---

67 Ibid., 16 March, 10, 11 September 1944. See Barton, *The blitz*, pp 265-83. 68 O'Brien made these statements at a meeting of the Ulster Unionist Council Executive Committee, 23 May 1950, in PRONI D1327/6. 69 See J.H. Whyte 'How much discrimination was there under the Unionist regime, 1921-68?' in T. Gallagher and J. O'Connell (eds), *Contemporary Irish studies* (Manchester, 1993) p. 19; also T. Wilson, *Ulster, conflict and consent* (Oxford, 1989) pp 126-7. Wilson writes 'no suggestion was ever made that [the Trust] operated in a sectarian manner ... Admittedly the houses it built were of a slightly higher standard than those provided ... by the local authorities and were, to this extent, less suitable for lower income Catholics.' It selected candidates not just on the basis of need but ability to pay. Thus it did less for Catholics than Protestants, D.P. Barrett and C.F. Carter, *The Northern Ireland problem: a study in group relations* (London, 1962) p. 112; P. Shea, *Voices and the sound of drums: an Irish autobiography* (Belfast, 1981).

introduce family allowances on the same basis as at Westminster, they were fully aware that the minority would benefit disproportionately from their proposed scheme.[70]

The introduction of family allowances touched a highly sensitive nerve in the unionist mentality. Stormont ministers had hopes, if not expectations, that social welfare measures combined with economic growth might in the long term deflect the minority from its aspiration to Irish unity. Indeed, in Brooke's opinion, expressed in 1944, the 'only chance for the political future of Ulster' was if it became 'so prosperous that the traditional political alliances [were] broken down'. In the meantime he and his cabinet regarded the relatively high Catholic birth rate with the most acute concern. Sir Basil recorded a wartime discussion with John MacDermott on this issue; both reached the for them depressing conclusion that there was no immediate 'solution' to the problem of the 'increasing disloyal population'.[71] The government did, however, respond indirectly to the perceived threat by regulating more closely the flow of southern labour into Northern Ireland. Brooke, of course, fully appreciated that 'even if we stopped all entries from Éire it would only scratch the difficulty'.[72] Nonetheless, a system of residence permits was strictly administered by Stormont departments, acting under powers derived from an imperial government order. Much thought was given to the possibility of differentiating Éire 'loyalists' (those who favoured partition) from the rest and facilitating their permanent settlement but no practicable scheme could be devised. Mounting anxiety that Westminster might refuse to sanction the continued monitoring of Éire migration after the war prompted the unionist leadership to consider whether the 1920 act ought to be amended. Some favoured reform in order to provide Northern Ireland with dominion status, so transferring to Stormont the necessary regulatory powers. All ministers regarded this issue as an important matter. Brooke himself regarded it as a 'burn-

---

70 For cabinet discussion of family allowances see cabinet conclusions, 28 June, 15 October 1945, PRONI CAB4/628, 650; education was considered in 25 July, 12 October 1944, PRONI CAB4/594, 601. The local family allowance scheme differed from the Westminster provision only in its inclusion of a modulated residence qualification. The 1947 education act provided Catholic voluntary schools with more generous support from public funds than was then available to comparable institutions in England or had been offered before in Northern Ireland. Patrick Shea, a middle ranking, Catholic civil servant in the Ministry of Education during the late 1940s, states that the voluntary sector made disproportionately good progress thereafter and that his department's 'reputation for generosity towards the Catholic schools' was 'well deserved', Shea, op. cit., pp 161, 179. Thus, the liberal sentiments expressed by ministers in cabinet were arguably translated into practical policy in this case. The 1947 act, nonetheless, 'suffered the venom of extreme Protestants while reaping precious little gratitude from the Roman Catholics', D.H. Akinson, *Education and enmity, The control of schooling in Northern Ireland 1920-50* (Newton Abbot, 1973), p. 180.   71 Brooke diary, op. cit., 11 July, 5 September 1944.   72 Ibid., 11 July 1944.

ing question'[73], having stated earlier that unless steps were taken to regulate southern labour and so ensure the Protestant ascendancy, the future of Northern Ireland was in jeopardy. Ministers generally agreed that Northern Ireland's constitutional powers needed to be increased; Maynard Sinclair was particularly concerned at the danger of mass unemployment in the North, if southern migration was not monitored closely. The question became more acute with the extension of social welfare legislation to Northern Ireland, post 1945, which it was feared would stimulate further cross-border population movement.[74]

This internal party debate on the merits of constitutional change was given additional impetus by the unexpected course of political events in Britain during the summer of 1945. As hostilities in Europe drew to a close, Brooke noted privately: 'I find I have no feelings of elation only thankfulness that others will not have to endure the losses that we have suffered. One realises also the vast and difficult problems which lie ahead'. No doubt with these thoughts in mind, with Glentoran and Andrews, he consulted his cabinet colleagues, amid the euphoria of VE Day (8 May 1945), and 'decided to go to the country at once'.[75] When the results were declared two months later, the Unionist party emerged with over 50 per cent of the votes cast, 33 seats and an overall majority of fourteen in the new parliament. The result was disappointing for the Unionist party, which had done particularly well in the previous election in February 1938. In all contests held between 24 June 1921 and 24 Feb. 1969, only once were fewer of its candidates successful (32 in 3rd April 1925).Table 1 details the 1945 results and compares them with those for 1938.[76]

Table 1 Results of elections to Northern Ireland parliament, 1938 and 1945

	14 June 1945		9 November 1938	
	Number	Percentage	Number	Percentage
Unionist	33	50.4	39	56.5
Unofficial Unionist	2	5.0	3	29.1
Northern Ireland Labour Party	2	18.6	1	5.7
Independent Labour	3	13.3	1	1.7
Nationalist and Republican	10	9.2	8	4.9
Others	2	3.5	0	2.1

Source: Elliot, *Northern Ireland parliamentary elections, 1921-1972.*

73 (CAB4/615).   **74** See cabinet discussions of Éire migration in cabinet conclusions, 10 July, 16 November 1944, 6, 15 February 1945, PRONI CAB4/592, 606, 614, 615. Also Brooke diary, op. cit., 2 May, 14 July 1944.   **75** Brooke diary, 7, 8 May 1945.   **76** See S. Elliot, Northern Ireland Parliamentary Election Results, 1921-72 (Chichester, 1973), passim.

The Labour Party's unexpected and historic victory in the British general election two months later caused the Unionist leadership deep consternation. However, the new warmth in Westminster-Stormont relations resulting from the shared experience of war, survived the change of government. The Labour leadership honoured fully Britain's wartime commitments by signing two agreements, in 1946 and 1949, which recognised Northern Ireland's right and funded its efforts to maintain its social services at the same levels as elsewhere in the United Kingdom. Furthermore, Labour ministers made another important, but more controversial contribution to the post-war stability of the six counties. The Ireland Bill, passed in 1949 in response to Éire's secession from the Commonwealth, contained a 'declaratory clause' which stated that the North would remain within the Union for as long as a majority at Stormont wished. Its inclusion is usually regarded as one of Brooke's foremost achievements. But, in fact, Attlee had needed no persuasion. He was anxious to assuage Unionist fears about the constitutional change, which he regarded as genuine. Also, he believed that the inclusion of the clause would be popular with the British electorate. Above all, he was convinced that it was in Britain's best interests. His leading officials advised him that, in view of Éire's secession and in the light of the recent experience of war, it was a

> matter of first-class strategic importance for this country that the North should continue to form part of His Majesty's dominions. So far as can be foreseen, it will never be to Great Britain's advantage that Northern Ireland should form part of a territory outside His Majesty's jurisdiction. Indeed it is unlikely that Great Britain would ever be able to agree to this, even if the people of Northern Ireland desired it.[77]

These sentiments stand in sharp contrast to the attitudes which had been traditionally shared by Westminster politicians. These Norman Brooke, the cabinet secretary, summarised in a letter to Attlee in January 1949 stating: 'For many years all political parties have been able to take the line over partition that there is nothing they would like better than to see a united Ireland.'[78].

In combination, these financial and constitutional developments provided the basis for the province's most harmonious and most promising years, the 1950s and early 1960s. They were years broadly characterised by economic growth, steady social improvement and a unique degree of peace and stability.

77 Report of working party of officials, 1 January 1949, in CAB21/1842 (PRO).   **78** Brooke to Attlee, 5 January 1949, in PREM8/1464 (PRO).

Neutrality and the volunteers: Irish and British government policy towards the Irish volunteers

Cormac Kavanagh

The invasion of Poland by Germany on 1 September 1939 and the subsequent outbreak of World War Two was to prove a testing time for the young Irish State and its citizens. It had developed an independent foreign policy under the guidance of Eamon de Valera and the ruling Fianna Fáil party which meant that Éire was to remain neutral for the duration of the war. The policy of neutrality was to prove problematic, as de Valera recognised, declaring, 'Problems much more delicate and much more difficult of solution even than problems that arise for a belligerent ... It is not ... sufficient for us to indicate our attitude or to express the desire of our people. It is necessary at every step to protect our interest, in that regard, to avoid giving any of the belligerents any due and proper cause of complaint ... A small state is always open to considerable pressure.'[1] Éire was of course particularly susceptible to pressure from Britain, not only because of its strategic value, historic links and the unresolved question of partition, but also due to the strong economic and social ties between the two countries. How de Valera's government dealt with these pressures was to have an impact on the lives of the state's citizens and in particular those who chose to serve with the British forces during the war. It is worth considering the various aspects of this declared policy of neutrality in order to understand how it was possible for many to contribute to the allied war effort despite Éire's neutrality.

It was always going to be difficult for the government to implement a policy of strict neutrality in any European conflict involving Britain. Not only had it to consider the diplomatic, economic and military implications of pursuing such a policy; it also had the problem of internal dissent from an IRA determined to take advantage of 'Britain's difficulty'. On the domestic front, government policy received widespread approval; as one commentator noted, 'Neutrality was the line of least resistance for any Irish Government.'[2] Perhaps the only significant

1 Quoted in T.P. Coogan, *De Valera: long fellow, long shadow* (London, 1993), p. 524.   2 J.J. Lee, *Ireland 1912-1985; politics and society* (Cambridge, 1985), p. 242.

political dissent came from James Dillon, the deputy leader of Fine Gael, who 'believed passionately in the moral rightness of the allied cause, whatever the domestic implications this may have meant for Éire'.[3] Dillon's principled stand was against the tide of public opinion and eventually led to his forced resignation from his party in 1942. Another source of dissent was the *Irish Times* under the editorship of R.M. Smylie. Its position on neutrality was to shift significantly during the course of the war; it had been broadly supportive of the policy in September 1939 but by May 1945 it criticised the policy while praising de Valera's handling of it, commenting that neutrality 'had its roots not ultimately in popular conviction, but in the dust of a buried feud'.[4] Perhaps some indication of the consensus in support of neutrality can be gained in the comments of the communist and anti-fascist Sean O'Casey, who wrote in the January 1941 edition of *Irish Freedom*, 'I can see no reason on God's earth or man's earth, why Irish bodies should mingle with the mangled squirming mass wriggling in pain here and in Germany'.[5] Even those who supported the British war effort in spirit or deed were inclined to view Éire's neutrality with some sympathy. Sir John Maffey, the United Kingdom representative in Ireland during the war, reported in 1940 that 'The policy of neutrality commands widespread support amongst all classes and interests in Éire. It is remarkable how even the pro-British groups, men who fought and were anxious to be called up again, men whose sons are at the front today, loyalists in the old sense of the word, agree generally in supporting the policy of neutrality for Éire.'[6] This observation was repeated by Herbert Shaw, a former Irish Unionist MP who wrote: 'I was surprised to discover that even former unionists, who were prepared without hesitation to send their sons into the British army, held no other policy to be possible.'[7] Even some of those who had joined the British forces indicated some support for the Irish government's policy. Brian Inglis, who enlisted with the RAF, recalls defending the 'right of the Irish to go their own way; for, as time went on, however we might care for the ideals and policies of Ireland's rulers, we adopted a kind of protective chauvinism, half serious half defense.'[8] Another RAF recruit, Fergus Duff from Santry, recalled having 'no problems with Irish neutrality' and believed that, while Churchill used to complain about being deprived of Irish ports, he had a secret understanding with de Valera. 'Most of the people he met (he said) in the RAF understood Ireland's position.'[9]

Of course, declaring neutrality was one thing; implementing it was another. The severest criticism and the greatest test of Éire's neutrality was to come from

3 R. Fisk, *In time of war* (London, 1983), p. 145.   **4** Editorial, 'Turning away wrath', *Irish Times*, 18 May 1945.   **5** Quoted in, C.D. Greaves, *Sean O'Casey: politics and art* (London, 1979), p. 158. **6** Quoted in J.T. Carrol, *Ireland in the war years* (Dublin, 1974), p. 30.   **7** Memorandum to Foreign office quoted in Fisk, *In time of war*, p. 356.   **8** Brian Inglis, *West Briton* (London, 1962), p. 60.   **9** A series of interviews with Joe Carroll entitled 'My VE Day', *Irish Times*, 1 May 1995.

the British government, its supporters and allies. The Irish government's resolve
was tested most severely during a series of crises between 1939 and 1941 over the
Treaty ports and again in 1944 over the 'American note' affair. This was reflected
in a number of damning criticisms directed at de Valera by Winston Churchill,
who wrote in September 1939: 'Three quarters of southern Ireland are with us,
but the implacable, malignant minority can make so much trouble that de
Valera dare not do anything to offend them.'[10] His criticisms were most famous-
ly repeated in the Victory broadcast of 13 May 1945 when he commented,
'Owing to the action of the Dublin Government, so much at variance with the
temper and instinct of thousands of southern Irish men who hastened to the
battle front to prove their ancient valour, the approaches which the Southern
Irish ports could so easily have guarded were closed by the hostile aircraft and U-
boats. This was indeed a deadly moment in our life, and had it not been for the
loyalty and friendship of Northern Ireland we should have been forced to come
to close quarters with Mr de Valera or perish forever from this earth.' Perhaps
criticism of the state's neutrality was most eloquently put by the Northern Irish
poet, Louis MacNeice who wrote,

> The Neutral island facing the Atlantic
> The Neutral island in the Heart of man
> Are bitterly soft reminders of the Beginnings
> that ended before end began ...
>
> ... But then look eastward from your heart, there bulks
> A continent, close, dark, as archetypal sin,
> While to the West of your own Shores the Mackerel
> are fat-on the flesh of your Kin.[11]

Central to these criticisms of Irish neutrality was the recognition of service of
many Southern Irish people for the allied cause. This highlights a number of
contradictions in both the British and Éire's position during the war. On the one
hand, Anglo-Irish relations were in a state of conflict over the Treaty ports
throughout 1939-41, and on the other Southern Irish citizens were losing their
lives in the service of the Royal Navy in the Atlantic. The *Irish Press* reported the
loss of 'several Irish seamen' with the sinking of the battleship *Courageous* during
September 1939.[12] Robert Fisk notes that while Churchill was making a speech in
the Commons on 5 November 1939 criticising Ireland's refusal to concede the
Treaty ports, Commander Fogerty from Ballinunty, Co. Tipperary, was steering
the armed merchantman *Jervis Bay* in a suicide attack against the German pock-

10 Winston Churchill, *The Second World War Vol. VI*, p. 667. 11 Louis MacNeice, *Collected
poems* (London, 1966) p. 202. 12 *Irish Press*, 'Some Irish victims', 21 September 1939.

et battleship *Admiral Scheer*, in mid-Atlantic. His action saved almost all 43 ships in the convoy he was protecting and earned him a posthumous Victoria Cross.[13] The overt adversarial nature of Anglo-Irish relations during the war was also to have a number of practical repercussions for those serving in the British forces. Brian Inglis recalled that many of those who served with him in the RAF and had homes in Éire 'speculated on what we should do if Churchill ordered the treaty ports to be re-occupied'.[14] There were also a number of restrictions imposed on travel between the two countries, particularly after the American note affair in March 1944 when the Home Office announced, 'No more permits or visas for travel between the two islands except for business or work of urgent National importance or on compassionate grounds of the most urgent and compelling nature' and that 'similar restrictions on leave of service personnel are being imposed'.[15] Additionally, both Britain and the United States restricted the availability of much-needed arms to the Irish defence forces as well as limiting commercial activity between the nations.

How we interpret Éire's wartime neutrality is crucial to our understanding of the contribution of its citizens to the British war effort. F.S.L Lyons argued that Irish neutrality psychologically isolated her almost totally from the rest of mankind:

> It was as if an entire people had been condemned to live in Plato's cave, with their backs to the fire of life and deriving their only knowledge of what went on in the outside from the flickering shadows thrown on the wall before their eyes from the men and women who passed to and fro behind them. Then after six years they emerged, dazzled, from the cave into the light of day, it was to a new and vastly different world.[16]

Yet Éire's contribution to the British war effort was significant in a number of areas. Its policy of neutrality was not conducted in a rigid sense; it took account of the realities of its relations with its nearest neighbour, Britain, and its historical benefactor, the United States. As R.M. Smylie put it in 1946, 'Éire was non-belligerent, but never neutral in the generally accepted sense of the term ... It may be argued that Éire was of greater assistance to the Allies as an official neutral than she could have been as an active belligerent.'[17] In fact the *Irish Times* listed the assistance given to Britain during the war, reporting, 'This country had no Foreign Enlistment Act, with the result that at least 100,000 – and probably more – of her sons joined the British forces. Their fighting record can bear

13 Fisk, *In time of war*, p. 252. **14** Inglis, *West Briton*, p. 63. **15** *Manchester Guardian*, 'Travel to Éire suspended' 13 March 1944. **16** F.S.L. Lyons, *Ireland since the Famine* (Fontana Press, 1973), pp 557-8. **17** R.M. Smylie, 'Unneutral neutral Ireland', in *Foreign affairs*, 24 (1946), pp 317-26.

proud comparison with that of any of the fighting men of any of the officially belligerent countrie.'[18] Indeed, there is now in process a reinterpretation of Anglo-Irish relations during the war. Dermot Keogh and Aengus Nolan note that Éire co-operated with the British government on several levels, including military collaboration, intelligence co-ordination, repatriation of Allied personnel and the internment of Axis personnel; and they argue that 'Those Irish people wishing to join British forces were not stopped from travelling to Northern Ireland or across the Irish Sea'.[19] This level of co-operation leads them to conclude that, 'At no time since the foundation of the State had the country been obliged to work so closely with the British at a range of different levels.'[20] However, during the course of the war the government was concerned to preserve the appearance of a strict and unyielding policy of neutrality. One of the principal measures taken to this end was the imposition of a rigid censorship.

The imposition of a draconian censorship under the Emergency Powers Act of 1939, particularly on the reporting of Irish involvement in the war, affected the international representation of the state abroad and also limited Irish citizens' perception of their country's contribution. The government's justification of its strict censorship was based, Keogh asserts, on 'the grounds that it was necessary to stop all communications endangering the security of the state or prejudicial to its good relations to other states'.[21] Of course, criticism of censorship restrictions could not be published during the war. What criticism there was came from publications outside the state. The *Belfast Telegraph* commented on 7 May 1945 that 'One of the marks of an illiberal regime is the denial of access to information and the close restriction of the liberty of the press.'[22] While censorship almost certainly impeded the awareness of Éire's citizens about events in Europe, it also severely restricted information about those fellow citizens who were serving with the British forces during the war. As R.M. Smylie commented later, 'There was never any secret about the enlistment of Irishmen into the British Army, though the censor would not allow a word of it to be mentioned. Obituary notices of men who fell in the war could not be published. Even the fact that Montgomery and Alexander were Irishmen had to be kept in the dark.'[23] This led, as Kevin Myers asserts, to an, 'absurd and inhumane situation' whereby the *Irish Times* 50 years ago was able to report the death of a Northerner in the war but not Southerners.'[24]

It was only after the lifting of censorship on 11 May 1945 that the national newspapers began to report the participation of Éire's citizens in the war effort.

---

18 *Irish Times*, 'Turning away wrath', 18 May 1945. **19** Dermot Keogh and Aengus Nolan, 'Anglo-Irish diplomatic relations in World War II' in *Irish Sword*, 19, nos 75 and 76 (1993-94), pp 107-30. **20** Ibid., p. 130. **21** Dermot Keogh , *Twentieth century Ireland; nation and state* (Dublin, 1994), p. 124. **22** *Belfast Telegraph*, 'Valera's blinkers', 7 May 1945. **23** Smylie, 'Unneutral neutral Ireland'. **24** Kevin Myers, 'Irishman's diary', *Irish Times*, 9 May 1995.

Both the *Irish Independent* and the *Irish Press* reported extensively on the military decorations received by Irish citizens during the war. The *Irish Times* was more brazen in its criticism of censorship, displaying a series of photographs entitled, 'THEY CAN BE PUBLISHED NOW, PICTURES STOPPED BY THE CENSOR DURING THE WAR.'[25] Perhaps one of the most poignant accounts published after the war were a couple of letters printed on the front page of the *Irish Times* from Irish officers who had been to German concentration camps. One officer with the Royal Army Medical Corps visited Belsen and wrote, 'When our troops arrived there were thousands of corpses lying on the ground and even now there are 8,000 seriously ill patients, with about 300 deaths a day ... These wretched prisoners were not criminals – just individuals whom the Nazis did not like – and for no crime were allowed to die in the coldest, most callous manner that the human mind could devise'. An Irish RAF chaplain also wrote of the horrors witnessed in these camps and added, 'All these facts that I have given you are true. Folks in Ireland have been slow to believe such things. They need to be shaken badly. They don't understand the horror of this war because it has not been brought home to them. They have spun their own cocoon, and have been indifferent to a great extent, to the suffering of humanity.'[26] Indeed, it was the *Irish Times* which reported on a less obvious consequence of censorship when it said that, 'In some ways, largely as we think, through the operation of press censorship, her neutrality was interpreted as *au pie de la lettre*. In its anxiety to avoid any suspicion of sympathy to one side or the other, the censorship often went to fantastic extremes. In actual fact, however, Ireland's neutrality, from the very start, operated in favour of the United Nations and particularly Great Britain.'[27] Thus the perception of a strict adherence to its declared policy of neutrality was created for public and diplomatic consumption. Nonetheless, the government could not ignore the fact that many of its citizens were serving with British forces and had to devise methods to deal with the potential embarrassment this could cause for an ostensibly neutral state.

Sir John Maffey recalls that after his appointment as United Kingdom representative to Éire, 'When I paid my official visit on the President, Dr Douglas Hyde, in the Phoenix Park, his secretary, Mr. McDunphy, hissed in my ear "Don't mention the War".'[28] This anecdote illustrates well the attitude of Éire's government and her officials to the war. They were aware that a war was taking place in which tens of thousands of the state's citizens were taking part, but this was not to be officially acknowledged for fear of breaching neutrality.

During the war travel permits issued by government were required by those wishing to travel to Britain. The need for such documents was a matter of con-

25 *Irish Times*, 12-20 May 1945. **26** *Irish Times*, 'Irish officers view German prison camps', 15 May 1995. **27** *Irish Times*, 'Turning away wrath', 18 May 1945. **28** Quoted in Keogh and Nolan, op. cit., p. 108.

cern for some of those serving in British forces returning to Ireland on leave. One officer wrote to the Department of External Affairs in December 1939 inquiring if he would be allowed to return to his unit if he 'visited Ireland to see his wife and family', to be told by an official that he could not return to his unit if he did not possess valid travel documents.[29] Such concerns were also expressed by one private who wrote to de Valera expressing his concern at the travel restrictions and asking if such restrictions were because 'we are British soldiers, or is it because we left our land of our own free will'. He added, that he hoped de Valera would not 'deprive a citizen of Éire, whether he wear a British uniform or not the liberty of free entry or departure from his native land'.[30] In the early stages of the war apparently there was some confusion surrounding what constituted a valid travel document for service personnel. After a number of inquiries were received, the office of the Irish High Commissioner in London intervened and agreed that service leave documents were acceptable as travel permits in Éire.[31]

Further complications arose over the restrictions under the Emergency Powers Act regarding the wearing of uniforms while on leave. Even in the early stages of the war, thousands of Irishmen were joining the British forces, and de Valera, alive to the political embarrassment which they could cause, requested that they should wear civilian clothes when they returned to Éire on leave. 'You could help us and help yourselves,' he told Maffey, 'if these men did not come into Ireland in uniform.' The British agreed to this request, and dumps of civilian clothes were provided at Holyhead so that servicemen travelling home could change into them.[32] Even the issue of how telegrams reporting the death of service personnel to relatives was seen as a threat to neutrality by some. During a session of the Dáil in November 1944, one Fine Gael TD asked the Taoiseach if he was aware that the British War Office, when notifying relatives of citizens of Éire who were killed in the British armed forces, referred to their 'having died for their country' and if he would 'make representations to the British on this point'. De Valera replied, 'I have no knowledge of the terms on which such notifications are made,' to which James Dillon interjected, 'we might leave the dead rest'.[33]

The Department of External Affairs received many inquires and requests for information from worried relatives of those reported missing during the war. Mrs Dora Bishop wrote to the Secretary of the Department in 1943, asking if he could make inquires through the Vatican about her son John Dillon Bishop,

29 National Archives, Ireland (NAI), DFA 202/557 File title, Travel permits 1939-45, Fitzpatrick letter, 7 December 1939.   **30** Ibid., Clark letter, 8 February 1940.   **31** Ibid., Correspondence between offices of the High Commissioner in London and Department of External Affairs, Dublin.   **32** Fisk, *In time of war*, p. 95.   **33** DFA, 241/32, Dáil report. 9 November 1944.

who was reported missing over Sicily.[34] Harry Lisney also wrote inquiring whether the Department could provide any information about his son, Lieutenant Leslie V. Lisney, reported missing from the Royal Inniskilling Rifles in Burma, and about his nephew, Ian Wells, from Co. Monaghan.[35] Actress Maureen Farrow (O'Sullivan) also contacted the Department about her brother, Major John O'Sullivan, reported injured and missing.[36] Most of these inquiries were referred to the Red Cross in Berne. On occasion the Department did intercede on behalf of servicemen. Sapper W. Coman from Cashel wrote to Dan Breen TD informing him that he had been sentenced to death after being found in France by the occupying German forces in civilian clothes and in possession of a revolver. He asked if Mr Breen could intercede with the German government on his behalf. His letter was passed to the Department, who reported the matter to the UK representative in Éire. His office reported back to the Department that the matter had been taken up by the Swiss government, who had made representation on his behalf, and that he had received a pardon. When Mr Coman returned to Cashel after the war, G2, the Army intelligence branch, kept him under surveillance for a brief period.[37] The Coman case was probably of exceptional interest to Éire's authorities because of his conviction for spying and the potential embarrassment this could cause to the state's policy of neutrality.

G2 was also active in monitoring the activities of those who wanted to provide assistance for Allied forces. In the early months of 1940 the Department of External Affairs was made aware by local Gardaí, of the activities of some citizens who were attempting to raise funds for the Allied cause. Such activities included a whist drive organised for 9 February 1940 in the Western Hotel Monaghan in aid of minesweepers and sailors. A dance was organized by Mrs Harold Goodbody in the British Legion Hall, Clara, on 2 February to provide comforts for the British forces.[38] The department objected to such activities, particularly an organisation set up in Dublin known as the Spitfire Circle which had raised funds for the *Belfast Telegraph*'s Spitfire Fund.[39] G2, estimated that £2,800 had been given in interest-free loans by Irish residents to 'the British government to help their war effort'. They also reported that 'The Spitfire Circle had collected £1,000 in Dublin and Cork.'[40] These reports concerned Frank Aiken, the Minister responsible for co-ordination of defence who believed that, 'unless the state checks or controls the number of these functions in future the "neutral" outlook of people in the country may become affected'.[41] The reality

34 DFA files series, 241/ 121-147 , Bishop letter, 2 August 1944. This file contains over 70 inquires of a similar nature. **35** Ibid., Lisney letter. **36** Ibid., Farrow telegram. **37** DFA 241/127/17. File contains a series of correspondence regarding the Coman case. **38** DFA 241/125. File Title, Comfort dances and functions to provide funds for British forces 1940. **39** Ibid., Memorandum 17 October 1940. **40** Ibid., G2 Memorandum, 30 October 1940. **41** Ibid. Aiken Memorandum, 18 March 1940

was that many were not neutral. Small groups across the country attempted, despite the attentions of the local authorities, to provide assistance for the Allied cause. One such was 'Men of Éire', which was set up by Lady Dunally of Kilboy, Nenagh, and whose aim was to do, 'welfare work for Éiremen in the British forces'.[42] It would appear such open support came largely from the minority Protestant and Anglo-Irish community. Gardaí from Co. Donegal reported a number of people including 'Protestants from Convoy and Tullyrap who were collecting funds to aid the British war effort'.[43]

It may be, as Browne argues, that, for many of the Anglo-Irish community, 'neutrality was a bitter pill to swallow. Many of them were still accustomed to think of the British forces as "our Army" and "our Navy". What others saw as sacred egotism, some of them were inclined to regard as a shameful indifference to the fate of their English kin.'[44] It would appear the government took little action to prevent its citizens from volunteering for service during the war, but was alive to the political embarrassment their participation could cause at home and abroad. It did not however, welcome the activities of the passive minority at home who were keen to support their endeavours on behalf of the Allied cause. Nor would it tolerate the desertion of service personnel from the state's defence forces to join the British armed forces. Such desertions were estimated at 7000 by the then Minister of Defence, Oscar Traynor, in 1946. Army intelligence and the military police were mobilised to apprehend these deserters. One volunteer recalled seeing, 'Redcap Spotters from the Irish army looking out for deserters'.[45] It would seem that many of these deserters were motivated by simple economics. A volunteer from Dublin left the Irish Army with his pay of 18s. for the British Army worth 22s. a week, as he recalled, 'nothing to do with anti-Hitler'.[46] Another recruit remembered meeting many deserters from the Irish defence forces and asserted that 'many of them were family men who could earn a pound a week with the British Army'.[47] However, many people were volunteering to join the British forces because they opposed neutrality and, in Aiken's opinion, they could have undermined public morale and furthered opposition to neutrality.

Violet McGuire wrote of leaving Westland Row railway station in 1942: 'Many others like myself were going to join the forces in Britain, compelled by a desire to help the war effort, and thus contribute to what, in those dark days, seemed a rather problematic Allied victory.'[48] A naval lieutenant from Dublin

---

42 Ibid., Leaflet Produced by Men of Éire, 1945. **43** Ibid., Garda Report, 8 April 40. **44** T. Browne, *Ireland: A social and cultural history* (Glasgow, 1982), p. 173. **45** Tommy Meehan, ex-Serviceman, Private, East Surrey Regiment, President, British Legion, Dublin Central. Interview 5 March 1996. **46** Myers interviews, *Irish Times*, 6 June 1984. **47** Meehan interveiw, 5 March 1996. **48** Violet Mc Guire, 'The departure', in Leslie Daiken (ed.), *They go: the Irish. A miscellany of wartime writing* (London, 1945), p. 83.

asserted, 'I was one of 160,000 who volunteered from neutral Ireland because we believed that that bloody little monster from Germany had to be stopped.'[49] It may be that there existed a certain residue of loyalty to Britain among the minority of Protestants who remained in Éire. Bernard Share describes thém as, 'a dwindling but still influential minority (who) were, though physically in occupation of decaying country houses and other crumbling enclaves, not living in contemporary Ireland at all. They talked of "our Navy" and "our Air Force" meaning those of England, though a great number of them had done what they saw as their duty and joined the British forces.'[50] This was certainly the case with Brian Inglis who recalled that many among his 'set' were inclined to join out of duty.[51] Peter Ross, who received a Military Cross while with the Royal Tank Regiment in North Africa, remembers joining up while still a student in Trinity College, Dublin, because it was 'the thing to do'.[52] It is difficult to assess the size and importance of the contribution from what might be called the Anglo-Irish middle class but it is worth noting that several leading figures in the British armed forces belonged to this group, including Field Marshals Montgomery and Alexander and Brigadier O'Donovan as well as the First Admiral of the Fleet, the earl of Cork and Orrery. Additionally there existed a plethora of small support groups committed to providing material and financial aid to the volunteers and the war effort.

It is probably fair to say that organised opposition to the government's policy of neutrality during the war did not exist in any real terms. But one could argue that many thousands showed their opposition to neutrality by joining the British armed forces, and by so doing helped to make Éire less neutral in fact. Churchill exploited this line of argument in his Victory speech when he referred to the action of the Dublin government being so much 'at variance with the temper and instinct of thousands of Southern Irishmen who hastened to the battle front to prove their ancient valour'. However, this ignores other factors which motivated volunteers – such as economic necessity and a thirst for adventure. Moreover, it ignores evidence suggesting that many of those who enlisted, even those with a residual loyalty to Britain, tacitly supported the position of the Irish government.

It would seem, as Myles Dungan has argued, that 'many of the Irishmen who joined the British Army could not afford the luxury of staying neutral'.[53] Unemployment in Ireland was relatively high in the late 1930s, the *Irish Times* recorded that the number of registered unemployed at labour exchanges on 28 August 1939 stood at 70,961. Emigration was also relatively high in this period,

---

49 Myers interviews, *Irish Times*, 6 June 1984.   **50** Bernard Share, *The emergency 1939-45* (Dublin, 1978) p. 71.   **51** Inglis, *West Briton*, pp 39-45.   **52** Peter Ross, *All valiant dust; An Irish man abroad* (Dublin, 1992) p. 18.   **53** M. Dungan, *Distant drums; Irish soldiers in foreign armies* (Dublin, 1993), p. 145.

at approximately 18,770 a year between 1936 and 1946; as Gerard Quinn notes, 'the great majority of whom were young and from the poorest sections of the population'.[54] De Valera's government was well aware of the realities of high unemployment and the benefits of emigration for the faltering wartime economy. A memo transmitted to de Valera by the Assistant Secretary of External Affairs reported the views of J.J. McElligott, the Finance Secretary, who was against restricting emigration to Britain. McElligott argued that, 'it [emigration] provides a safety valve against revolution, and the resulting inflow of ready money – he put as high as £100,00-£150,00 thousand a week – did a great deal to relive distress and maintain economic activity.'[55] It is highly likely that the exodus of volunteers to the British armed forces and those who went to work in Britain during the war did much to alleviate economic pressures in Éire. However, due to the censorship restrictions of the Emergency Powers Act, reporting on emigration and enlistment with the British forces was prohibited. As the Controller of Censorship, T.J. Coyne, rather sarcastically put it, 'picturing thousands of starving Irish workers flocking across to the bombed areas of England or to join the British forces, or maybe to throw themselves into the sea, have simply got to be stopped if public morale is not to be hopelessly compromised'.[56] It would appear that Éire's government and her officials were all too aware of the economic realities which encouraged tens of thousand of its citizens to enlist with the British armed forces and how potentially embarrassing publication of these facts was for the neutral state.

To portray the service of Éire's volunteers as being primarily driven by economic deprivation would however be a gross simplification. Whatever the motivation of the volunteers, there is little or no evidence to suggest that the Irish government took any concerted action to prevent them joining the British forces. Of course, the fact that the government did not officially record their movements and censored any reporting of recruitment and enlistment of volunteer activity suppressed any recognition of the size of Éire's contribution to the Allied war effort. This in turn led to a great deal of confusion and inaccuracy regarding the size of Éire's contingent in the British armed forces. Figures range from the *Manchester Guardian*'s estimate of over 300,000 (reported on 13 March 1944) to a Dominion Office document entitled, 'Southern Irish who joined in Belfast', which puts the figure at 38,554. The Dominion Office provided a variety of figures for Éire's volunteers who served with the British Forces.[57] Another was given in reply to a question put by the Earl of Cork and Orrery in the Lords, the Secretary of State for Dominion Affairs, Lord Addison replied on the 19th of March 1946, that 42,665

54 Gerard Quinn, 'Changing pattern of Irish society 1938-51' in Kevin Nowlan and T.D. Williams (eds), *Ireland in the war years and after* (Dublin, 1969), p. 107. 55 NA S11582a May 1942. 56 Donal Ó Drisceoil, *Censorship in Ireland; neutrality, politics and society* (Cork, 1996) p 256. 57 PRO DO 35/ box 1228, 'Southern Irish who joined in Belfast'.

including, 4,695 women volunteers from Éire had served in the British Armed Force. These figures were compiled on the basis of the place of birth provided by the volunteers. Addison admitted that these figures were unsatisfactory and argued it was 'impossible to give more accurate figures'.[58] There is little doubt that tens of thousand of Éire's citizens fought for Britain during the war.

In 1945 Sean O'Casey wrote in the following terms of the legacy of those Irish who had fought on behalf of the British and other armies: 'These fighters have stretched out to the present day, and, I daresay, will go on for ever. Looks like there'll always be blossoms of blood on our sprig of Green. Are we proud of these men? Not a bit; all but a few know anything about them, and their names are never mentioned at home.'[59] O'Casey's lament was written before he could have known of how Second World War veterans would be remembered or honoured in Éire. There is some evidence that in the immediate post-war period many were inclined to take pride in the achievements of the state's wartime volunteers. Carrol notes, 'There was pride in the revelation that the contingent of Southern Irishmen serving in the British forces won a total of 780 decorations including eight Victoria Crosses.'[60] Indeed, the *Irish Times* reported extensively on honours received by 'Irish Heroes' commenting, 'During the recent War brave deeds won honour for Ireland's name although the nation was officially neutral. Great numbers of Irishmen fought with the Armed forces and where ever they fought their fighting quality was outstanding.'[61] The *Irish Independent* also reported on the bravery of Éire's citizens; during November 1945 it told of the 'Priest Hero', a Fr Duffey from Cork who had, during action in the Rhur, 'crawled under shellfire to a number of wounded men including two Germans and one by one carried them to safety'.[62] But despite the extensive reports of the bravery of some, most volunteers were to return to Éire not as conquering heroes but, quietly and almost unnoticed, to an uncertain future.

Lady Hanratty's welfare association, Men of Éire, expressed concern that the volunteers 'have no status in their native land and therefore have a poor chance in the post-war rush for employment. They may even be boycotted and refused employment on their return home.'[63] A memorial petition sent to Clement Atlee on behalf of Irish volunteers worried that on their return to Éire, those who demobilised would not receive unemployment benefit rights, and thus be deprived of 'valuable protection against the evils of unemployment', arguing that this 'clouds the prospects and effects the plans of all volunteers'.[64] One volunteer who returned to Dublin in 1946 recalled no difficulties in receiving bene-

58 Document contained in file headed, 'Irish contribution to the Second World War', D/T S15262 NAI. entitled 'How many?' by H.H. **59** Daiken, op. cit., p. 17. **60** Carrol, op. cit., p 163. **61** *Irish Times*, 'Editorial', 10 November 1945. **62** The *Irish Independent*, 'Priest Hero saved wounded underfire', 12 November 1945. **63** DFA 241/125 'Men of Éire' Pamphlet 1945. **64** D/T S15262 'Memorial Petition', 1945.

fits: 'We were on Insurance stamps which were paid until they ran out.'[65] There
is also evidence that many companies with historical links to Britain were quite
supportive to returning volunteers – most notably Guinness. This is an assertion
confirmed by another volunteer who was employed by 'good old uncle Arthur',
where he remained for over 40 years and who recalled that there were 'quite a
few ex-service men working there'.[66]

Nonetheless the Allied victory was not universally welcomed in Éire. Perhaps
the most infamous illustration of such sentiment was the incident in College
Green on VE day and the subsequent rioting involving some Trinity students
and nationalists. One consequence of these disturbances became apparent when
the British Legion applied to hold a Remembrance Day procession from St
Stephen's Green to the War Memorial at Islandbridge on 11 November 1945. The
procession was not permitted (on the advice of Garda Commissioner on the
grounds that it may constitute a 'breach of the peace').[67] This ban caused widespread indignation. An *Irish Independent* editorial called for 'some explanation of
the Garda action'.[68] James Dillon spoke passionately in the Dáil in support of
the constitutional right of the British Legion to hold their procession and asked
Mr Boland, the Minister of Justice, 'If a body of law-abiding decent citizens
were to be made responsible for the action of one isolated, ignorant brat, who
from the top of Trinity College burnt the national flag'.[69] In the event a service
did take place at Islandbridge, where about 6,500 servicemen marched passed
the Memorial.[70] The following year a cabinet meeting decided that permission
would be given for a British Legion procession on 10November 1946.[71] Any overt
display of commemorative militarism by ex-British Army volunteers was liable
to cause offence to those who persisted with anti-British sentiments. The government had to thread a fine line between upholding constitutional rights of
assembly and association while avoiding offending some nationalist elements.

Many volunteers kept quiet about their wartime service. One veteran interviewed in 1984 expressed the view that 'there are odd folks around here; it is
acceptable to be a first World War veteran but the Second World War is different. It is fashionable to have been in the Somme but not in France 40 years
ago'.[72] Another volunteer felt that he could not 'wear his poppy on remembrance
day' and recalls that on several occasions remembrance services he attended 'were
picketed by republicans'.[73] After 1969 the British Legion suspended their street
collections.[74] Perhaps the irony is that many from both north and south of the

65 Meehan interview, 5 March 1996. 66 Meehan, interview 5 March 1996. 67 *Irish Times*, 9
November 1945. 68 *Irish Independent*, 9 November 1945. 69 Dáil Debates, 15 November
1945, vol. 98, no. 5, col. 1240. 70 *Irish Times*, 12 November 1945. 71 S 3370c D/T File title,
'Armistice day commemorations 1932-46'. Cabinet memorandum 15 October 1946. 72 *Irish
Independent*, interview with unnamed veteran of D-Day landing, 6 June 1984. 73 Meehan
interview, 5 March 1996. 74 Grogan interview, 4 March 1996.

border served together during the war in the Ulster regiments. Brigadier Pat Scott, who commanded the Irish Brigade in Italy, wrote: 'What we hope is that all the magnificent deeds wrought by the sons of Éire in this war against the barbarism of Germany and her allies, may be remembered to her credit. It is sometimes overlooked that the services of every Irishman from any part of Ireland are given of their own free will for the good of the cause'.[75] Sam McAughtry, who estimates that one fifth of the Royal Ulster Rifles were from the South, recalled how 'A ceremony took place in which Field Marshall Montgomery awarded two riflemen with military medals, illustrat(ing) the all-Irish aspect of the regiment. Side by side, accepting their decorations, were Riflemen Feeny of Dublin and Gilliand of Newtownards, Co. Down'.[76]

It is worth recalling the words of Conor Cruise O'Brien while commenting in an editorial of the *Trinity College Journal* (the *TCD*), during 1939. in which he wrote, 'Those of us who are not glad to be neutral in Ireland will, we hope, speedily depart to help which ever belligerent they favour. Most of us are heartily glad to be outside, if only just outside, this tremendous futile catastrophe'.[77] Many of the state's citizens did as O'Brien suggested and departed to fight for the Allies during the war. They went to war, for a variety of reasons. Neutral Éire did nothing to prevent or encourage their decision to contribute to the British war effort. Nonetheless their action could possibly have compromised the State's neutral status. Thus, the State choose to disregard their contribution, by a variety of means. Censorship prevented publication of any reference to the activities of these volunteers. Special powers were introduced to prevent the wearing of uniforms on leave. Action was taken to prevent the collection of funds in the State on behalf of the British war effort. Protecting neutrality meant the state was unable to act on behalf of its citizens who were embroiled in a war from which it stood apart. And yet Éire's neutrality was not absolute. Éire was, as one historian notes, 'on the side of the Allies ... but quietly'.[78] Thus neutrality was pursued in a manner that took heed of diplomatic realities. Nonetheless, by the end of the war Éire had a major credibility problem in a post-war world shaped by victors. Churchill took delight in contrasting the bravery and valour of those Southern Irishmen who 'hastened to the battlefront' with de Valera's governments action in refusing to concede the Treaty ports.[79] If, as some have suggested, Éire's neutrality was primarily borne out of 'national self-interest', it is conceivable that such interests would have been equally served in the post-war period by vigorously promoting the contribution made by at least 40,000 of its citizens to the war effort.[80]

75 Quoted in Richard Doherty, *Clear the way. A history of the 38th (Irish) Brigade, 1941-47* (Dublin, 1993), p. 160. **76** *Irish Times*, 6 June 1984. **77** Quoted in Bernard Share, *The emergency, 1939-45* (Dublin, 1978), p. 9. **78** Keogh and Nolan, op. cit., p. 124. **79** W. Churchill, *The Second World War Vol. 1: The gathering storm* (London, 1948), p. 582. **80** J.P. Duggan,

Duggan notes that, 'Éire has nothing to be ashamed of in its crusading record in combating it (Nazism). Thousands of Irishmen died at the tip of the spear – that's where they generally were – on the battle fields. Éire got eight Victoria Crosses to prove it. It is an extraordinary and unsung contribution.'[81] In order to understand why these volunteers' contribution remained unsung in the post-war period, it is necessary to consider the State's policy of neutrality beyond its declaration of self-interest. Éire's neutrality was also an expression of national sovereignty and independence. More particularly, the ability to pursue a foreign policy independent of Britain. The fact that tens of thousands of the State's citizens chose, for whatever reason, to join the British forces during the war was an uncomfortable reminder of Éire's social, economic and traditional links to Britain. Moreover, since the question of partition remained a matter of dispute between the two states there was little possibility of any recognition of a shared wartime heritage. The presence of the British Army in Northern Ireland since 1969 has meant that any official recognition of the contribution of the State's citizens to the British war effort was anathema to many nationalists, both north and south of the border. It may well be that by ignoring the contribution of Éire's volunteers in the Second World War, the State has been guilty of the convenient pursuance of a one dimensional national identity. Perhaps it is time, as former Taoiseach John Bruton asserted at a commemorative service at Islandbridge on the 50th anniversary of VE, to acknowledge 'a shared experience of Irish and British people ... to remember a British part of the inheritance of all who live in Ireland.'[82]

Neutral Ireland and the Third Reich (Dublin, 1985), p. 258. **81** Ibid., p. 259. **82** *Irish Times*, 29 April 1995.

Irish heroes of the Second World War

Richard Doherty

The story is told of the occasion in the Anzio beachhead in 1944 when a prisoner taken by the Irish Guards demanded to know why neutrals were serving with the Allies in Italy.[1] Shortly afterwards, during the battles around Lake Trasimene, 1st Royal Irish Fusiliers took a number of Germans prisoner. These men were bemused by the phenomenon of Irish soldiers fighting, as they saw it, for England, since they believed that a permanent state of hostility existed between the two nations. Their confusion could not have been helped by some of the responses they received to their questions about the existence of Irish regiments in Britain's Army. Typical were remarks such as 'We took pity on them' and 'Sure, we wouldn't want to see them beat, now.' The bewilderment of the prisoners was considered worthy of recording by regimental officers.[2]

Most of those officers were Irishmen themselves, from every corner of the island. Unlike the German prisoners they saw no contradiction in neutral Irishmen fighting for Britain. And they were often emphatic about their Irishness: the Irish Brigade songbook includes the 'Soldier's Song', 'The Wearing of the Green', 'The Minstrel Boy' and 'Kelly, the Boy from Killane'.[3] Irish officers visited Dr Kiernan, the Irish minister to the Vatican, who took a proprietorial interest in the Irish Brigade and presented it with a pennant bearing the harp on the white of the tricolour; that pennant flew from the brigade commander's staff car on a number of occasions thereafter. One officer spent a pleasant afternoon in Dr Kiernan's home singing Irish ballads with the minister's wife, the singer Delia Murphy.[4]

The Irish Brigade was the largest Irish formation of the Second World War. The Royal Artillery had 3rd (Ulster) Anti-Aircraft Brigade, but this formation was broken up soon after the outbreak of war; its various units went to different theatres of operations. Throughout the Army there were other Irish units. The Royal Air Force had No. 502 (Ulster) Squadron but the idea of a Shamrock

1 D.L. Fitzgerald, *History of the Irish Guards in the Second World War* (Aldershot, 1949), p. 339. 2 T.P.D. Scott, *An account of the Irish Brigade* (private account written for the Colonel of The Royal Irish Fusiliers, copies held by Royal Irish Fusiliers' Museum, Armagh). 3 *Irish Brigade songbook*, copy in author's possession. 4 The pennant is in the Royal Irish Fusiliers' Museum, Armagh; Colonel K.G.F. Chavasse DSO and Bar, in correspondence with author.

Wing, espoused by Churchill in October 1941, came to naught. In the Royal
Navy Irishmen served as individuals with no Irish groupings.[5] No large formations of Irishmen existed, unlike the Great War when Ireland provided three
infantry divisions, the equivalent of an army corps, without taking into account
either the many Irish units or individuals not serving in those divisions.

No one has yet produced a definitive figure for the Irish, from both sides of
the border, who served in the 1939-45 war. The very subject has often been the
cause of controversy, eliciting heated debate that sometimes takes on a political
hue, reflecting the political differences between Northern Ireland and the
Republic. Late in the war, figures as high as 300,000 were being quoted in newspapers, this particular claim appearing in the letters' column of the *Manchester
Guardian*. That figure was halved in a *Daily Telegraph* letter while, in the United
States, the *New Yorker* put the figure at 250,000.[6] In 1946 the Dominions Office
informed Sir Basil Brooke, Northern Ireland's Prime Minister, that 37,282 men
and women from Northern Ireland had served in the forces during the war.
Based on that information, even the lowest of the three figures quoted in the
previous paragraph indicates that a neutral country, perceived to be anti-British,
had made a much higher contribution to the war effort than had Northern
Ireland, so noted for its loyalty to the crown. It is interesting to note that by
January 1942 the then Northern Irish Prime Minister, John Andrews, was claiming that 23,000 Ulstermen had joined the forces, a figure that Spender, the head
of the Northern Ireland civil service, thought a rather optimistic estimate.[7] In
early 1945 the Admiralty, War Office and Air Ministry produced figures indicating that 42,665 men, and women, from Éire were *serving*: 27,840 men and 3,060
women in the Army; 715 in the Royal Navy; and 11,050 in the RAF. A year later
this figure had been reduced to 38,000 with no explanation provided for the
reduction. Perhaps some civil servant decided to make the two figures more balanced; but this can only be speculation.[8]

Joseph T. Carroll provides a further figure, giving a breakdown from
Dominion Office files: Army 28,645; Royal Navy and Royal Marines 483; and
Royal Air Force 9,426 for that revised total of 38,554. Carroll also quotes a letter
from General Sir Hubert Gough – of Curragh incident fame – in *The Times* in
August 1944, claiming that there were 165,000 Irish next-of-kin addresses for

5 R. Doherty, *Clear the way! A history of the 38th (Irish) Brigade, 1941-47* (Dublin, 1993); R.
Doherty, '3rd (Ulster) Anti-Aircraft Brigade (SR)', *Irish Sword*, 18, 71 (Summer 1991), pp 120-
8; W. Churchill, *The Second World War*, vol. VI (London, 1948), p. 329.   **6** *Manchester
Guardian*, 13 March 1944; *Daily Telegraph*, 18 October 1944; PRO, Kew, DO35/1230
WX132/1/140, Sedgwick to Costar, 3 November 1945.   **7** PRO, Kew, DO35/1230 WX132/1/124
Machtig to Maxwell, 12 March 1946; PRONI, Spender Diaries, D715/18/ 21 January 1942.   **8**
PRO, Kew, DO35/1230 WX132/1/124; R. Fisk, *In time of war, Ireland, Ulster and the price of
neutrality, 1939-1945* (London, 1983), p. 523.

British servicemen and women.[9] However, the files of *The Times* show no such letter although there is a note from Gough regarding the 200,000-plus Irish who were involved in the UK war effort, either in the armed forces or in industry. One assumes that the letter referred to by O'Carroll appeared in another paper but the author has, as yet, been unable to find it. If Gough had such information – and he was in a position to have it – its significance is worth considering. Gough had been a supporter of the unionist cause and so there is no reason to suspect him of bias in favour of nationalists, especially of de Valera. The fact that he refers to next-of-kin addresses would also cover the many Irish who joined up in Britain, and those from Éire who crossed the border to enlist in Northern Ireland. The figure supplied to Sir Basil Brooke of 38,282 personnel from Northern Ireland serving in the forces during the war must also include a significant proportion of individuals who had crossed the border to enlist. Brian Barton points out that between September 1941 and May 1945, 11,500 individuals volunteered from Northern Ireland while recruiting centres there approved a further 18,600 Éire recruits.[10]

At Islandbridge in April 1995, Taoiseach John Bruton suggested that 150,000 Irishmen, from both sides of the border, had served in Britain's forces during the war, of whom 10,000 had died. Ascertaining the true number of Irish dead is difficult; the Commonwealth War Graves Commission insist that there is no mechanism for establishing nationality, or place of birth, from their records. However, the recent (late-1998) placing of their files on the internet would allow detailed, if laborious, research on that subject.[11]

Another method of arriving at a figure for Irish dead in the British forces is to trawl the lists of dead for all three services to ascertain places of birth. This raises the interesting question: what is an Irishman, or Irishwoman? The purist definition is someone born in Ireland which omits those of Irish parentage born elsewhere but includes those of non-Irish parentage born in Ireland. Two Victoria Cross winners illustrate this point. David Lord, VC. was born in Cork of Welsh parents – his father was a Royal Welch Fusiliers' warrant officer – while Eugene Esmonde, VC was born in Yorkshire of Irish parents and moved back to Tipperary as an infant.[12] However, such cases are probably not statistically significant and would mean that trawling the rolls of honour should give an accurate number for the Irish dead. One problem remains: there is a roll of honour for the Army at the Public Record Office in Kew, but no parallels for the Royal Navy and Royal Air Force. The latter is especially difficult as the records of their dead appear to have been kept in three separate ways and only a correlation of all three would provide an accurate answer. A trawl of a cross-section (50 per cent)

9 J.T. Carroll, *Ireland in the war years* (Dublin, 1975), p. 182. 10 B. Barton, *Northern Ireland in the Second World War* (Belfast, 1983), p. 54. 11 Commonwealth War Graves Commission, letter to author. 12 The Military Historical Society, Lummis Files E.21 and L.40.

of the Army roll of honour at Kew provided the following: of 84,489 dead, a total of 1,709 were Irish, which suggests that the Irish death toll was about 2 per cent. Adjusting this to represent the entire Army, and the higher Irish death toll in Irish regiments, the total of Irish dead comes to 4,468. From this it is possible to calculate the number of Irish soldiers: 171,000 British soldiers died from a total enlistment of 3,778,000, representing one dead to every twenty-two who served. Applying that ratio to the Irish dead gives a total of 98,296 Irish in the Army.[13]

Unfortunately, the figures for the other two services are much cruder estimates: as the Army, with 2 per cent Irish enlistment, had the highest proportion of Irish personnel, a figure of 1 per cent was assumed for both Royal Navy and Royal Air Force to give an Irish enlistment of 9,230 sailors and 11,850 airmen.[14] Thus the total of Irish serving in the British forces would have been about 120,000, most of whom enlisted during the war. Based on the place of birth information in the Army's roll of honour, about 67,826 were from the present Republic and 52,174 from Northern Ireland. A fully accurate figure for Irish involvement in the war may never be agreed upon. But, whether or not that happens, there remains a fascinating story: the part played by those Irishmen – and women – in the most horrific and cataclysmic war in human history.

Irishmen were serving from the beginning to the end of the war. We cannot claim that the first shots were fired by an Irishman, nor that the first VC was won by an Irishman, but there are still some claims that can be substantiated. The Royal Air Force's first VC of the war was to an Irishman – Donald Garland from Ballinacorr, Co. Wicklow, who died in his obsolete Fairey Battle in a suicidal attack on the bridge over the Albert canal at Veldwezelt. (His three brothers also died during the war, two on active service and one from ill-health while in the RAF). And Captain Harold Marcus Ervine-Andrews, of the East Lancashire Regiment, born in Keadue, Co. Cavan, was the Army's first gazetted VC of the war, although actually the last of the campaign in France and the Low Countries in 1940. The first Military Cross – Britain's third highest military gallantry award – awarded to a chaplain in the war went to Fr Thomas Duggan, a Great War veteran, and a member of the staff of St Finbarr's College, Cork. Interestingly, the third clerical award went to a Dubliner, the Revd Richard Newcombe Craig, at Calais in May 1940.[15]

The range of Irish service was comprehensive: from high commanders to lowly private soldiers, from chaplains to commandos, from doctors to despatch riders, from vets to air gunners. At least 161 priests from Irish dioceses served in the British forces, not counting those who volunteered from dioceses in Britain

---

13 PRO, Kew, WO304; J. Ellis, *The World War II databook* (London, 1993), p. 254.   14 Ellis, ibid.   15 The Military Historical Society, Lummis Files, G. 8; C. Bowyer, *For valour* (London, 1992), p. 215; The Military Historical Society, Lummis Files, E. 20; R. Doherty, *The sons of Ulster* (Belfast, 1992), pp 48-49; Anon, *Volunteers from Éire* (Dublin, 1944), p. 22.

and a number from the Irish College, following the liberation of Rome in 1944.[16] The Church of Ireland contributed 66 chaplains from Irish dioceses, plus some from English dioceses.[17] The Presbyterian Church in Ireland and the Methodist Church also provided chaplains. Many Irish doctors served with the Royal Army Medical Corps. Desmond Whyte, from Co. Down, ought to have been awarded the VC in Burma in 1944 but instead received the DSO, the highest gallantry award made to an Irish doctor in the war.[18] There were many MCs and a large number of awards in the Order of the British Empire, which may have seemed ironic to some of the recipients.

There were also the ordinary servicemen, sailors, marines, gunners, sappers, craftsmen, stretcher-bearers and, suffering most of all, the poor bloody infantry-men. Their war was often boring, they were poorly paid, and they spent long hours moaning about food, NCOs and officers; and then they were ordered to risk their lives in pursuit of a strategy that they often did not understand, and which, in its operational guise, occasionally seemed to make no sense at all. There were times when they rebelled. Some deserted, some cracked up in the face of what they were called upon to endure; but most did endure and either died in the enduring or survived the war. Those who survived, having been at the sharp end, were, to borrow from Yeats, 'changed utterly'. I have in my pos-session two photographs of a soldier of the London Irish Rifles: one was taken in January 1942, not long after he joined up, and it shows a fresh-faced lad, little more than a boy; the second was taken in Italy in December 1944 but the man in it has matured by many more than the three years between the two pictures.

It would be impossible to catalogue all the experiences of Irishmen during the war but three men may serve as examples. They are not typical in that two won the VC while the third was also highly-decorated with two DSOs, a DFC and an AFC. They are typical in that they represent Ireland, and that they served at sea, on land and in the air. Although born in Yorkshire in 1909, where his father practised as a doctor, Eugene Esmonde was an Irishman and the family returned to Co. Tipperary later that year when his grandfather died and Doctor John Joseph Esmonde inherited the family home at Drominagh. Esmonde's great-uncle, Captain Thomas Esmonde of the 18th (Royal Irish) Regiment, had won the Victoria Cross in 1855 during the Crimean War. Another ancestor, John Esmonde, was executed for his part in the 1798 rebellion.[19]

Having decided that the priesthood was not for him, Eugene Esmonde joined the RAF in 1928 and later became a pilot with Imperial Airways with

16 T. Johnstone and J. Hagerty, *The cross on the sword* (London, 1996), p. 195; Bishop Edward Daly and Mgr John Shortall to author. 17 *Church of Ireland Gazette* office to author. 18 J. Masters, *The road past Mandalay* (London, 1961), p. 278; Doherty, *The sons of Ulster*, pp 110-11. 19 Military Historical Society, Lummis Files, E. 21; C. Bowyer, *Eugene Esmonde, VC, DSO* (London, 1983), p. 17.

whom he flew for five years until 1939. He was then offered a regular commission in the Fleet Air arm as a lieutenant-commander and re-enlisted on 14 April. After refresher training he took command of No. 754 Squadron before being appointed to command 825 Squadron, equipped with Fairey Swordfish torpedo-bombers. By May 1941 Esmonde's was a highly-efficient squadron, superbly led, with tremendous morale and considerable operational experience.[20] No. 825 was then operating from the aircraft carrier HMS *Victorious* in Admiral Tovey's Home Fleet pursuing the German battleship *Bismarck*. In atrocious weather conditions, Esmonde led 825 Squadron in a strike intended to slow *Bismarck's* progress and allow Tovey's ships to engage it. Six of Esmonde's aircraft returned safely. For his part in that operation, Eugene Esmonde was awarded the Distinguished Service Order. *Victorious's* captain described his leadership as 'skilful and gallant' and commended his unbounded enthusiasm, which inspired the whole squadron.[21]

At the end of May, 825 Squadron transferred to *Ark Royal* to operate with Force H in the Mediterranean. In November, *Ark Royal* carried out an aircraft delivery mission to Malta. After flying the fighters off, the carriers – the old carrier *Argus* accompanied the *Ark* – and their escort turned for Gibraltar. Next day *Ark Royal* was struck by a torpedo. Strenuous efforts were made to save the carrier but fire in a boiler room stopped salvage efforts for two hours and, as the ship listed to 35 degrees, it was clear that *Ark Royal* was finished. The 'abandon ship' order was finally given, and the last 250 men slid down ropes to the destroyer HMS *Laforey*. Except for the captain, Eugene Esmonde was the last to leave. He had volunteered to stay with the skeleton crew and, appointing himself catering officer, arranged food and refreshments for the men who struggled to save their ship. After leaving the ship he, 'continued to see to the welfare of his men, including their spiritual needs in the case of fellow Roman Catholics by arranging for a local priest at Gibraltar to attend them'.[22] His work on board the carrier, and during *Ark Royal's* death throes, earned a Mention in Despatches that spoke of Esmonde's 'courage, enterprise and resolution in air attacks on the enemy'.[23]

The bulk of 825 Squadron's crews were transferred to Lee-on-Solent to re-equip. By now Esmonde had commanded 825 for 18 months with most of that time on front-line operations. In the RAF he would probably have been 'rested' at this stage with a non-operational posting, but the Fleet Air Arm was short of pilots with Esmonde's experience and rank which probably played a part in his continuing to command 825 Squadron. In January 1942 he had only six aircraft, although there was no shortage of Swordfish, and only two of his pilots and four observers had seen operational service; all six telegraphists/air gunners (TAGs) had been on operations. This part-trained half-strength unit was soon to be

20 Ibid., pp 67-9.   21 *London Gazette*, 16 September 1941.   22 Bowyer, *Eugene Esmonde*, pp 105-6, 108.   23 *London Gazette*, 20 Jan. 1942.

launched on an impossible mission, from which most of them would not return. The mission was against the German battleships *Scharnhorst* and *Gneisenau* which had sunk some 115,000 tons of Allied shipping in three months before docking at Brest in March 1941, where they were later joined by the heavy cruiser *Prinz Eugen*. The presence of three major German surface units was a considerable headache to the Admiralty as the ships threatened both Atlantic and Africa-bound convoys and added to the overstretching of Royal Naval resources.[24]

The RAF was asked to deploy bombers against the German ships. Bomber Command's supremo, Air Marshal Sir Richard Peirse (an Irishman), issued a directive stating that, should they attempt to move, the ships would be attacked by surface vessels and aircraft by day, but no aircraft would attack by night. The Germans were happy to keep all three ships at Brest since their presence there caused considerable diversion of British naval and air effort. However, Hitler, convinced that the Allies intended to invade Norway, delivered an ultimatum to Admiral Raeder, the Kriegsmarine commander, to move *Scharnhorst*, *Gneisenau* and *Prinz Eugen* from Brest, or have the ships dismantled and their heavy guns moved to the Norwegian coastal defences. Raeder, with little choice, began planning for the move from Brest to a German port and then to Norway. Admiral Otto Ciliax, who was assigned the task, decided to leave Brest after dusk on a moonless night to gain maximum cover for the first stage of the voyage. Moon, tide and current conditions combined to make 11 February the date chosen for Operation CEREBUS; *Scharnhorst*, *Gneisenau* and *Prinz Eugen* would slip their moorings at 7.30 p. m. and, with their escort force, sail through the night towards the English channel, entering the straits of Dover around noon the following day. Sailing in darkness reduced the chances of detection and allowed the opportunity to cover much of the route to Germany without being intercepted.[25]

British planning for a possible escape from Brest by the German ships was based upon a daylight sailing although Air-to-Surface-Vessel (ASV) radar-equipped aircraft flew regular nocturnal patrol routes off the French coast. During early February, Bomber Command mined the possible routes of a German dash from Brest and three squadrons of Beaufort torpedo-bombers stood ready to attack the German ships. The Beauforts were seen by senior naval and air officers as the principal weapon against Ciliax's force. Remembering the *Bismarck* attack, and the damage wrought earlier on the Italian fleet at Taranto by Swordfish torpedo-bombers, it was believed that the Beauforts could damage the enemy ships enough to leave them at the mercy of Royal Navy surface vessels. Almost as a postscript, a force of Swordfish was added to the attacking air units by Vice-Admiral Bertram Ramsay at Dover. Ramsay shared the belief that the Germans would leave Brest in daylight and pass through the Dover straits in the darkness before dawn, thus providing cover for the Swordfish, and the

24 Bowyer, *Eugene Esmonde*, pp 109, 112. **25** Ibid., pp 115; 118-19.

Beauforts, to attack without a fighter escort. The Swordfish 'force' was to be Esmonde's 825 Squadron which moved to RAF Manston in Kent in readiness for the operation.[26]

On 11 February Eugene Esmonde travelled to Buckingham Palace to receive his DSO for his part in operations against the *Bismarck*. That evening he was a guest at a dinner given by Admiral Somerville. Across the Channel, Admiral Ciliax had issued an order to his command to leave harbour for a night exercise between La Pallice and St Nazaire before returning to Brest the following day. The order was a cover for Operation CEREBUS: the breakout was about to begin. The German ships were delayed for almost two hours by an RAF bombing raid. At 9.14 p.m. Ciliax gave the order to slip anchor. *Scharnhorst*, as Ciliax's flagship, led the ships out of harbour. By midnight they were passing Ushant, sailing at best speed through a thin haze on a clear, starlit night. A combination of circumstances allowed the Germans over twelve hours of undetected sailing before the alarm was raised at 11.35 a.m., an hour after a sighting had first been broadcast by a Spitfire pilot. Ciliax could not have asked for better luck.[27]

It was 12.15 p.m. before Esmonde and his crews climbed aboard their Swordfish to attack the German ships. An escort of five fighter squadrons had been promised and Admiral Ramsay had told Esmonde that the decision to go was his and his alone. He was *not* being ordered to lead his squadron in a daylight attack. Assured of protection by five fighter squadrons, however, Esmonde made the decision to go, having asked 'for the love of God' that the fighters be with 825 Squadron on time. At 12.25 p.m. he led his Swordfish off Manston's frozen grass runway for the rendezvous with the Spitfires. At 12.32 p.m. ten Spitfires of 72 Squadron met Esmonde's planes over Ramsgate. No more fighters appeared. Esmonde could, justifiably, have called off the attack since he had accepted the daylight mission only on the understanding that his highly vulnerable biplanes would have 60 fighters in support. Instead of ordering his squadron back to base, Esmonde, with a wave of a gloved hand, led them to their rendezvous with Admiral Ciliax's force. Why did he choose to do so? His biographer, Chaz Bowyer, suggests that, since he had given his word to Ramsay that 825 Squadron would attack, he felt duty bound to carry out the operation as:

> by his very nature [he] would have felt totally obliged to honour his word – honour and duty had been the lynchpins of the Esmonde family lineage and Eugene particularly exemplified those ideals throughout his life. His devout Catholic faith undoubtedly softened the all-too human fear of death and its aftermath. But, whatever his actual thoughts at that crucial moment, Esmonde's decision became instantly plain.

26 Ibid., p. 121.   **27** Ibid., pp 124, 132.

At fifty feet above the waves the Swordfish made for their target at less than 100 m.p.h. Above them their escorts flew a weaving flightpath at about 2,000 feet altitude. As the biplanes flew across the Channel, the missing escorts arrived over Ramsgate some fifteen minutes late, and in two separate formations, before heading across the Channel and engaging enemy aircraft, but without sighting 825 Squadron.[28]

Esmonde's aircraft first met enemy fighters ten miles out from Ramsgate. Two *Staffeln* of Messerschmitt Bf109 fighters pounced on the biplanes and raked them with cannon- and machine-gun fire, causing damage to most of the Swordfish but no injuries. Before the Bf109s could make a second attack the Spitfires beat them off. At 12.50 p.m. the German fleet was spotted, as was the mass of fighters in the air above. The Swordfish closed to within two miles of the battleships and German fighters swarmed in for the kill, having to drop flaps, and even undercarriages, to reduce their speeds to those of their victims. Once again the Spitfires dived to protect their charges. Several Royal Navy motor torpedo boats had just attacked the German giants, each firing its two torpedoes in a vain effort to damage the enemy vessels. The MTBs remained close by, lest they be needed to rescue the Swordfish crews. Esmonde had reached the outer screen of destroyers and E-boats, his aircraft trailing fabric torn by the fire of the German fighters. He flew on through a blizzard of tracer fire, and the huge, frightening spouts of water thrown up by the battleships' heavy armament, the other two aircraft of his sub-flight close behind. A further fighter attack forced them to weave and dodge to avoid being shot down. Then they were back on a steady course, heading for *Prinz Eugen*.

Charles Kingsmill, flying the third machine in Esmonde's sub-flight, watched his leader fly steadily on with tracer fire all around him. So intent was Kingsmill on watching Esmonde that he had no recollection of being aware of danger; and, apart from one fighter, hardly noticed the German aircraft. He kept his gaze on Esmonde even when his own plane shook as cannon shells hammered into it. Then Esmonde's plane lurched upwards and Kingsmill lost sight of it. It must have been at that stage that Esmonde's Swordfish was attacked by two Bf109s. The Swordfish's tail caught fire and the TAG, Jack Clinton, calmly crawled out along the fuselage, beat out the flames with his hands and returned to resume firing his machine-gun. *Prinz Eugen*'s heavy guns blasted forth at the leading Swordfish, tearing away most of the port lower wing. Although the biplane dipped a wing seaward as it staggered from the force of a shell strike, Esmonde regained control, brought his doomed machine back on course, and kept flying towards the huge warship.

Then the two Bf109s came in again from behind, their bullets killing Clinton and the observer, Lieutenant William Henry Williams, and hitting Esmonde in

28 Ibid., pp 141-5.

the back and head. The aircraft's nose tipped up slightly and its torpedo was seen to fall away, presumably released by the dying Irishman. The battered aircraft fell seawards and disintegrated on hitting the surface. Fighters also brought down the other two Swordfish of the sub-flight and *Prinz Eugen*'s captain changed course to avoid Esmonde's torpedo. All six Swordfish were shot down. Only five men survived, and were rescued by the waiting MTBs. Esmonde's last moments had been witnessed by at least three RAF pilots. When the sole unwounded survivor, Edgar Lee, returned to Manston, he was met by Wing Commander Tom Gleave, who had watched the Swordfish depart, saluting each as it passed him for he had seen in Esmonde 'the face of a man already dead' and had known that 825 Squadron would not return. Gleave then wrote a report in which he recommended Esmonde for a posthumous award of the Victoria Cross.[29]

Gleave's recommendation – the first time a RAF officer had recommended a naval officer for the VC – was supported by Admiral Ramsay. Concluding his recommendation Ramsay wrote that Esmonde's, 'high courage and splendid resolution will live in the traditions of the Royal Navy and remain for many generations a fine and stirring memory.'[30] Ramsay was highly critical of the planning and operational errors that had led to the deaths of Esmonde and so many of his squadron. They had died in vain for their effort made no impression on the Germans. No impression that is except to note the gallantry of the airmen who, in their antiquated biplanes, had taken on the might of the Kriegsmarine and Luftwaffe and died in so doing. Ciliax wrote that they were men 'whose bravery surpasses any other action by either side that day', reflecting Ramsay's comment that it was 'one of the finest exhibitions of self-sacrifice and devotion that this war has yet witnessed' and Gleave's succinct summary of the Swordfish crews as 'courage personified'.[31]

There could be little doubt that Eugene Esmonde would be awarded the Victoria Cross and an announcement appeared in the *London Gazette* on 3 March 1942. On Saint Patrick's Day, his mother and two of his brothers – Owen, an RAF officer, and Patrick, an Army doctor – received the Cross from King George VI whose suggestion it was that this posthumous investiture of an Irishman with the VC should take place on Ireland's national day. The Esmonde family had decided that Eily Esmonde, although infirm, should be the one to receive her son's award at Buckingham Palace. To Eugene Esmonde duty was always his paramount consideration. In 1940 he wrote to his family that 'I can think of no greater honour, nor a better way of passing into Eternity than in the cause for which the Allies are fighting this war.' Less than two years later, in the English Channel, he demonstrated that those words summarised his own devotion to duty and his outstanding personal courage, rooted in a deep faith.[32]

29 This account is based on Bowyer, op. cit., pp 150-67. **30** London Gazette, 3 Mar 1942; PRO, Kew, ADM1/12460. **31** Bowyer, *Eugene Esmonde*, pp 167-8; Bowyer, *For valour*, p. 278. **32** Bowyer, *Eugene Esmonde*, pp 170, 66.

Many Irishmen volunteered to serve in the forces of their adopted countries. Those in Australia's forces were all volunteers as the 2nd Australian Imperial Force was a volunteer formation. Although Australia had conscripts, these were in the home defence Militia. (The Militia did, however, serve outside continental Australia from 1942 when Militia forces stopped the Japanese advance in Papua and New Guinea, both of which were Australian-administered territories and, therefore, considered part of Australia for the purposes of the Defence Act.)[33]

During the fighting in New Guinea, an Irish soldier of the AIF. won the Victoria Cross. Richard Kelliher was a 33-year-old private in 2/25th (Queensland) Battalion and he earned his VC on 13 September 1943 as Australian forces were pushing the Japanese back in New Guinea. Born in Ballybeggan, Tralee, Co. Kerry, he had emigrated to Australia in the 1930s and was working as a labourer in Queensland when he volunteered for service with the AIF in early 1941. In June he was posted to 2/12th Battalion and embarked for the Middle East to join the battalion but transferred to 2/25th Battalion in October when that unit was carrying out garrison duties in Syria after the campaign against the Vichy French.[34]

Japan's attack on Pearl Harbour in December 1941 brought war much closer to Australia and caused the withdrawal of Australian troops from the Middle East to meet the threat of a Japanese attack on Australia. In March 1942 Richard Kelliher's 2/25th Battalion returned to Australia to prepare for a move to New Guinea. After Pearl Harbour the main thrust of Japanese aggression had been to the south-west of Japan itself, aimed towards Singapore. However, Japanese commanders realized that, ultimately, they would have to defend their gains from American attack from the east; this led to the Japanese consolidating the island chains to the south, including the Marianas, Carolines, Solomons and Marshalls.[35] The establishment of this defensive belt of island fortresses brought war to Australia's mainland.

The first Japanese troops to land in New Guinea did so unopposed in March 1942 but then spent weeks preparing the base for an attack southwards. This delay allowed the Australians a breathing space to build up their strength. Australian troops were sent to Milne Bay, on the south-eastern tip of the island with a further two battalions being ordered to push over the Owen Stanley mountains by the Kokoda trail to Buna on the north coast where an airfield was to be built from which to attack the Japanese positions.[36] Thus began a tough and bloody campaign that stopped the Japanese on 25 August. A further Japanese landing at Milne Bay was repulsed and evacuation followed on 6 Sept-

33 John Conor, Australian Defence Academy, letter to author.   **34** The Military Historical Society, Lummis Files K. 8.   **35** B. Pitt (ed.), *The military history of World War II* (London, 1986), p. 164.   **36** Ibid.

ember, the first occasion on which the Imperial Japanese Army had been forced to retreat. The Milne Bay repulse was followed by another on the Kokoda trail. Two Australian divisions – 6th and 7th – had been concentrated on Papua. On 23 September General Sir Thomas Blamey took command of the Australian force and began an offensive. At the end of the campaign 7th Division withdrew to rest, re-equip and re-organize for further operations in New Guinea. By September 1943 Kelliher's battalion was preparing for another phase of operations against the Japanese in New Guinea as the Australians moved against enemy positions at Nadzab and Lae.[37]

In early September both 7th and 9th Divisions began to advance on Lae from different directions. The leading troops of 2/25th Battalion, still in 7th Division, had advanced more than one-third of the way to Lae before meeting their first serious opposition, at Jensen's plantation, on 10 September. Overcoming this hurdle the battalion pressed on to reach Whittaker's plantation two days later where Japanese marines were encountered, well dug in, with strong defensive positions, and fighting with the usual Japanese tenacity. But the determined Australians intensified the pressure and two companies of 2/25th reached high ground overlooking Heath's plantation, their next objective, by nightfall on 13 September, repelling several determined counter-attacks during the night. During that advance towards Heath's plantation Richard Kelliher won his Victoria Cross.[38]

On the morning of 13 September Kelliher's platoon of B Company came under sustained fire from a camouflaged machine-gun position on a slight rise some fifty yards away. Five soldiers died and three were wounded, one of them Corporal W.H. Richards, Kelliher's section leader. The Irishman's reaction was to say to another soldier,

> 'I'd better go and bring him in', then suddenly got up, rushed the post and hurled two grenades at it. When he ascertained that some, but not all, of the enemy had been killed he returned to his section, seized a Bren gun, and again dashed forward to within thirty metres of the post and with accurate fire completely silenced it. He then went forward again, through heavy rifle fire, and successfully rescued his section leader who had been wounded in the shoulder.[39]

The citation for Kelliher's VC states that his action, 'electrified everyone who saw it and his company as a whole, besides directly resulting in the capture of the enemy position, which was later found to contain one officer and eight other ranks enemy dead'.[40]

37 L. Wigmore, *They dared mightily* (Canberra, 1946), pp 154-5.   38 Military Historical Society, Lummis Files K.8.   39 Wigmore, op cit., p. 155.   40 Anon, *Reconquest – an official*

Kelliher's version of the action differs slightly from the official account and is worth recording:

A party of Japanese marines – and well-fed they were too – occupied a small ridge in Heath's Plantation near Lae and were able to overlook our positions along the track. The opposition was pretty stiff, because it was apparently headquarters and we were held up. When we cut a telephone line leading from the headquarters, the Japanese became a bit demoralised. Our section leader, Cpl 'Billy' Richards, went down with a bullet through his shoulder, and appeared to be losing a fair amount of blood. Another man was shot through the ankle, and a third was wounded. All lay out in No Man's Land.

I wanted to bring Cpl Richards back, because he was my cobber, so I jumped out from the stump where I was sheltering and threw a few grenades into the position where the Japanese were dug in. I did not kill them all, so I went back, got a Bren gun and emptied the magazine into the post. That settled the Japanese.

Another position opened up when I went on to get Cpl Richards, but we got a bit of covering fire and I brought him back to our lines. I also helped the section to bring back the other two.[41]

Kelliher's company went on to take its objective which fell to 2/25th Battalion in the early afternoon. The Japanese defenders left almost 300 dead behind. Thereafter 7th Division turned its attention to Markham Point across the river which was subjected to frontal assault, mortar and machine-gun fire for some days until, one night, Australian patrols found that the enemy had abandoned the strongpoint and slipped away in the night. The fugitives were later mopped up by Australians moving up the coast. Kelliher subsequently fought at Markham Point, in actions in the Ramu valley and then at Balikpapan in Borneo. The announcement of the award of his Victoria Cross was made on 30 December 1943. Unlike many winners of the award, Richard Kelliher lived to learn that he had been decorated. He survived the war and went to London in 1946 as a member of the Australian contingent for the Victory parade. In 1956 he made another visit to London for the centenary celebrations of the Victoria Cross. He died in Melbourne as the result of a stroke in January 1963, aged 52 years.[42]

The third and final individual is Victor Francis Beamish, born in Dunmanway, Co. Cork in September 1903. His family later moved to Coleraine from

record of the Australian Army's successes in the offensives ... September 1943-June 1944 (Canberra, no date). p. 49.   **41** Ibid., pp 49-50.   **42** *London Gazette*, 30 Dec 1943; Military Historical Society, Lummis Files K. 8.

where Victor joined the RAF, qualifying as a pilot. Invalided out of the service as a result of T.B. in 1933, which seemed to spell the end of his career, he managed to rejoin the RAF as a civilian adjutant in 1936 and was later restored to his commission. He returned to flying duties and took command of the Meteorological Flight at Aldergrove, Co. Antrim. In 1938 he was awarded the Air Force Cross for his work in establishing the flight. Beamish was commanding 504 Squadron soon after war broke out, having turned down a staff appointment. He was an excellent leader and was described as 'having the gift of leadership with an Irish charm, and very friendly'.[43] Although a tough taskmaster who imposed high standards on his pilots, he never asked them to do anything he would not do himself.

At the end of May 1940 Beamish was appointed to command RAF North Weald in Essex. This was a job that was principally ground-based, but Beamish did as much flying as he possibly could. He had already been in action over the beaches of Dunkirk and in the battle of Britain he refused to stay on the ground, frequently taking off in his own Hurricane after the station's squadrons had scrambled and joining in the aerial battles. This was a dangerous practice as he had no wing man to cover him. Now aged 37, twice as old as some of his pilots, Beamish flew an incredible 126 fighter sorties in the battle of Britain. He shot down several enemy aircraft, although the exact figure cannot be ascertained as he would never make a claim unless he was absolutely positive that the other aircraft had gone down. Nonetheless, he was decorated with the DSO in July 1940, followed by the award of the Distinguished Flying Cross in November.[44]

Although posted to another staff job he managed to persuade the authorities to return him to the command of a fighter station, RAF Kenley, where he resumed his practice of flying operationally when he took command there in January 1942. By then he had been awarded a Bar to his DSO for operations over Britain in late 1940 and in fighter sweeps over France in 1941. The latter were often suicidal missions and led to high losses among the RAF's pilots. The citation for Beamish's Bar noted that he had carried out 71 operational sorties between October 1940 and March 1941. During that time he had destroyed three enemy aircraft for certain and had probably destroyed three more as well as damaging several. He was now one of the RAF's most decorated fighter pilots; and one of the most decorated Irish servicemen of the war.[45]

In February 1941 No. 11 Group had begun the practice of flying sweeps, or circus operations, over France. This policy was initiated by Operational Instruction No. 7 which stated that, 'the object of circus operations, from a fighter point of view, is to destroy enemy fighters enticed up into the air, using the tac-

43 D. Stokes, *Wings aflame, the biography of Group Captain Victor Beamish, DSO and Bar, DFC, AFC* (London, 1985), pp 16-59; Quotation at p. 65. **44** Ibid., pp 69-81; *London Gazette*, 23 July 1940. **45** *Volunteers from Éire*, p. 47.

tical advantages of surprise, height and sun'.[46] In fact, the nature of the operations often surrendered at least two of those tactical advantages: surprise was rarely achieved. Often the Germans would not rise to the bait, or, alternatively, they would be up at a great altitude, holding the advantage of height. Small groups of bombers were used as the bait for these missions, attacking a selected target while many squadrons of Spitfires supported them; those Spitfires were escorted by other Spitfires at an even higher altitude. Most of Fighter Command's heavy losses in 1941 resulted from these sweeps with the greatest toll falling on the escort squadrons. The offensive was a reversal of the battle of Britain situation with the RAF making the same mistake as the Luftwaffe had made in 1940, when Göring had given in to his bomber pilots' pleas for closer fighter protection. Fighters left to wait for attackers were always tactically disadvantaged.

In February 1942 Beamish flew a patrol to check if *Scharnhorst, Gneisenau* and *Prinz Eugen* were heading for the channel. Having established that they were, he flew back to Kenley and then tried to pass the news on to 11 Group HQ. He has been criticised for doing this: as a former staff officer he knew the contingency plans for the break-out, and it has been suggested that he ought to have broken radio silence to report what he saw. However, a pilot who did break radio silence did so in vain as his transmission was not picked up.[47] With the radio sets fitted to the Spitfire it was unlikely that any message from Beamish, or anyone else, would have reached Britain. Climbing to transmit might have had a better chance of getting through but also raised the chances of being shot down. There was no real alternative to flying back fast and low; that is exactly what Beamish did. Even then he had difficulty persuading others of what he had seen. A radio message could so easily have been ignored even if it had been received.

On 28 March 1942 Beamish was flying with 485 Squadron of the Kenley wing on a fighter 'rodeo' over Calais. At 19,000 feet he spotted a force of about 50 to 60 Bf109Fs and FW190s and turned his wing to engage them. In the ensuing battle he lost his wingman, whose radio was out of action, and was jumped by a 190 which inflicted considerable damage on his Spitfire before being shot down. Beamish was probably injured and was last seen heading for England, with smoke trailing from his aircraft, entering a cloud layer at about 12,000 feet.[48]

Victor Beamish was never seen again.

Eugene Esmonde, Richard Kelliher, and Victor Beamish were only three of Ireland's contribution to the Allied war effort. As with the minstrel boy of old, they had gone into the ranks of death and death claimed two of them. Many

46 Stokes, op. cit., p. 114.   **47** Ibid., p. 147; Bowyer, *Eugene Esmonde*, p. 132.   **48** Stokes, op. cit., pp 171-3.

others went with them: some died, most survived; some were highly decorated, most received only campaign medals; but all made a lasting contribution to the Allied cause and to the final victory. They deserve to be remembered, for their native land can be very proud of what they did.

The oral history of the volunteers

Aidan McElwaine

This chapter examines the factors which motivated the Éire volunteers to enlist, using the oral evidence of the volunteers themselves.[1] My use of oral sources was facilitated by the Volunteers Project at University College Cork. The aim of the project was to investigate the role, contribution and experience of Irish citizens who volunteered and served in the British and Allied armed forces during the Second World War. Oral history interviews with surviving veterans have been a central focus of the project, as well as my own research in Irish and British government and military archives.[2] Ms Tina Neylon, the project's research assistant, conducted the interviews with Irish veterans of World War II. In all, 52 veterans were interviewed. These taped interviews, along with relevant documents and memorabilia are to be used in establishing an archive which will be open to all researchers.

There was a great variety of reasons motivating Irish citizens joining the British armed forces. Of course, with any individual volunteer it was never just one particular reason; rather there were usually at least two or three contributing factors. There was a long tradition of Southern Irish men serving with the British armed forces. In many ways the high rate of enlistment of volunteers from Éire in World War II was merely a continuation of this trend. When asked what motivated them to enlist, 17 of the veterans interviewed revealed that close relatives of theirs had previously served in Her Majesty's Forces. The importance of a family connection varied from case to case. Some Anglo-Irish families, in particular, had a strong tradition of military service with the British crown and men from these families were sometimes more or less expected to join the colours. James Hickie from Dublin came from a distinguished military family. Two of his uncles had commanded the First Battalion of the Royal Irish Fusiliers, one of them went on to command the 16th Irish Division during the First World War. Hickie maintained this family tradition by enlisting in the Royal Irish Fusiliers in September 1940. In his own words he would have 'been given the white feather' by his family had he not enlisted.

---

1 Unless otherwise indicated, all quotations in the text are from the Volunteers Oral Archive in University College Cork. 2 See Aidan McElwaine, 'The forgotten volunteers: Irish service in the British armed forces during World War II', M.Phil. thesis, 1998, University College Cork.

Basil Baker from Fermoy seemed destined for a military career from an early age. Both his mother's and father's family were involved in the army. He felt it was in his blood. His paternal grandfather had been a general in the Connaught Rangers. Baker recalls how as a child he used to go to the Georgian house in Fermoy where his grandfather lived: 'All his braid, his gold braid and his medals and his sword and anything that involved the army, I tried it on and walked around in it. I knew from then on that it was the life for me.' He attended school at Middleton College until 1937, when his headmaster suggested to him that he should join the RAF. He attempted to do so but failed the medical, joining the North Irish Horse in Enniskillen instead. Three of his classmates from Middleton also joined the North Irish Horse.

John Jermyn from Cork was also partially motivated by family tradition. His mother's only brother had been killed in Gallipoli during World War I. He was only 19 years old and had served with the Royal Munsters. This affected Jermyn's decision, 'In some foolish way I thought that perhaps I should take his place'. Jack Harte, who was born in the Dublin tenements, joined the British Army to stay out of trouble as much as anything else. He too came from a family with strong military ties. His father had been in the Royal Dublin Fusiliers in World War I. His mother had six sisters who were all married to British soldiers who had been stationed in Ireland. One of his brothers had been in the British Army since 1928. Coming from such a background it was no surprise that Jack himself also wanted to be a soldier. When he began getting 'into some difficulties with the law' in Dublin as a teenager, his father suggested that this might be a good time to think of joining up. Not tall enough to join the Irish Guards, he joined the Royal Irish Fusiliers in 1938.

Maureen Deighton, from an Anglo-Irish background in Co. Limerick, joined up primarily because all her friends and relations had joined up. 'It was the done thing ... it was accepted in my circle in Co. Limerick in those days'. Mark Downey from Killiney, whose mother was English, had quite a few relations who had joined up. One of his cousins, who was also one of his best friends, had narrowly escaped death at Dunkirk, and went on to become the youngest major in the British army for a time. His numerous dramatic escapades were 'quite a strong influencing factor' on Downey. Although by his own admission he wasn't 'all that wise about what was happening' he felt that 'a lot of people did realise that something had to be done about the Nazis'.

Brother Columbanus Deegan from Dublin, who joined the Franciscans after the war, was the son of a World War I veteran. Br Columbanus' mother had lost her youngest brother in the GPO in 1916. So there was a 'conflict between Republicanism and Royalty' [sic] in his family. Ailsa Jones from Cork was pressurised by her father into enlisting. Her family were living in Kent when war broke out. She recalls her father used to say 'I'm not having any children of mine being conscripted, you must volunteer'. She was only 17 when her father said that it was time for her to join up. Although her father's family were Irish Catholic, they were very pro-British. Her grandfather had been MP for Douglas, while other relatives had served in World War I.

Eamon O'Toole from Antrim (now living in Limerick) was a nephew of three men who had served in Irish regiments in World War I. As a child, Eamon 'was enthralled by the stories they used to tell about the trenches, it was horrible and disgusting. And they also had various souvenirs like helmets and German Mausers', which he used to play with. Then in 1930 his father took him to Empire Air Day at RAF Aldergrove where he saw warplanes for the first time, and was absolutely intrigued. From then on he determined that he should join the Royal Air Force. He did consider joining the Irish Air Force at one time but, 'found that they had three aeroplanes and they were confined to Baldonnel so I didn't see an awful lot of excitement in that prospect.' He enlisted in 1938.

For the majority of Irishmen at this time, however, probably the most enticing aspect of the British armed forces was that it was a relatively well-paid job which did not always require a high standard of education or training. There were high levels of unemployment in Ireland during the war and pre-war period. Of the 503,000 male employees in the country in April 1936, 35 per cent experienced unemployment in the twelve months April 1935 to April 1936.[3] In the words of John O'Regan, in the late 1930s 'as a young unqualified man, prospects were not good.' 'Life was grim' and for O'Regan, the son of a large West Cork family, the Royal Navy was one of the best options someone in his position had. He enlisted in 1936 and served throughout the war years.

Stephen Mulcahy, also a Corkman, recalls that 'times were very difficult then'. He joined the RAF. Following demobilisation in 1946, he found it impossible to obtain work either in Ireland or in Britain, so he promptly re-enlisted. As well as the basic level of pay, there were attractive pension benefits for dependants. Patrick Dennehy recalled with pride that his mother got a pension of two pounds a week from his service in the RAF. For Dennehy however, this turned out to be something of a double-edged sword. Bored at the lack of action (he had been posted to Scotland for six months) his mind turned to thoughts of desertion. But the lodge in which his mother lived was owned by a former World War I officer and she would have been thrown out had her son deserted. He was therefore stuck in the RAF. Happily for him, however, he was later posted overseas which cheered him up immensely.

Richard Philips from Cork had been working for Clyde Shipping company before the war. In the early days of the war the ships had been taken over by the admiralty and he was laid off. After a month having been unable to gain other employment, he took the quite natural step for an unemployed shipping clerk and joined the Royal Navy. John Jacob, from Kinsale, although not unem-

3 Joseph Lee, *Ireland 1912-1985, politics and society* (Cambridge, 1989), p. 192.

ployed, did not see a promising future in his job. As he describes his own situation in the early years of the war, 'for me, a qualified accountant, working in an import business being slowly strangled by hostilities abroad, involvement was an option. Being footloose and fancy free and above all a competent seaman and lover of the sea, the option became compelling.' He joined the Royal Navy in February 1941.

James Farnan from Co. Meath joined the Fleet Air Arm of the Royal Navy. Although he had reservations about fighting for Britain, due to his nationalist views, in 1939 there were not many job opportunities in Éire. Denis O'Brien from Cork gained employment in the Royal Navy shortly after becoming redundant from his previous job. William Condon had gone to England at a young age to seek employment. He was called up under the terms of the National Service Act but as an Irish citizen he had the option of returning to Ireland. However, he saw little prospects for himself in Ireland, therefore he allowed himself to be conscripted. For this reason he always saw himself as a volunteer. Patrick Hamilton from Sligo, could not find work in Ireland either and also allowed himself to be conscripted in England. David Cronin volunteered purely because he could find no other employment, either in Ireland or in Britain.

Donald MacPherson, one of six children from a working-class Dublin family, also had limited prospects in Ireland, and resented this. He was unable to find work at home 'so the only thing for a young man like that was get out of this benighted bloody country. De Valera's government didn't think we existed – export our youth and let them sweat in their own juice, and that's what they done [sic] to their shame.' His two eldest brothers left home in 1930 and were soon serving in India with the army. In 1932, Donald himself left home, at the age of 17. He tried to join the British Army, but was not tall enough. He remained unable to find work. A year later he joined the Lancashire Fusiliers Territorial Battalion, for no other reason than to get a pair of boots and an overcoat. Over the following years he managed to pick up various menial jobs. In August 1939 he was called up to the regular army. According to him, men joined up because they had no money and no future, 'half of them did it for the shilling, not because they loved King George'.

Peter Ward-Quinn, who was himself in the Navy, was acquainted with a volunteer from Galway who had developed TB at the age of 19, but later enlisted in the RAF in Belfast. They failed to detect the TB at his medical. After two years service in the RAF his condition worsened. The RAF assumed he had developed the disease while serving, and he was pensioned out of the service as a consequence. He received a good pension for the rest of his life, along with all the other benefits which service entitled him to, including grants for his family's education. Some of the volunteers were quite mercenary in their approach. Brother Columbanus claims 'I think most people of my vintage joined for the excitement and the money', because according to him, 'it wasn't our war'. Displaying admirable honesty, he goes on to say 'We were mercenary, in it for the adventure, in it for the training'. Quite frank, he even goes on to say 'if a German officer had offered me 10p a day more I would have thought about it.'

A large proportion of those enlisting were virtually apolitical. The vast majority were young men (or women) in their late teens or early twenties (some were as young as 16). Many were ill-informed or had little interest in the political climate in Europe. It was not until after Germany's surrender and the liberation of the death camps that the attempted genocide in Nazi-occupied Europe was a matter of public knowledge. Jack Harte, from Dublin, had enlisted in 1938 and spent much of the war in the front line, and was even captured by the Germans. Yet it was not until 1945, when at home on leave in Dublin he saw a film about Belsen, that he had any inkling of the horrific crimes perpetrated by the Third Reich. In his own words 'I couldn't believe it.' And this from someone who presumably was exposed to allied propaganda for the duration of the war. How much less was known therefore by the average young man back in Ireland, where one of the strictest regimes of censorship in the world was in operation?

Of those veterans interviewed who listed employment as one of their primary motives, almost all were from low income backgrounds. Generally their education had ceased at between 14 and 16 years of age, if not earlier. Scarcely any of these people claim to have had any real knowledge of Nazi Germany or the persecution of minorities there. Even those from more privileged backgrounds, with access to third-level education, knew little more. David Baynham, from Dublin joined the Royal Engineers in 1944. While in college in Trinity he had read the 'Brown Book' which described ill-treatment of Jews in Nazi Germany before the war. This had been seen by many as Jewish propaganda at the time. It wasn't until he visited Belsen in 1945 that he saw the reality of it.

Many of those from low-income backgrounds saw service as one of their few chances to get a decent job. What's more, for many it was a very exciting job. Several of those already referred to as enlisting primarily for pecuniary reasons also specifically referred to a sense of adventure as being a contributory factor. Service with the armed forces offered these young people a chance to experience a completely new way of life and to travel to countries they would not otherwise have been able to visit. According to Brother Columbanus, 'Danger didn't seem to enter into it at all'.

Romie Lambkin from Dublin was finding her job as an office secretary very boring. She had always been an adventurous sort of person, and during the Battle of Britain she decided that she wanted to get involved. She subsequently enlisted in the ATS. David Baynham also saw service as an exciting opportunity to do something completely different. He had been studying engineering in Trinity College, Dublin 'but was getting somewhat bored and was facing some rather hard exams and which encouraged me to join; also I had the feeling that the war was going to be over long before I was ready so I thought I better get ready'.

For Brian Bolingbroke from Cork 'it was excitement, not knowing what war was all about'. Stephen Mulcahy admitted that being young he had joined partly on impulse. Richard Philips, who was out of work anyhow was also influenced by the opportunity for adventure- 'at twenty-one years of age most fellahs want a bit of excitement'. George Forde from Arklow joined 'out of pure divilmint'. Arthur Smith from Glasnevin found Dublin 'a very boring small place' and 'was itching to get away'. John Rowland from Dalkey similarly saw his situation in Ireland as being 'very constrictive'. 'You couldn't do any foreign travel, and somebody leaving school would normally have an ambition to do a bit of travelling. Joining one of the Forces was a way of getting out of a very restrictive situation and seeing a bit of the world.'

Michael Connell from Dublin had an older brother who was on the Reserve list as war approached, having previously served for seven years in the Lancashire Fusiliers, and the Irish Army before that. In August 1939 he was recalled, and asked Michael to come back with him to enlist. Michael, who at that time was 'hanging around with not much to do', agreed. As he described it himself, 'because at that time, you see, it wasn't just for the love of King or country, the British Army was somewhere to be. You'd see a bit of the world and as your father would say, they'd make a man of you.' Delia Dooley from Clondalkin had trained as a nurse. Wanting to travel, she was attracted by the prospect of enlisting. Her father warned her to keep away from the army but she ignored him and joined up anyway.

Éire at this time had no real navy or airforce to speak of. She possessed merely a few old gunboats and an insignificant number of outdated training aeroplanes. For anyone with an interest in aviation or a love of the sea there was little attraction in the Irish armed forces. Joseph Neylon from Clare was intrigued by aeroplanes, and the RAF afforded opportunities not readily available in civilian life 'This was a time when flying was in its infancy. I thought I had the ability to fly.' He enlisted in 1938. Similarly, those with a love of the sea were often drawn to the Royal Navy. Brian Bolingbroke 'had always loved the sea, messing around in boats.' John Jacob was 'always fond of the sea' and was a competent seaman. Cornelius Glanton from West Cork, traditionally a strong recruiting ground for the Royal Navy, was himself the son of an ex-RN sailor. Two of his brothers also served, as did an uncle. Many men from around his native Skibbereen also joined the RN and he 'used to watch these lads coming home in their uniforms. I liked the sailors suit.'

Dermot Clarke from Dublin joined the Merchant Navy. 'I always loved the sea. I loved adventure. I was an adventurous sort.' Michael D'Alton from Killiney chose the Navy ahead of the other services as he had sailed since he was a child and loved the sea. Kevin Gibney from Dublin wanted a career at sea. He was a little too old for the Merchant Navy and as Éire didn't have a navy his next option was the Royal Navy. He joined in January 1939. He was annoyed by the outbreak of war as it upset his career plans. Unsurprisingly, the majority of Irish who served in the Royal Navy at this time were from coastal areas, particularly the southern counties Cork, Waterford and Wexford, as well as Dublin. Coastal towns in these counties, such as Skibbereen, Youghal and Dungarvan, had always had relatively high levels of enlistment in the Royal Navy, and this trend continued during World War II.

In an article entitled 'The logic of collective sacrifice: Ireland and the British Army, 1914-18', David Fitzpatrick makes a compelling argument linking enlistment with 'group affiliations and collective pressures'. These might take such forms as 'communal patriotism, local traditions of soldiering, or prior enlistment of comrades from one's school, club or workplace'. Enlistment in World War I was affected regionally, both by 'the efficiency with which different fraternities and societies were mobilised' and by the effectiveness of British recruitment methods. The advantage of examining these factors is that they, 'unlike the effects of adventurousness or personal patriotism, are to some extent capable of historical verification'. The effects of adventurousness and personal patriotism may not be capable of historical verification using documentary sources only, but they certainly can, and have been, verified using oral history sources. This point reinforces the importance of oral history sources when dealing with an issue such as motivation of individuals in enlistment.[4]

Unfortunately, compared to the abundance of data on Irish recruitment during World War I , material on southern Irish enlistment patterns during World War II is much more sparse. During the First World War records were maintained of a recruit's address, religion, and profession or trade, amongst other data. The police and military both kept separate records of recruits. Various other sources such as 'Z8' returns submitted by the industrial firms to the Board of Trade give additional information on the trades from which recruits were drawn. In contrast, many of the Éire volunteers who 'joined up' during World War II are not even listed as being from southern Ireland in British military records. There is not enough data to assess the 'impact of group affiliations and collective pressures' on recruitment during World War II. Even if there was, a comparative study such as Fitzpatrick's (based on comparisons between British and Irish recruitment rates during 1914 and 1915, before conscription was introduced in Britain) could not be carried out on recruitment during World War II, as conscription was introduced in Britain as soon as war began.

However, some of his conclusions may prove useful to a study of the Second World War. He discounts the sometimes exaggerated influence of politics or religion on recruitment patterns, by showing 'the spatial similarity, at county level,

4 David Fitzpatrick, 'The logic of collective sacrifice: Ireland and the British Army, 1914-1918', *The historical journal* 38:4 (1995), pp 1017-30

of Protestant and Catholic levels of enlistment in 1915'. He refers to a thesis on the Royal Munster Fusiliers during World War I which demonstrates that many recruits came from families with previous experience of soldiering. However, 'such was the flood of enlistment after August 1914, that only a small proportion of recruits could have followed any path towards a military "career"'. And he rejects 'the hypothesis that enlistment would be heaviest among those with insecure employment.' In the early days of World War I, 'the heaviest outflow of recruits and reservists emanated from the industries most in demand for war production, and least affected by pre-war unemployment'.

However, from the limited relevant evidence on the issue, it would appear that the 'group affiliations and collective pressures' which were so influential in World War I, did not apply in the same degree in Southern Ireland during World War II. Of those interviewed, even where there was a family history of service in the British forces, no more than a handful felt that this had in any way obliged them to enlist. For the majority of those interviewed, enlistment appears to have been very much an individual decision. Many of them were not influenced in any way by people they knew to enlist and most travelled to the recruitment centres alone.

Some volunteers were motivated primarily by idealism. Desmond Fay, for example, was a committed anti-fascist. Born in London, of Irish parents (his father was a co-founder of the Abbey Theatre), he always considered himself Irish – 'the fact that you were brought up in a foreign country doesn't seem to me to alter your nationality.' He had regretted not fighting with the International Brigades in the Spanish Civil War. He had been too young at the time. He 'seized the opportunity when World War II started because our war effort was the same, to fight the evil system of fascism'. Dr Richard Barry, from Cork felt that it was a just war, 'I think the war to prevent the Germans overrunning Europe was justifiable, especially led by Hitler.' His father had been a Major-General in India, his grandfather also served. His mother was Anglo-Scottish which presumably also influenced his pro-British views. He reasoned 'I felt you can't really go and get jobs over there and then when England gets in difficulties not lend a hand and help her.' Other Irish shared this sense of indebtedness to Britain for having provided them with a livelihood in peacetime. Simon Corkery from West Cork had been working as a male nurse in England since 1938. He joined the RAF at the end of 1939. He felt 'that if you're earning a living in a country you should join the colours of that country' in the event of a war. Michael Ryan had also found employment in pre-war Britain. Upon the outbreak of war he felt that he should do the 'honourable thing, especially after witnessing the exodus of my panic-stricken countrymen in 1939'.

Others realised that if Britain was defeated and Hitler turned his attentions on Ireland, there would be no hope of survival. Some of these men felt that possibly the best way of defending Ireland was in fighting for Britain. According to

John Jermyn, 'it was sticking out a mile that if he came into England and conquered England that Ireland would be next … he only had to send a platoon of girl guides to take Ireland because we had a tiny army at the time, utterly dependent on England for their cast-offs in the way of arms and things and not really capable of defending anything. I mean I thought I should do something about it.'

Brian Bolingbroke had similar views: 'genuinely I thought Nazi Germany was a terrible thing and I would hate to have thought that we would have been living under Nazi rule for the rest of my life and that it was something worth fighting for. I genuinely believed that I was fighting on the right side.' Larry O'Sullivan, from Cork saw the war as 'a fight of civilisation against the dark ages'. At home on leave, he was 'shattered' to find out that the majority of Irish people 'didn't give a damn about the war'. Although he had joined two years before war began, thus ruling out idealism as a motive, there is nevertheless no doubting the strength of his convictions. At home on leave during the war, his mother forbade him to go back. As an Irish citizen, he could of course desert without any fear of retribution. His mother pleaded with him to 'let the English fight their own battles, after all they have done to us'. She argued that 'It's nothing to do with us'. He tried to argue that it had everything to do with Ireland. He duly returned to the Navy.

William Clarke from Dublin remembered the morning he heard that German troops had invaded Russia, 'I could see the Nazis taking over everything, so I wanted to do my little bit.' He recalls with amusement some of the English conscripts calling him a 'bloody fool' for coming back to Britain and the war having gone home on leave to Ireland. Denis Murnane was almost unique amongst his peers in that he was one of the few who had experienced the uneasy atmosphere of pre-war Nazi Germany. He had visited Germany in 1937 and was 'rather surprised to see on people's faces a look of fear if you even asked directions on the street from somebody, they would sort of look around and just point, but they wouldn't actually talk to you'. According to Murnane, it was obvious to anyone visiting Germany at this time that they were gearing up for war. Following the outbreak of war, he thought to himself 'in the name of God, if the Germans do decide to invade what are we going to fight them with, so I decided I'd rather fight with what little the British had' so he went up to Belfast to join the RAF. Murnane's father, grandfather and three uncles had all fought in World War I but apparently this did not influence him. In fact his father, who died in 1939, had worried that Denis would join up and thus not finish his studies in Trinity College, Dublin. He was proved right in this regard.

Michael D'Alton from Killiney describes himself as 'coming from what you might call, or some people might call, a West British background.' But he dislikes this label, preferring to describe himself as pro-British. This, however, did not entail being anti-Irish, 'which it frequently seems to do in many people's thoughts here.' Due to this background, loyalty to the Crown did have a bearing on his decision to enlist. More importantly, he 'was thoroughly convinced that Hitler and the Germans organised by him were a menace that simply had to be resisted or we would end up the same as the rest of Europe.' John Jacob echoes this view, 'like many others I was certain that if the Germans did conquer Britain, they would not stop at Holyhead or Fishguard.' Elisabeth Dobbs also came from a 'West British' background. All her friends had joined up, while her uncles had served in the First War. Her religion and background were the main factors in her decision to enlist in the WRENs. 'Most Protestants felt a kinship, sort of something to do with England'. Similarly Brian Inglis, self-styled 'West Briton' joined out of duty, as did many of his 'set'.[5]

However, it would appear that almost 20 years of Irish independence had to some extent loosened the ties that the Anglo-Irish felt towards Britain. In the early days of the war, the 'Irishman's Diary', a daily column in the *Irish Times*, discussed what it considered to be a complete change of attitude on the part of the younger generation, compared with the early days of World War I:

> what most of us have forgotten is that the young men who are now of military age never lived under the British regime in this country, that they never learned the kind of history that we learned at school, and that the British Empire, which to us twenty five years ago was almost a personal possession, to them is little more than a vague abstraction, which has no direct bearing on their lives ... I have nephews and nieces who to-day are about the age at which I faced the last war. They have the same traditions as I had, but I have been shocked – and very wrongly shocked as I realise now – to find that their attitude towards the present war is utterly impersonal. They really are neutrals, although they have not a very high opinion of Messrs. Hitler and Company![6]

Although the author does not explicitly refer to his tradition as being an Anglo-Irish one, his referral in the same article to feelings of emotion upon seeing the Union Jack or hearing 'God Save the King' would seem to indicate this.

The evidence of George Forde and David Baynham would seem to confirm changes in the attitudes of many Anglo-Irish. George Forde made reference to his Protestantism, but felt no allegiance towards England whatsoever. As seen already he was mainly motivated by a spirit of adventure. David Baynham also made reference to the fact that he is Church of Ireland, 'which I suppose has historically some association with Britain, but I don't think that was any influence on me'. There is no comprehensive data regarding the religious backgrounds of the Éire volunteers, but what little relevant data there is suggests that religion

5 Brian Inglis, *West Briton* (London, 1962), p. 43. 6 *Irish Times*, 24 September 1939.

had little impact on enlistment trends. The Anglo-Irish community does not appear to have been over-represented amongst the Éire Volunteers.[7]

Sean Drum from Tullamore served in the Irish Army Air Corps until 1943. By this time the threat of a German invasion had more or less disappeared. To him it now seemed a waste of time to remain in the Irish Army as there was little for them to do. According to Drum, 'most of the Army Air Corps men would have been fairly sympathetic to the British'. There was a close relationship between the RAF and the Irish Army Air Corps at this time. For example, the Air Corps bought all their planes from the British. The RAF supplied the Air Corps with instructors and there was a couple of RAF liaison officers based at Baldonnel. Air Corps personnel were often sent to RAF training schools. The Air Corps even used British manuals, called Air Ministry Orders (AMOs). As Drum saw it, life in the Irish Army Air Corps wasn't very much different from life in the RAF.

He took 'French Leave' (that is, deserted) from the Irish Army along with quite a few of his comrades and they travelled up to Belfast to join the RAF. In regard to his motives for joining the RAF he makes the point that 'when there was very heavy bombing of British cities and towns many of our friends and relations were actually living and working in these towns in Birmingham, Coventry and London so our sympathies were with them by and large.' Several of his uncles had fought in the various different Irish regiments during World War I and this also influenced him. His home town, Tullamore, was a garrison town, and 'there was certainly no vestige of anti-British consciousness there at all. Even after the Armistice Day parades, which were quite extensive then, when they would march to the local cenotaph in slow time and lay poppy wreaths and that, even the old IRA men joined them in the British Legion club afterwards for a drink, because after all they were their brothers, their cousins and their neighbours.' Drum feels that the Irish population 'in general had no wish to see a British defeat'.

The British Empire had always offered ambitious or adventurous young Irish men exciting career opportunities, either in the civil service or in the armed forces. The sheer size of the Empire meant that there were unrivalled opportunities for travel and career advancement. Even after the Free State came into existence, many Irish continued to look to Britain to provide them with employment. In this way, the motives of Irish people entering the British forces were probably not entirely different from the motives of any soldier who has served in the army of his own country. It is probable that patriotism plays only a small part in any individual's decision to join the military. In his book, *The history of warfare*, John Keegan categorises soldiers from pre-history to the modern era. Describing twentieth-century soldiers he notes, 'regulars are mercenaries who

7 See interviews and other data collected by the Volunteers Project, UCC.

already enjoy citizenship or its equivalent but choose military service as a means of subsistence. In affluent states, regular service may take on some of the attributes of a profession'.[8] An English or Scotsman joining the British Army was probably just as motivated by career considerations as any Irishman.

It may be that the desire of young men for adventure and excitement is universal, as is man's propensity for warfare. Keegan criticises a book by another author for 'discounting the allure that the warrior life has over the male imagination'. Unfortunately, Keegan himself makes little effort to examine this allure. He also writes that he is tempted, after a lifetime's involvement with the British Army, to argue that 'some men can be nothing but soldiers.'[9] While few of those interviewed spent the rest of their careers in the armed forces, there is no doubting the attraction which soldiery held for them when they were young. As Patrick Manson from Co. Down has pointed out, 'the attitude of most 19- or 20-year-olds had not changed much since the fifth century BC when Thucydides wrote "there were great numbers of young men who had never been in a war and were consequently far from unwilling to join in this one."'

In assessing the evidence we must be aware that oral history has certain limitations. As with any primary source, the historian must ask certain questions about the evidence. With oral history, as Valerie Raleigh Yow points out, one must ask how the passage of time and self-selectivity have affected the sample of narrators.[10] This self-selectivity may have restricted those who had very negative experiences from coming forward. Almost all of those interviewed seem to have viewed their wartime experience as a positive thing. There is no way of knowing how many of the Éire volunteers would have disagreed with this view.

In this project, begun 56 years after the outbreak of World War II, the passage of time probably has had a significant impact on certain aspects of the evidence. Virtually all those interviewed were in their late teens or early twenties when they enlisted. Being so young, many of them were at least partially motivated by the desire for adventure and excitement. However, we have little evidence of the experience of those who were older when they enlisted. A 30-year-old who enlisted at the outbreak of war would be 90 years old at the time of writing. Unsurprisingly, few veterans of this age participated in the project. If such a project had been undertaken 30 years ago, perhaps their evidence would have differed in some respects, though of course it is impossible to say. Another factor which requires consideration is that all those interviewed for the project lived in Ireland and had returned to the country at some time after the war. It is likely that a significant body of volunteers remained in Britain, though at this point in the research it is impossible to conclude that this group would have different experiences to report.

---

8 John Keegan, *A history of warfare* (New York, 1994), p. 228.   **9** Ibid., p. 226.   **10** Valerie Raleigh Yow, *Recording oral history* (Beverly Hills, 1994), p. 17.

John Tosh points out the influence which the interviewer has on the evidence gathered. Not only does the interviewer select the informant and indicate the area of interest, but:

> the presence of an outsider affects the atmosphere in which the informant recalls the past and talks about it. The end product is conditioned both by the historians social position *vis à vis* the informant and by the terms in which he or she has learnt to analyse the past and which may well be communicated to the informant.

In other words, 'historians must accept their share in creating new evidence'.[11] One should not, however, overestimate the relevance to the veteran interviews of Tosh's reservations about oral history. Firstly, the Volunteer Project did not 'select the informants'; they selected themselves, by answering notices in the press. These notices appeared nationally, thereby making the sample more representative. Secondly, skilled interviewing can help reduce the 'historians share in creating new evidence'. In order to avoid disturbing the natural flow of the interview, the number of questions were limited, thereby giving more control to the interviewee in telling his or her own story. Thirdly, the oral historian no more creates new evidence by 'indicating an area of interest' than the documentary historian does by selecting which document he will examine. Finally, the act of interviewing should not be seen purely as the creation of new evidence. The evidence already exists. Skilful interviewing merely records it, catalogues it, but should not create it.

Tosh points out further difficulties even after the historian has been taken into account. Not even the informant is in direct touch with the past, 'His or her memories, no matter how precise and vivid, are filtered through subsequent experience'. Making reference to the writings of Paul Thompson, Tosh states:

> whatever the evidence it rests on, the notion of a direct encounter with the past is an illusion, but perhaps nowhere more than in the case of testimony from hindsight. The 'voice of the past' is inescapably the voice of the present too.[12]

Unquestionably this is true, but it misses the point. Oral sources are by their nature different from documentary sources, but that does not mean we should discount their value in reaching a richer and truer understanding of history. Because they are different, they must be approached in a different way. The 'usefulness of any source depends upon the information one is looking for, or the questions one seeks to answer.'[13]

---

11 John Tosh, *The pursuit of history* (London, 1984), p. 178.   12 Ibid., p. 179.   13 Ronald J.

The precise date which someone enlisted, or was promoted, or left the services; the accuracy of North African placenames; the exact details of training schedules; these are all relatively insignificant. Psychological research has shown that the memories of people in the 'Reminiscence' phase of their lives (from the age of around 70 on) can be remarkably accurate in recalling their youth, but this point is not central to the argument. There is no doubt that some of the 'insignificant details' described in the interviews are inaccurate. Memory can be unreliable after even short periods of time. But the Volunteer project is concerned with broad issues rather than specific detail; their attitudes now to how they were treated then, and how they are being treated now; the general circumstances which influenced their actions, rather than particular events in which they were involved. There may be much that has been forgotten, but it is what they remember, and why they remember it that is significant.

Documentary sources, too, have their limitations. Personal memoirs, diaries and letters, all important documentary sources, are subject to many of the same qualifications as oral testimony. Newspaper reports, another important documentary source, are usually based on the testimony of individuals, who sometimes have had only a peripheral view of the given event. Jan Vansina notes that 'the study of memory teaches us that all historical sources are suffused with subjectivity from the start'.[14] Restrictions to access of documents for 30, 50 or even 100 years, render access to other sources even more important. The strength of oral history 'is the strength of any methodologically competent history. It comes from the range and the intelligence with which many types of source are harnessed to pull together.'[15]

The Volunteer Project is part of the new 'history from below'. One of the main weaknesses of documentary history, as Thompson points out, is that as 'the nature of most existing records is to reflect the standpoint of authority, it is not surprising that the judgement of history has more often than not vindicated the wisdom of the powers that be.' In relying exclusively on documentary sources, there is a danger that a narrow and one sided (and therefore weaker) history is produced, which fails to take into account some of the most important participants. In fact it is inconceivable that one should undertake a study on a topic such as the Éire Volunteers without research into the experiences of the Volunteers themselves. The interviews give an important personal dimension to the subject. Oral history 'provides a more realistic and fair reconstruction of the past, a challenge to the established account'.[16]

Grele, *Movement without aim: methodological and theoretical problems in oral history*, in Robert Perks and Alistair Thomson (eds), *The oral history reader* (London, 1998), p. 41.   **14** Jan Vansina, *Memory and oral tradition*, in J.C. Miller *African past speaks*, p. 276. **15** Peter Burke, *New perspectives on historical writing* (Oxford, 1997), p. 135. **16** Paul Thompson, *The voice of the past – oral history* (Oxford, 1978), p. 5

Irish workers in Britain during World War Two

Tracey Connolly

The Second World War was a watershed in twentieth-century Irish emigration. As a result of the war the volume of Irish emigration increased substantially and Britain was established as the main destination of migrants. According to census data net emigration was 189,942 for the period 1936-46, an annual average net emigration increase of 13.9 per cent since the 1926-36 census.[1] Britain as a destination for Irish emigrants had increased in popularity during the 1930s, primarily as a result of the depression in the United States. Although Britain was experiencing its own depression, Irish migrants viewed Britain as a more favourable place to emigrate to. Migrants knew that if they didn't make good in Britain they could return home with little difficulty. The establishment of Irish networks in Britain in the 1930s was important for intending emigrants in choosing Britain as a destination in the 1940s. These networks eased the strain of finding accommodation and employment, and helped new arrivals to settle in. Chain migration also played an important part in the decision to go to Britain.

When the war broke out, Britain launched a major campaign in Ireland to recruit workers for the British labour force, which greatly influenced and increased migration There were certain terms under which Irish emigrants were allowed to migrate to Britain during the war. As a means of monitoring migration, passengers to Britain were required to obtain travel permits and those going for work had to arrange employment before leaving Ireland. Travel identity cards for employment in Britain were not issued to persons who already had jobs in Ireland or those who had left their employment voluntarily. Thus, the Irish government intended only unemployed persons to emigrate to Britain. Restrictions were placed on persons with skills considered essential for the Irish State, such occupations included turf cutters and persons involved in food production. Intending emigrants had to apply for travel identity cards through the Gardai. They had to supply a certificate from the Department of Social Welfare, which stated that they were exempt from emigration restrictions and a written offer of employment in Britain with their application.

From 1940 to 1945 Irish workers going to Britain were classified as 'conditionally landed'. This implied that Irish workers were excluded from conscrip-

1 Census of Population 1946, *Preliminary Report* (Dublin, 1948), p. 13.

tion if they returned home after two years. If they remained in Britain after this deadline they were liable for conscription. Increased IRA activity during the war heightened the British Government's fears concerning the activities of some Irish migrants in Britain. The IRA had embarked on a campaign of letter bombs, bombing the Underground and other locations, while along the border dividing the north and south of Ireland several custom checkpoints were destroyed in 1938. In January 1939 the IRA sent an ultimatum to the British Foreign Secretary demanding the withdrawal of British troops. A wave of explosions and fires followed in British cities including London, Manchester and Birmingham. The British responded by enacting the Prevention of Violence Bill in July 1939, whereby newly arrived migrants in Britain were required to register with the police. Irish immigrants also had to report to the police if they changed their address or job.

The number of Irish workers in Britain who contributed to the war effort and the number who emigrated during the war were certainly quite considerable, but it is impossible to calculate a definitive figure. The number of travel permits issued for those travelling to Britain during the war provides the best data into the extent of emigration, but these figures are by no means completely reliable. A memorandum on emigration by the Department of External Affairs showed that a total of 172,574 permits were issued for persons travelling to Britain and Northern Ireland from 1941 to 1945, an annual average of 34,514.[2] The Home Office official statistics indicate that in July 1943 there were about 100,000 Irish labourers (from northern and southern Ireland) in Britain.[3] Table 1 shows the number of new travel permits issued from 1940 to 1945.

Table 1 Numbers of new travel permits issued for travel from Éire to Britain and Northern Ireland. 1940-45

Year	Male	Female	Total
1940	17,080	8,884	25,964
1941	31,860	3,272	35,132
1942	37,263	14,448	51,711
1943	29,321	19,003	48,324
1944	7,723	5,890	13,613
1945	13,185	10,609	23,794

Source: *Commission on emigration and other population problems*, p. 128.

2 National Archives of Ireland. D/T S11582. Department of External Affairs Memorandum. 30 August 1947. **3** PROL. DO.35/1230. WX.132/1/124.

There are several reasons why these statistics are unreliable. A proportion of those who went to Britain as visitors may have taken up permanent employment there, while many workers who went to Britain were seasonal workers and cannot be properly classified as 'emigrants'. It was also possible for the same person to hold more than one travel permit, which inflated statistics. In addition, it is also impossible to know how many actually utilised their travel permits, so figures may have inadvertently been exaggerated.

Wartime Britain witnessed unprecedented demands for labour. In 1940 the British Manpower Commissioner, Lord Beveridge, examined the labour force. According to his findings over 8.5 million men would be needed in the forces and munitions factories by the end of 1941.[4] As a result of this demand, employment agencies were set up throughout Ireland to recruit workers for the British labour force. The Ministry of Labour was responsible for this labour recruitment. Thousands of Irish emigrants were employed in aerodrome construction, the manufacturing of armaments and other equipment necessary for the war. As a result of the urban location of such employment, Irish emigrants tended to settle in cities such as London, Birmingham, Manchester and Liverpool. Many British employers sent intending emigrants their travel fares which eased their emigration and hastened their arrival. However, there were cases where firms sent money to intending emigrants who subsequently never emigrated. To counteract this some firms sent travel vouchers as opposed to cash. So systematic was the whole emigration process that many emigrants arrived in Britain wearing their employer's name on their lapels as means of identification and in order to speed up the whole process.

Of the four provinces, Connacht had the greatest population loss through emigration during the 1940s. Data from travel permits issued to persons going to Britain indicate that there were 17.2 external migrants per 1,000 of the population from 1940 to 1951 compared with the national average of 11.1. Ulster (3 counties) had 11.8, Munster had 11.4 and Leinster had the smallest number at 8.4.[5] Table 2 shows the number of travel permits granted from 1940 to 1951 in counties, which received large numbers.

There is a clear indication of high urban migration throughout the period. Dublin experienced 20 per cent of the country's outflow according to this table. Large numbers of recruits for the British forces during the war came from Dublin, which may be represented here and responsible for the hike in figures. Urban employment was falling off at this time, which may have been reason for Dubliners signing up with the forces or going to Britain for work. Dublin had a reservoir of unskilled and semiskilled workers – the type of worker in demand in

---

4 James Wolf, 'Witholding their due: The dispute between Ireland and Great Britain over unemployment insurance payments to conditionally landed wartime volunteer workers', *Soathar: journal of the Irish labour history society*, 21 (1996), p. 39. **5** *Commission on emigration and other population problems* (Dublin, 1954.) Statistical Appendix. Table 36. p. 327.

Table 2 Number of persons, classified by province and county of residence granted travel permits for employment in Britain. 1940-51

	Males	*Females*	*Total*
Ireland (26 counties)	213,420	149,558	362,978
Leinster	75,125	48,553	126,678
Munster	62,490	51,325	113,815
Connacht	55,391	37,286	92,677
Ulster (3 counties)	20,414	12,394	32,808
Dublin	46,512	24,779	71,291
Mayo	27,957	15,484	43,441
Cork	22,876	16,431	39,307
Galway	13,950	10,295	24,245
Donegal	15,965	7,508	23,473
Kerry	12,076	10,356	22,432
Limerick	10,666	8,446	19,112
Tipperary	5,958	6,245	12,203
Waterford	5,854	4,624	10,478
Clare	5,060	5,223	10,283

Source: *Commission on emigration and other population problems*, p. 327.

Britain during the war and after. It is also likely that given the relative ease with which Dubliners could travel to Britain that they viewed their migration as temporary. The other counties dealt with in Table 2 were predominantly rural and traditionally lost much of their populations through emigration. Emigration from the Western seaboard counties was colossal. For instance Mayo lost 27.8 per 1,000 of the population, Donegal lost 16.2 and Kerry lost 16.1. Other counties not shown in the table had smaller numbers emigrating but remarkably high in proportion to the population. Amongst such counties was Sligo, which lost 9,455 through emigration representing 14.2 per 1,000 of the population, 6,171 left Leitrim or 13.6 per 1,000 of the population, and 9,335 emigrated from Roscommon 12.5 per 1,000 of the population. Neighbouring counties Offaly, Laois and Carlow had the slightest losses of 3,120, 3,356 and 3,488 respectively. The counties with the smallest proportion per 1,000 of the population immigrating to Britain were Kildare (5.3), Offaly (5.4), Monaghan (6.0) and Laois (6.3). On the whole emigration during the war was primarily from rural areas, which was in line with the pattern of emigration in previous decades, but there was a noticeable increase of emigration from Dublin.[6]

6 Ibid.

Female domination of Irish emigration has been the norm, with the exception of three wars involving Britain, namely the Boer War, the First World War and the Second World War. The large number of male Irish recruits to the British forces during these wars was the main cause for the rise in male emigration, coupled with the great demand for male labour in Britain during these periods. Female emigration was strictly controlled and limited throughout the Second World War. Table 3 deals with Irish emigration to Britain according to sex from 1941 to 1945.

Table 3 Number of Irish males and females going to Britain and Northern Ireland 1941-5

Year	Male	Female
1941	31,860.	3,272
1942	37,263	14,448
1943	29,321	19,003
1944	7,723	5,890
1945	13,185	10,609

Source: National Archives D/T S11582. Department of External Affairs Memorandum. 30 August 1947

The flow of Irish emigrants was particularly high from 1941 to the end of 1943. Traffic slackened in 1944, probably as a direct result of security and travel restrictions prior to the invasion of Normandy. By 1945 migration had resumed at a higher rate, which seems to indicate that developments in the war in 1944 were responsible for the fall-off in that year.

Male emigration was more prevalent than female during these years and outnumbered female emigration by a ratio of 268 to 100. Britain intensified its drive for recruits during these years. As the size of the British armed forces swelled, the gap in the labour supply at home widened. British employers looked to Ireland to fill this gap and the volume of Irish immigrants in Britain inflated rapidly. Once employment controls for females in Britain were removed on 30 June 1946, followed by the Irish government's removal of female emigration restrictions from 27 July 1946, female emigration to Britain took a sharp upward turn. By 1946 female emigrants once more outnumbered their male counterparts. This indicates that the controls had a serious effect on female emigration and highlights the fact that Irish males were more inclined to emigrate in larger numbers during wartime than during peacetime. Youth emigration has been typical of the Irish experience and this was also the case during the war, as the majority were in the 16- to 24-year-old age cohort. Table 4 deals with the ages of travel permit recipients from 1943 to 1945.

Table 4 Age-distribution of recipients of travel permits 1943-5 (percentage by age groups)

	Year	16-19	20-24	25-29	30-34	35 +
Males	1943	6.9	26.4	20.9	14.5	31.3
	1944	12.3	28.8	18.1	13.1	27.7
	1945	12.8	33.8	17.9	12.5	23.0
Female	1943	20.3	39.3	18.5	9.1	12.8
	1944	22.2	38.8	18.1	8.9	12.0
	1945	29.2	40.7	14.7	6.9	8.5

Source: *Commission on emigration and other population problems*, p. 129

There was a greater incidence of males over 30 years of age emigrating than that of females. Throughout the war an increase in older male emigration was noticeable. This was the norm during times of war. While in the case of those under 25 years of age, it is evident that more females than males emigrated. The growth of young female emigration over the three years dealt with in Table 4 is remarkable. Of all females emigrating in 1943 59.6 per cent were 16 to 24 years of age. 1944 saw a slight rise at 61 per cent and in 1945 the figure took a substantial leap to 69.9 per cent. Male emigrants were also young but their proportion was not as great as in the case of females, as males in the same age cohorts were 33.3 per cent, 41.1 per cent and 46.6 per cent respectively for the same years. There are many possible explanations for the large presence of young female emigrants. Most of the work on offer in Britain for females required young workers, for factory work and domestic service. Emigration gave females greater autonomy, particularly for those who didn't earn a wage as they worked at home. It was generally the younger females who were the most disillusioned about lack of social outlets in the rural areas. In fact it has been argued that the search for a husband was the cause of some female migration. It was common for rural bachelors to wait until they were middle aged and had inherited the family farm before marrying. Much tension in rural households grew out of the presence of two females, as the arrival of a daughter-in-law was often seen as a threat to the older woman's authority. To encourage early marriages, boost the marriage rate in the countryside and prevent female emigration de Valera established an inter-departmental committee in 1943 to examine the setting up of dower houses. The scheme however, was rejected on the grounds that two houses could lead to subdivision of farms. Reporting to the Land Commission in 1944 R.M. Duncan wrote of rural girls unwillingness to remain in their localities and marry. For those whose families were poor, girls generally wanted to escape the drudgery while better off girls who had 'generally been sent to good schools ... will not contemplate becoming farmers' wives even when an adequate staff of servants is available.'[7] This indicates that social advancement, wanderlust and the desire to escape the boredom of rural life were important factors in female migration, both internal and external.

There were several obvious reasons for the large outflow of emigrants from Ireland during the war. Employment opportunities and economic advancement were not least among these reasons. Unemployment was a continuing problem in Ireland, although by 1943 male unemployment had dropped by 36 per cent. Female unemployment on the other hand, increased, doubling between 1939 and 1943.[8] Clearly the restrictions placed on female emigration had an impact on unemployment levels at home. Wages in Britain were higher than in Ireland; this must have had an impact on the decision to emigrate. Between 1941 and 1945 wages in Britain increased by 20 per cent. Comparing industry-wide levels in 1938 and 1946, the difference between Irish and British wages rose from 16 to 32 per cent for males, and for females it increased from 8 to 31 per cent. Emergency orders in Ireland restricted wages. Indeed, pre war wage levels were not achieved again until 1949.[9]

Social reasons for emigrating existed throughout the war, as they had in peacetime. Chain migration continued because contact with those who had already emigrated from a family or locality was important to those emigrating for support in all aspects. Emigrants returning on holidays continued to influence many in Ireland to leave. Brody observed that 'by 1940 Irish culture had evolved the double nostalgia that has been one of its hallmarks: emigrants in Chicago sang heartfelt laments about home, while their younger brothers and sisters at home talked wistfully about the wonders and riches of America'.[10] This was one contradictory aspect of emigration – those who hadn't left often felt that their lives would improve as a result of leaving, whereas some who had emigrated may have been consumed with homesickness and regretted emigrating. Often as a result of pride they didn't return home, as to do so was perhaps to admit their failure to succeed in another country. Many never communicated the difficulties in living abroad to intending migrants, as this was an admittance of failure. Frequently emigrants home on holidays glorified their lives abroad and exaggerated their success, which was again a product of pride. An article written in 1943 highlighted the sense of wonderment that a returned emigrant aroused within a family and community, 'To have a son back from America with silk

7 National Archives of Ireland. D/T S13413/1. 8 Mary E. Daly, 'Women in the Irish Free State, 1922-1939: The interaction between economics and ideology' in Joan Hoff and Maureen Coulter (eds), *Irish women's voices past and present: journal of women's history* (Winter/Spring 1995.) p. 111. 9 Cormac Ó Grada, *A rocky road; the Irish economy since the 1920s* (Manchester, 1997), pp 21, 17. 10 Hugh Brody, *Inishkillane: change and decline in the west of Ireland* (London, 1973), p. 10.

shirts, and all such gear, came as near as makes no difference to having a priest in the family.'[11] O'Faolain observed a greater quest for social and economic advancement in 1943 as 'men are leaving home who were content enough to stay hitherto.' It appears that the abundant opportunities that the war presented was the reason behind what O'Faolain termed, 'the wholesale exodus from the countryside'. There was a perception that financial advancement in Britain during the war was realisable, consequently more people were inclined to emigrate and seize such fortunes. While economic improvements were evident abroad there was a growing dissatisfaction in Ireland which O'Faolain felt was 'just as likely to be inspired by the meretricious appeal of streets – glorified by the movies' coupled with the 'seed of ambition'. Among the multitude of other social motives for emigration during the war, as at other times, were wanderlust, a desire for adventure and escape from personal problems.[12]

In Britain Irish females were primarily engaged in the sectors that Table 5 deals with, namely factory, domestic and agricultural work and nursing.

Table 5 Areas of work for Irish female emigrants in Britain and Northern Ireland, 1939-45

	Agriculture	*Nursing*	*Domestic*	*Other (including factory work)*
1939 (Sept.-Dec.)	57	3,132	5,396	1,350
1940	492	1,634	5,285	1,125
1941	176	785	1,343	789
1942	657	2,2838	6,037	5,060
1943	422	2,838	9,125	6,255
1944	302	1,125	2,760	1,591
1945	466	3,523	4,719	1,694

Source: Trinity College Dublin, March Papers 8300/1-31.

Although Irish female emigrants were predominantly engaged in domestic work, the war presented them with greater opportunities to branch away from domestic employment, into areas such as clerical work, factory work and nursing. Increasingly Irish females became more upwardly mobile and this was particularly evident after the war as the development of the welfare state in Britain

11 Peadar O'Donnell, 'The Irish in Britain', *The Bell*, 6, 5 (August 1943). **12** Sean O'Faolain, 'Silent Ireland', *The Bell*, 6, 5 (August 1943), p. 464.

expanded their scope for advancement. During the 1940s female emigrants engaged in domestic service had declined by up to 60 per cent and those nursing had risen to nearly 14 per cent of the total outflow.[13] Female migration differed from that of men during the war (and in other periods) as they frequently emigrated alone; this was normally the case with those going as domestics, whereas men usually emigrated in a group. Males who emigrated during the war tended to be less skilled than their female counterparts. The volume of unskilled male emigration as shown in Table 6 was very high. Not only do both tables reveal the occupational profile of the emigrants and the areas of work in Britain with demand for labour but they also reveal an obvious hike in the numbers emigrating from 1941 and 1943, which were the highest years of Irish emigration during the war.

Table 6 Areas of work for Irish male emigrants in Britain and Northern Ireland, 1939-45

	Agriculture	Building Construction	Clerks and skilled work	Unskilled workers
1939 (Sept-Dec.)	843	956	2,266	3,251
1940	5,408	1,180	2,278	5,901
1941	1,773	2,655	3,156	21,035
1942	4,767	1,172	3,873	23,830
1943	3,584	1,473	3,468	18,310
1944	1,361	226	1,414	4,340
1945	3,148	632	2,085	6,244

Source: Trinity College Dublin. March Papers 8300/1-31

Opinion in Ireland about the large-scale emigration which took place during the war, tended to be rather vague and somewhat contradictory. Emigration was accepted as part of Irish tradition but at the same time it was condemned as a bad thing. Given the closeness of Britain and Ireland people believed that their emigration would be brief. Because of this perception that emigrants would return, the significance of emigration was seemingly reduced. At the same time, emigration was seen in official circles as a safety valve for economic and social problems, which could be exported, to Britain. Emigration contributed to the reduction of Irish unemployment figures, which dropped from 15 per cent in

---

13 NESC 90, *The economic and social implications of emigration* (Dublin, 1991), p. 82.

1939 to 10 per cent in 1945.[14] In 1941, the Department of Industry and Commerce greeted the 'placing of Irish unemployed workers in employment in Great Britain' as it 'would provide a very welcome mitigation of the difficulties at home.'[15] The government acknowledged the benefits of remittances as it claimed 'the worker employed at good wages in Great Britain is in a position to send substantial contributions to his dependants at home, and thereby break for them the monotony of continuous poverty.'[16] Emigrants' remittances were very important to the whole Irish economy and dramatically increased during the war. Over £1 million of postal orders and money orders were received from Britain and Northern Ireland in 1939 alone and by 1941 this had doubled.[17] Healy in *No one shouted stop* dealt with the contradictory reactions that emigration elicited, 'while fathers, sons and daughters cried all the way to the train and the bus and ship, the flow back of emigrant cheques and money orders evaporated the maternal and wifely tears so that on the threshold of the Post Office or Hibernian Bank below in Main Street you could smile a little more with every passing week'.[18]

The main difficulty that the government had in acknowledging or encouraging emigration was that in doing so, they might be admitting to their inability to ameliorate the economic and social issues which were causing emigration. It appears that while the government opted not to dwell on the large outflow, the fear of a mass return of emigrants after the war was taken seriously. Amongst those who stressed the need to halt this return this was F. Boland, the Assistant Secretary of External Affairs. With much exaggeration, Boland warned that the return of Irish emigrants 'who have no doubt imbibed a good deal of 'leftism' in Britain' would upset the status quo in Ireland and may even produce the 'danger of social revolution'.[19] However, the government's greatest fear was the further increase in unemployment figures on account of returned emigrants. As early as 1942 the government began to take action to avoid such a situation arising, with a plan to arrange with Britain the, 'spreading out this return in such a way as to facilitate this country in coping with the problem of their re-employment and re-settlement.'[20] The Irish government was anxious to reach some agreement with the British on reciprocity, but when the war ended no arrangement was made as the British government argued that as emigrants did not return to Ireland that their social insurance funds should remain in Britain. Irish emi-

14 Ellen Hazelkorn, '"We all can't live on a small island": the political economy of Irish migration' in Patrick O'Sullivan (ed.), *The Irish World Wide. vol. 2 The Irish in the New Communities* (Leicester, 1992), p. 189.   15 National Archives of Ireland. D/T S11582. 'Memorandum for the Government from the Department of Industry and Commerce', 13 March 1941.   16 National Archives of Ireland. D/T S11582. 'Memorandum for the Government from the Department of Finance', 19 September 1941.   17 National Archives of Ireland. D/T S12865. Remittances from emigrants. 'Department of Industry and Commerce Memorandum', June 1942.   18 John Healy, *No one shouted Stop!* (Achill, 1988), p. 16.   19 National Archives. S11582. May 1942.   20 Ibid.

grants were entitled to unemployment insurance in Britain and Wolf has dealt with this issue in detail arguing that this may be the reason why many Irish stayed on in Britain after the war.[21] While the Irish government couldn't directly help emigrants as it could be viewed as an endorsement of emigration, the Catholic church and other voluntary bodies took care of emigrants. The Archbishop of Dublin, John Charles Mc Quaid, established the Emigrant Section of the Catholic Social Welfare Bureau (later called Emigrant Advice) in 1942, with the primary aim of looking after emigrants, especially female emigrants who tended to be young and often emigrated alone. The Bureau planned to arrange 'proper introductions' and to secure emigrants with 'the opportunity of continuing the religious life they have led at home.'[22] The Bureau investigated if employment in Britain was suitable for Catholics, if they were able to carry out their religious duties and often put emigrants in contact with other Catholics, including the local priest in the emigrant's intended destination.

The Catholic church in Ireland was concerned that emigrants would lose their faith in a foreign country. Considering that the majority were young, it was felt that they were more vulnerable to moral dangers. With this in mind the Catholic church sought to safeguard emigrants. However their involvement with emigrants wasn't confined to religious and moral issues as they also endeavoured to help emigrants overcome an array of social difficulties which they encountered abroad. In addition, the presence of church organisations in Britain such the Legion of Mary helped to unite emigrants. It provided them with a contact point where they could meet other Irish emigrants. After the war reconstruction and the development of the Welfare State resulted in further Irish emigration to Britain. So great was the labour demand after the war that the British Ministry of Labour claimed that it would not be necessary 'to require any substantial numbers of Éire workers transferred to this country during the war to return to Éire because of unemployment in this country.'[23] Given the choice of remaining in Britain where employment was plentiful and wages high or returning to Ireland where unemployment prevailed, it is little wonder that the number of emigrants who returned to Ireland was only marginal. An article in *The Bell* claimed that if there were jobs in Ireland for emigrants 'to return to at wages on which houses can be rented ... they will be back in droves.'[24]

In the immediate post-war era, Britain remained the most popular destination for Irish emigrants. The absence of large-scale overseas (outside of Britain and Europe) Irish emigration for over 15 years meant that chain migration was no longer as strong and that contact with other migrants had weakened. Irish emigrants usually depended on emigrant family members, neighbours and

21 Wolf, 'Withholding their due' p. 44.   **22** Kate Kelly and Triona Nic Giolla Chiolle, *Emigration matters for women* (Dublin, 1990), p. 12.   **23** PROL. DO35/1230/WX132/62.   **24** Peadar O'Donnell, 'Call the exiles home', *The Bell,* 9, 5 (February 1945).

friends for support. Given the large Irish emigration to Britain of the war years, such support was more available there than in other destinations. By 1951 the number of Irish persons living in London was 241,000 and nearly 481,000 had settled in other cities in Britain.[25] Although emigrants continued to be predominantly unskilled and semi-skilled, the presence of Irish emigrants in white-collared work in Britain began to grow in this period. For example, Irish civil engineers were employed for reconstruction, while the establishment of the National Health Service meant that more Irish doctors and nurses were employed. In the late 1940s the Atlee government commenced a campaign to get more females into the workforce, which sharply contrasted with the ethos in Ireland. The utopian Ireland, which de Valera described in his 1943 St Patrick's Day speech was not a dream shared by everyone. While de Valera dreamt of an Ireland which was 'the home of a people who valued material wealth only as the basis of right living, of a people who were satisfied with the frugal comfort and devoted their leisure to the things of the spirit' tens of thousands who aspired for more than frugality were emigrating to Britain on a permanent basis.[26]

25 Revd Jeremiah Newman (ed.), *The Limerick rural survey 1958-1964* (Tipperary, 1964) p. 160.
26 Maurice Moynihan (ed.), *Speeches and statements by Eamon de Valera 1917-73* (Dublin, 1980), p. 565.

MI5's Irish memories: fresh light on the origins and rationale of Anglo-Irish security liaison in the Second World War

Eunan O'Halpin

Anglo-Irish political relations during the Second World War defy easy character-isation. Depending on the period chosen and on the issue addressed, they can be described as unavoidably tense or perilously fractious. The matters at issue in relations between Dublin and London changed over time, but the underlying problem was that of Irish neutrality and its strategic consequences for Britain. As the British director of naval intelligence lamented after a visit in August 1941, the Irish:

> cannot see that they and ourselves are like two houses on the edge of a cliff, which will both fall into the sea unless something is done to stop coastal erosion. This argument is too realistic for them, and they invari-ably slide off into politics.

Yet politics lay at the heart of the policy and the practice of neutrality. The principle that independent Ireland should stay out of other peoples' wars had been common cause amongst the political leadership of the independence move-ment even after the treaty split. This had become policy after 1922, although in 1925 W.T. Cosgrave added the personal gloss that defence policy and organisa-tion should be predicated on the desirability of close co-operation with British forces in the event of an invasion threat.[1] De Valera's alternative draft of the 1921 treaty displayed somewhat greater ambitions for Irish defence, but it too recog-nised the legitimacy of Britain's Atlantic security concerns:

> So far as her resources permit, Ireland shall provide for her own defence by sea, land and air, and shall repel by force any attempt by a foreign power to violate the integrity of her soil and territorial waters, or to use

---

1 E. O'Halpin, *Defending Ireland: the Irish state and its enemies since 1922* (Oxford, 1999), pp 90-1.

them for any purpose hostile to Great Britain and the other associated
States [of the British Commonwealth].[2]

When agreement was reached in 1938 on the removal of Britain's defence rights
to key ports and facilities under the treaty, de Valera explicitly coupled his welcome for this radical change with a reiteration of the commitment that the state
would never permit Ireland to be used by foreign powers to harm Britain's strategic interests.[3] That statement laid the basis for the security understandings
reached during the next seven years, a collaboration which sufficiently softened
the blow of neutrality to provide the British with a tangible reason not to take by
force the facilities which the Irish would not grant voluntarily.

   This chapter sets out to place some of the more subtle aspects of those relations within the wider set of transactions and understandings of which they were
part, drawing largely on the extant records of one of the British agencies
involved in Anglo-Irish security affairs – if such a bilateral term can be used to
describe relations which were to an extent triangular because they also embraced
the police and military services in Northern Ireland. It also reflects on the way in
which security and intelligence policy and operations in retrospect can acquire a
logic and coherence which was not at all evident at the time, and on the degree
to which an organisation's version of the past may be conditioned by its ongoing
interests in the policy system. This is true in respect both of the Irish and the
British authorities. There is, however, no doubt that interagency confusion,
rivalries and friction, those familiar handmaidens of secret bureaucracies, were
rather more prevalent on the British side because of the number of organisations
which took an interest at one time or another in Irish affairs, because of their
sometimes conflicting operational aims, and because of the vastly wider set of
problems facing British intelligence and security organisations.

   The chapter re-appraises aspects of Anglo-Irish security relations in the light
of recently released British material. These releases add additional pieces to but
do not complete the full picture of such relations, which remains incomplete for
a number of reasons. The first, clearly, is the obvious one that in matters of security and defence policy, not everything was written down. This was particularly
understandable in the Irish case, where from June 1940 until the end of 1941,
there was an entirely rational fear of invasion by either set of belligerents.
Furthermore, the Irish officials most closely involved in covert security and
defence negotiations and cooperation had learned their trade in the under-

---

2 'Document No. 2', presented to Dáil Eireann, undated, January 1922, in R. Fanning, M.
Kennedy, D. Keogh and E. O'Halpin (eds), *Documents on Irish foreign policy volume I: 1919-
1922* (Dublin, 1998), p. 368. **3** N. Mansergh, *The unresolved question: the Anglo-Irish settlement
and its undoing, 1912-72* (London, 1991), p. 302; text of de Valera's statement to the Dáil, 27
Apr. 1938, National Archives of Ireland (NA), Department of the Taoiseach (DT), S. 10701A.

ground IRA of the War of Independence, were conscious that not all of their colleagues and masters would be happy with developing any understandings with the British, and so were not inclined to commit too much to paper. Finally, such co-operation was an extremely sensitive matter in terms both of Ireland's relations with Germany and of domestic political opinion – it is clear that within the army as well as in the wider political sphere there were sharp differences as to the most desirable outcome of the war and the appropriateness of helping out the British (particularly when it looked likely that they would emerge the losers against Hitler), and that one of the army's two most senior field officers, Major General Hugo MacNeill, was in sympathy with the Germans and had some contact with the only significant German agent dispatched to Ireland, Dr Herman Goertz. On the British side, too, there were sensitivities about the secret understandings on security reached with Ireland, not least because they continued on into the post-war world, as well as a general reluctance to acknowledge the clandestine intelligence activities of secret agencies, be they the codebreakers of the Government Code and Cipher School (GC&CS), the spies of SIS or the sabotage planners and black propagandists of Special Operations Executive (SOE).

Analysis of the intricacies of Anglo-Irish security co-operation (and competition) is complicated by the multiplicity of agencies involved. One would expect to find Irish-related intelligence and security material in the records of, at a minimum, fourteen British agencies and units: the Dominions Office and the papers of its Dublin representative Sir John Maffey and his staff; the security service MI5; the Scotland Yard Special Branch; the secret intelligence service MI6 or SIS; GC&CS, responsible for codebreaking; the naval intelligence division of the Admiralty; the intelligence directorate of the Air Ministry; the military intelligence division of the War Office and the intelligence and planning sections at the headquarters of British Troops in Northern Ireland (BTNI); the Political Warfare Executive (PWE); the SOE; and the escape and evasion service MI9. At the highest levels of policy, the records of the Security Executive – which supervised the work of all the security and intelligence agencies and civil departments insofar as the security of the British Isles was concerned – and of the Joint Intelligence Committee (JIC), which produced the all-source intelligence assessments provided to the chiefs of staff and to the government – also come into the frame. So too do those of the chiefs of staff committee. To this list must be added the RUC and, possibly, the Northern Ireland Ministry of Home Affairs.

On the Irish side, matters are somewhat less complicated: the two organisations which dealt directly with security work and Irish/UK liaison were the army's intelligence directorate G2 and the Garda Siochána's headquarters security section C3. A good deal of work was done at their behest by other bodies, including the postal and telephone services and the media censorship machinery. Policy matters were handled respectively by the Department of External Affairs and the Department of Justice, and very few issues were referred upwards to the cabinet for consideration although Mr de Valera was kept very fully in the picture. Thus the all-party 'Defence Conference' hastily improvised in June 1940 in response to the German invasion threat following the collapse of France proved to be an exercise in window dressing rather than a deliberative or decision-making forum.[4] A lot is now known about the evolution of Irish security policy and practice after 1939, as both the Department of Foreign Affairs and the Department of Defence have adopted a generally liberal approach to the release of records since 1991, although we still await the release of Garda security records. What was largely missing until now was what might be termed the Whitehall perspective on Irish security affairs.

There have been considerable developments in recent years which facilitate detailed appraisal both of security relations and of British clandestine activities concerning Ireland. Most importantly, the situation has been transformed in respect of the security service MI5, which had the primary responsibility for security liaison and for ensuring that neutral Ireland did not become a source of information leakages and of enemy espionage directed against Britain. The Department of Foreign Affairs records released in 1991 include a good deal of MI5 correspondence with G2, providing concrete evidence of cooperation but not much on the British calculations underpinning it. In February 1999, however, a start was made on releasing MI5's wartime records. To date (May 1999), the most significant records opened are the in-house omnibus history of the 'The Security Service: its problems and operational adjustments 1908-1945', referred to hereafter as the Curry history after its author Jock Curry, and a number of departmental histories including that of its Irish section, referred to hereafter after Cecil Liddell, the founding head of the Irish section in 1939 and the author of its history.[5] That section's working papers have yet to see the light of day, although it is believed that some will be opened once they have been weeded to remove references to SIS operations and personnel. We should note that there have also been other significant releases of British material since 1997: a number of Dominions Office files dealing with security matters dating from 1939-40; the minutes of meetings and supporting memoranda of the Security Executive, the committee which had overall responsibility for the security of the British Isles and which oversaw the work of MI5 and that of SIS 'in respect of Great Britain and Eire'; and the surviving policy and management records of the GC&CS codebreakers; and two of the three surviving SOE Irish files, both of which deal with substantive matters and cast a good deal of light on the high politics of clandestine operations.[6] This analysis , however, concentrates on the Curry and Liddell MI5 histories prepared in 1945-6.

---

4 These are in NA, DT, S. 11896. **5** The Curry history is at KV4/1 and the Liddell history at KV4/9, Public Record Office, London (Private information). **6** F.H. Hinsley and C.A.G. Simkins, *British intelligence in the Second World War volume 4: security and counter-intelligence* (London, 1990), p. 65.

It is here that the fresh material adds considerably to knowledge both of the *raison d'etre* of security co-operation involving Ireland and of the manner in which conflicting policy objectives were mediated within the Whitehall war machine. It reinforces the view that Irish security was a matter of very high concern in London both during the dark days of 1940 and 1941 and in the months preceding Operation Overlord in June 1944, drawing in not only middle-ranking desk officers but the heads of SIS and of MI5. Commenting on the Liddell history in 1946, the head of MI5 Sir David Petrie wrote that 'I have been kept in pretty close touch all along' with Irish matters, 'particularly in the anxious months preceding D-day.'[7] Furthermore, the new material highlight the inadvisability of taking published official histories prepared with privileged access to secret records, even when written by so eminent and upright a scholar and wartime intelligence officer as Sir Harry Hinsley, as gospel in every detail and every nuance.[8] Finally, while the Irish-related records of SIS, of the RSS and of the escape service MI9 remain out of bounds, the new MI5 material adds substantially to what was already known of the activities of two of those organisations from Irish sources. This is particularly significant in respect of SIS, reliable though incomplete material on whose clandestine Irish activities up to 1945 was hitherto available only from interviews with the wartime head of G2 Dan Bryan, and from a confidential Irish source.[9] The Curry and the Liddell histories not only provide more information on SIS operations, but also cast considerable light on debate within Whitehall in 1945-6 about which organisation should be responsible for the future collection of secret intelligence in Ireland.

Useful though they are, these in-house histories have to be treated with some caution. Begun before the war was over and completed during its immediate aftermath, they reflect a combination of operational experience from the years 1939 to 1945 and rather more problematic departmental folklore from pre-war days. Furthermore, they do not provide a complete picture either of security liaison or of British clandestine activities because they are based simply on events, activities and discussions of which MI5 had knowledge. While MI5 had the lead role in developing a close understanding with the Irish security authorities, its knowledge of what other British agencies did concerning Ireland was limited. This was the case both for sound 'need to know' reasons, and because neither SIS, its principal partner in protecting British interests in Ireland, nor other secret organisations told it everything that they knew or every operation that they had attempted involving Ireland. This phenomenon was not peculiar to the Irish theatre of Britain's secret war.[10]

---

7 Petrie to Curry, 11 Feb. 1946, PRO, KV4/9. 8 Hinsley and Simkins, *British intelligence*, pp 72-3. 9 O'Halpin, *Defending Ireland*, pp 225-9, 237-9. 10 Hinsley and Simkins, *British intelligence*, pp 131-7.

While they were never intended to be published in any form, the histories consequently had a very important propaganda function for MI5 within the secret world. This is abundantly clear from an exchange of minutes between Curry and Petrie in the last days of the war. It was agreed to use early drafts of the first chapters of the Curry history in an attempt to persuade Sir Findlater Stewart of the Security Executive, responsible for settling questions of post-war intelligence organisation, to find in MI5's favour in a protracted and crucial jurisdictional dispute with SIS which had waxed and waned since 1939. The issue was which organisation had the primary responsibility for counterintelligence, that is the study of and penetration of the enemy's intelligence system in order to determine what he knows or wants to know, and the personnel, methods and organisation he uses:

> I have been led to suggest this mainly by the idea that they will serve to rebut the view which 'C' [as the head of SIS has always been styled after its founding chief Sir Mansfield Cumming] is evidently going to put forward in favour of bringing the intelligence functions of the Security Service and of SIS within the orbit of a united Intelligence Service, the corollary of which would be to separate the 'getters' and the 'users'. I think that these two draft chapters show that the Security Service has certain responsibilities which could not be discharged by them if the getting of all secret intelligence was taken out of their hands and put into those of SIS while the Security Service was left – as I believe 'C' intends – to deal with the actual cases of arrested agents and their prosecution without having any part in the direction of means for obtaining intelligence in this country or abroad.

Petrie replied that 'I entirely agree about showing these … chapters to Sir F Stewart …' The Liddell history, in Curry's view 'as a Section History … one of the three or four most impressive records', was also drawn on in this dispute, for the reason that it provided evidence that in the Irish case the two contending agencies MI5 and MI6 had co-operated effectively. In Ireland, Curry observed, SIS had played an 'important part … in assisting the Irish Section', and this provided 'a suitable opportunity for a gesture which might help to build up the good relations with SIS in other directions which are very much to be desired in the immediate future'.[11] It may be, consequently, that any wartime disagreements between the two organisations on Irish matters were played down in the Liddell history in the interests of promoting future harmony.

A more obvious limitation of the Liddell history is the straightforward one that limited excisions have been made from the text released, occasionally

---

11 Curry to Petrie, and reply, 28 and 29 Apr. 1945, KV4/1, and undated and 11 Feb. 1946, KV4/9.

involving whole paragraphs but more usually only the names of individuals. Most importantly, the name of the head of SIS's wartime Irish section is blanked out, although the accompanying pronoun discloses the interesting fact that this was a woman working within Section V, the division of SIS responsible for counterintelligence. Who was this dark lady of the in-house histories? One plausible candidate is the Anglo-Irish writer Elizabeth Bowen, whose known Irish work for the British Ministry of Information could also have provided cover for more secret activities. Whoever she was, her main Irish role is not clear: counterintelligence against Axis agents and sympathisers was undoubtedly the principle function of the SIS organisation established in Dublin in June 1940, but that tedious on the ground work was done under the supervision of the British passport control officer Captain Collinson. It may be that the SIS woman was concerned with higher political intelligence.[12]

Amongst other names blanked out in the MI5 histories, in this case pointlessly since his involvement is already well known, is that of the maverick Irishman and would-be German spy turned MI5 double agent Joseph Lenihan. His name was also withheld from the Hinsley volume in 1990 at the insistence of the Cabinet Office, in the mistaken belief that his nephew Brian, who was by then reaching the end of a long ministerial career in Ireland, would be embarrassed at publicity about his uncle's colourful past. In fact the contrary has always been the case.[13] The Liddell history's description of Joseph Lenihan's intellectual attributes might equally have been said of his distinguished nephew: 'though of rough appearance, he was fairly well educated, intelligent and with a phenomenal memory for facts and faces. He gave more fresh and accurate information' about the Abwehr (the German foreign intelligence agency) 'in the Netherlands and Paris than any other single agent'.[14] Such futile excisions reinforce the case for a more liberal approach to the release of official records more than fifty years after the events with which they deal occurred.

Anglo-Irish security relations on the eve of the Second World War presented a number of peculiarities. Although in British eyes a dominion, Ireland was not a participant in the machinery of imperial defence planning. Nor was she involved in the parallel security system created after the First World War, which MI5 maintained through the posting of liaison officers in the various dominions and colonies, to monitor the movements and activities of supposed subversives and other suspects throughout the empire. Yet the British Isles was a common travel area, Ireland and the United Kingdom shared a completely open 180-mile border, Irish people had uncontrolled access to the British labour market and,

12 O'Halpin, *Defending Ireland*, pp 238-9; John Bowman, *De Valera and the Ulster question, 1917-1973* (Oxford, 1982), p. 207. 13 Information from Sir Harry Hinsley, 1990. By a further irony, Brian Lenihan's last two ministerial posts were respectively Foreign Affairs, and Defence. 14 Liddell history, pp 52-3.

while after 1922 Irish and British immigration services had co-operated amicably on the admission of foreigners to either jurisdiction, this relationship was managed entirely by the occasional exchange of correspondence and was not very effective.[15] So vague was the arrangement that the Liddell history was unable to determine when it had been agreed (in fact it dated from 1924). The consequence was that there was an obvious danger that foreigners bent on espionage or sabotage could slip into or out of the United Kingdom via Ireland unknown to the authorities of either state. The same factor applied in respect of the IRA, whose record showed that they would hurt Britain whenever they could and who might well be wooed by German for sabotage and intelligence gathering purposes.

For a combination of reasons including, paradoxically, contiguity and familiarity, as well as political sensitivities after de Valera came to power in 1932, when Britain relinquished her defence rights under the treaty in 1938 there was no Anglo-Irish liaison machinery to address such problems. It is known that Britain attempted to meet the consequent deficiencies in her knowledge of Irish political affairs by clandestine means. Within weeks of de Valera's forming his first government in March 1932 British codebreakers began to decrypt Irish diplomatic cable traffic, not that it told them much.[16] Thanks to the Liddell history, we now know that in 1932 MI5 was also asked to collect intelligence on Ireland, but 'after consideration, declined to do so'. SIS then agreed:

> to provide, not an Intelligence Service, but a very restricted information service. The reports furnished by this service did not do more than give a limited cross section of private opinion on current events of political or public interest in Éire. It has always been understood that the authority given to SIS to establish an organisation in Éire was an exclusive one. This meant that the Security Service had no right to run agents in Éire without the knowledge and approval of SIS.[17]

SIS had also established a link with the RUC, 'through whom they received information about events and suspect individuals' in both parts of Ireland, although in 1938 'at the request of SIS, it was arranged that this information should in future be passed by the RUC' to MI5. The reality, however, was that the RUC knew little about matters south of the border other than republican affairs and was not organised to collect and appraise political or security intelligence – assessing its wartime performance in these roles, Liddell wrote that it was 'jealous of its rights and responsibilities ... and not inclined to welcome

---

15 Ibid., pp 75-7. 16 E. O'Halpin, ' "Weird prophecies": British intelligence and Anglo-Irish relations, 1932-3', forthcoming in M. Kennedy and J. Skelly (eds), *Irish foreign policy, 1919-68* (Dublin, 2000). 17 Liddell history, p. 3.

what it calls "the amateur interference of Intelligence Officers, who lack local knowledge" '. So pronounced was this attitude that, even after a visit to Northern Ireland in August 1940 disclosed alarming security problems, it was decided 'not to send a Regional Officer ... though in other circumstances, he could have performed valuable services', both for MI5 and the RUC, which:

> as a Police Force, with its experience and training concentrated on local problems, above all the everlasting problem in Northern Ireland of the IRA ... was not well equipped to study foreign organisations and activities in Éire. As far as is known, no one ... had any knowledge of German or was familiar with German names. They were not, therefore, in a position to assess the accuracy of information they received about Germans in Éire or to study German activities there.[18]

The consequence of these weaknesses in security organisation and liaison was that, as European war became a likelihood and as evidence accumulated of German interest in Ireland as a natural base for espionage against Britain, MI5 had no worthwhile information on Ireland, was debarred from taking any clandestine initiatives to remedy this because such covert work in Ireland was technically SIS's exclusive preserve, had no channels of communication with the Irish authorities, and did not have a single officer specialising in Irish matters. Furthermore, until Sir John Maffey was sent to Dublin with the anomalous title 'British Representative' in September 1939 to set up what was in effect an embassy, the United Kingdom had no diplomatic presence in Dublin whatsoever apart from an overworked trade commissioner.[19] How, consequently, was the threat to British interests posed by the political and intelligence activities of the Axis powers in Ireland to be assessed and dealt with?

The answer lay in de Valera's 1938 pledge on British strategic interests, which was not so meaningless an undertaking as, given Ireland's almost complete defencelessness, it might have appeared. Its practical significance is underlined in the Curry history:

> Perhaps the most important political factor was the policy of neutrality qualified by Mr de Valera's guarantee that his Government would not allow Éire to be used as a base for operations against this country. This guarantee was the only safeguard against a potentially dangerous consequence of the neutrality policy ... At the time the guarantee was given it appeared to relate only to military operations, but in practice it was given a wider interpretation.[20]

18 Ibid., pp 9-10.   **19** Mansergh, *The unresolved question*, p. 309.   **20** Curry history, undated [?1946], Public Record Office, London (PRO), KV4/2, pp 264-5.

The first indication of this was the result of an Irish initiative. On 31 August 1938, as the Munich crisis unfolded, Joseph Walshe, the secretary of External Affairs, approached the Dominions Office on 'the question of liaison on counter-espionage matters'. At a meeting with the head of MI5's counterespionage branch Guy Liddell – who was to bring his brother Cecil into MI5 in 1939 to establish its Irish section B9 – he explained that 'the Éire Government was anxious about the NSDAP Group in Dublin', that is the Nazi political organisation designed to maintain control on Germans living abroad: 'they felt that it virtually infringed their sovereign rights'. Some days later Liddell gave the Irish high commissioner 'a copy of our memorandum on the NSDAP', together with another outlining recent British experience in investigating German espionage activities. These preliminary exchanges were crucial. They set the pattern for what followed, with Anglo-Irish security collaboration being mediated in Dublin by the Department of External Affairs rather than by Defence or Justice, and on the British side by MI5. A parallel link was also established between the Garda and the RUC – the Liddell history states that this was set up after war broke out, although there were clearly some pre-war contacts between the two police forces at local if not at headquarters level

It is not clear that the British ever appreciated the particular significance of the Irish approach of August 1938: in the published Hinsley history Walshe is described as the 'Minister' rather than the secretary of the department, and the year of the meeting is given as 1939. Furthermore, the Liddell history assumes that the success of the subsequent collaboration was largely due to the willingness of Irish officials to take risks by co-operating far more extensively than their political masters would have sanctioned: it comments that Archer, who as head of G2 dealt with MI5 from October 1938 until the summer of 1941, was initially hampered by 'an internal political situation in which a factor was a divergence of views within the Éire Government itself', while after the war Sir David Petrie wrote that 'the one factor indispensable to success was the good will of the Éire Officers'.[21] While the growth of goodwill and mutual confidence was indeed essential to the development of effective security relations after 1938, the key point which the British accounts miss is that the liaison had in effect been established by the Taoiseach, Eamon de Valera, who was also minister for external affairs and who through Walshe exercised a tight personal grip on all aspects of external relations. He personally directed that G2 rather than the Garda be briefed to handle espionage and related problems on the grounds that it was the practice 'in almost all other States' that defence ministries dealt with such problems and he authorised the establishment of a new 'Defence Security Intelligence Section' under Dan Bryan; he sanctioned an arrangement whereby the Department of Justice provided G2 with postal interception warrants; and he

21 Petrie to Curry, 11 Feb. 1946, KV4/9.

approved visits to Britain by a Post Office official to study new methods of postal interception.[22] In short, from its inception Anglo-Irish security liaison enjoyed de Valera's personal benediction, and the Irish evidence indicates that this continued to be the case even during the most strained period of Anglo-Irish relations in 1940-1.

The reasons for Irish interest in the link were clear enough: it provided a channel for the exchange of information on Axis activities which benefitted Ireland as well as Britain, increased British confidence in Irish security and *bona fides*, and gave an incentive not to work too much behind the back of the Irish government. Furthermore, as the Liddell history observed, 'the Dublin link was not always favourable to British policy; its existence provided de Valera with an answer to the British complaint about the presence and activities of the German Legation' in that MI5 were 'fully informed of the measures taken by the Éire government. to watch and control the Legation's activities'. The Éire government made full use of this argument in private when the American note requesting them to expel the Axis Legations' was presented in 1944. The liaison also provided a secure link for other purposes: it was through his MI5 contacts that Archer in May 1940 passed on the proposals for military discussions on joint action against a German invasion which led to the establishment of a British military mission in Dublin, and the Curry history claims that arguments advanced to MI5 by Archer in May 1941 on the likely impact of the imposition of conscription in Northern Ireland had a decisive impact on the Lord Privy Seal Sir John Anderson, himself an old Ireland hand, who then successfully pressed the case against conscription in the cabinet: 'Thus, at a moment of great political tension the personal link between ... Liddell and Colonel Archer again provided a friendly and unofficial channel for the transmission of information on a political matter which went far beyond the usual scope of an intelligence liaison'.[23]

This brings us to the second crucial point about the Irish side which the MI5 histories miss, that the Irish were not starting completely from scratch. However ignorant they were of the particular ways of German or Italian intelligence and related secret organisations in the late 1930s, Bryan, Archer and many of the army and Garda officers and Post Office officials involved in security and counterespionage work in one way or another between 1938 and 1945 already had very considerable experience both as invesigators and as clandestine operators. Liam Archer had been a crucial cog in Michael Collins' intelligence machine during the War of Independence as a Post Office telegraphist with access to official

22 Memorandum on 'Defence Security Intelligence', with Bryan to minister for defence, 21 June 1945, NA, DFA A8/1. **23** Liddell history, pp 7 and 43; Curry history, p. 263. Anderson had been sent to Dublin Castle in June 1920 to reform the Irish administration, and was an advocate of conciliation. E. O'Halpin, *The decline of the union: British government in Ireland 1891-1920* (Dublin, 1987), pp 208-13.

communications. Dan Bryan had spent most of his career since joining the IRA in 1919 in intelligence work, firstly against the British and after 1921 as an army man – between 1922 and 1926 army intelligence had had primary responsibility for watching both the republican movement and other political, labour and social organisations regarded as potentially subversive, it had investigated suspected British and Northern Irish agents, it had run its own agents within the republican movement in the United Kingdom, and it had done some spying on the new Northern state and on the RUC.[24] It is, consequently, not entirely accurate to write of the initial efforts of the 'Éire military and civil authorities, hampered as they often were, by their political superiors, lack of experience, and primitive means' in 1938-9.[25] As the Admiralty's director of naval intelligence commented in his unpublished memoirs, furthermore, the Garda, 'having only recently emerged from a … civil war … were particularly good at detecting underground conspiracies'.[26]

The assumption in the MI5 histories that the British taught the Irish from scratch after 1938 is reflected in the assessments of the successive heads of G2 with whom they dealt. Archer,

> though at all times friendly and absolutely straight in his dealings, was a strong Irish Nationalist and inclined to limit his co-operation rather strictly. He was a conscientious, but not an enthusiastic Intelligence Officer. Colonel Bryan, while just as mindful of his duty to his country, was wrapped up in Intelligence work for its own sake. Once personal relations and mutual confidence had been established, his enthusiasm for the work produced a degree of co-operation from the Irish which increased steadily as the war went on.[27]

These comments are in themselves a fair reflection of the two men. Archer was regarded as a steady, cautious officer, who was promoted to assistant chief of staff in July 1941 and who became chief of staff in 1949. Bryan, his G2 deputy and successor as director of intelligence was considered as an oddity, whose favourite hours of work were between 1 a.m. and 4 a.m. when nobody was about and contacts could be met in safety.[28] What the British seem never to have realised is that Irish competence in security operations between 1938 and 1945 extended to uncovering not only IRA and Axis intrigues but also the clandestine activities of

---

24 O'Halpin, *Defending Ireland*, pp 53-9. **25** Liddell history, p. 18. **26** Quoted in O'Halpin, *Defending Ireland*, p. 206. **27** Liddell history, p. 54. **28** Interviews with Colonel Bryan, December 1983, and with Dr Cleveland Cram, the CIA officer responsible for liaison with G2 for much of the 1950s and 1960s, January 1998; comments of Douglas Gageby, who served as a lieutenant in G2 under Bryan, 12 May 1999. Gageby later became editor of the *Evening Press* and of the *Irish Times*.

British and American agencies. This is reflected in Liddell's discussion of SIS' Irish activities:

> the service of SIS (Irish Section) have been valuable, both as a source of original information and as a check on reports received from other sources. It will be realised that this information had to be kept secret, not only from the enemy in Éire, but also from the Éire authorities. Had it come to the knowledge of the latter, the effect on our political relations with Éire would have been very serious and irreparable harm would have been done to the general security co-operation which had been built up with the Éire Government both by the Security Service and the Royal Ulster Constabulary.[29]

How wrong he was. G2 was concerned not to stamp on SIS's Irish network but rather to monitor it, to feed off the intelligence which it was collecting for London, and to leave it undisturbed lest the British start a new one which might not be so permeable. G2 had a man inside Captain Collinson's SIS organisation in Dublin within months of its establishment, a former civil war opponent of Bryan's from Ballsbridge who provided a continuous stream of information up to the network's last days in 1945.[30]

Curiously, the exception to this general tendency to underestimate the capacity of Irish security officials was in the realm of codebreaking, ironically one area of intelligence where technical, linguistic and personnel issues outweigh sovereignty and local knowledge and make it highly unlikely that a small unaligned state could develop any serious competence. In the course of the war both the British and the American governments came to believe that the Irish could read their diplomatic traffic to and from Dublin. That conclusion stemmed largely from Anglo-Irish collaboration on German agent codes after 1941, when British codebreakers had been taken aback by their encounters with Dr Richard Hayes, the director of the National Library and the only code expert on whom G2 could draw. Described by the American minister in Dublin in a 1944 telegram to Washington as 'a very skilled cryptographer' who had 'broken … code messages from London' to Sir John Maffey, the Liddell history goes even further in its estimation of 'his gifts', which 'amounted almost to genius'.[31] Yet in reality Hayes never paid any serious attention to Allied diplomatic messages: his initial brief was to study German legation traffic, and his great achievements lay in his single-handed mastering of German agent ciphers which had defeated GC&CS.[32]

29 Liddell history, pp 4-5. **30** Interview with Colonel Bryan, December 1983; confidential Irish source. **31** Gray to Washington, 22 Feb. 1944, quoted in O'Halpin, *Defending Ireland*, p. 186; Liddell history, p. 71. **32** O'Halpin, *Defending Ireland*, pp 228-9, 243.

Discussion of codebreaking brings us to perhaps the most striking fresh vin-dication of the Irish policy of covert security liaison with the British (and from 1942 also with the American OSS). By 1944, when Irish security became a public issue in February through the American note demanding the closure of the Axis legations in Dublin, both MI5 and the OSS were so convinced of Irish efficien-cy that Sir David Petrie and a senior OSS officer lobbied the Allied governments not to press the Irish publicly. Thanks to the Liddell history we now also know that, when the American demarche was in contemplation, the British Joint Intelligence Committee 'submitted a report on the dangers of leakage through the Axis legations ... and on the pros and cons for expulsion'. This appraisal was, 'entirely based on a note prepared by Captain Liddell [Guy, head of MI5's coun-terintelligence division and brother of Cecil of the Irish section] setting out these pros and cons, but clearly indicating that ... there would be very little, if any, security advantage in the removal of the German Legation whose communica-tions we then controlled'. If the legation were closed, it

> might be replaced at the most critical moment by enemy agents with means of communication which it would take time to discover, all the more so as our relations with Éire would be so strained that it was at least doubtful whether we should continue to enjoy the assistance we had hith-erto received in matters of this kind. It was eventually decided that an American Note should be presented to the Éire Government and that Sir John Maffey was to inform Mr de Valera verbally that the British Government had been consulted and concurred. The American Note was presented on the 21st February, and on the 7th March the Éire Minister in Washington replied that it was impossible ... to comply with this request.
>
> The presentation of the American Note was regarded with great mis-givings by the Security Service, who feared that at a most critical period the intelligence co-operation with the Irish might be seriously prejudiced. Fortunately this did not occur. It is believed that the Irish realised that the move was inspired by the Americans, although it had British support.[33]

One of the perennial difficulties for Britain in her relationship with neutral countries during the Second World War was the tension between the desirability of security and intelligence understanding and the temptation to mount secret intelligence gathering, propaganda and other types of clandestine operations in such states, whether directed against them or aimed at Axis targets there or in adjacent countries. The one desideratum of good relations with the local security organs did not completely exclude clandestine activities, but there was a difficult

33 Ibid., pp 230-1; Curry history, p. 271.

equilibrium to be struck. The difficulty in the case of Ireland was that in 1939 there was no great bank of experience on which to draw within Whitehall and the armed services. We have seen that SIS had been providing only a limited 'information service' since 1932, which one suspects was based entirely on Anglo-Irish dinner table gossip: there is nothing to suggest that it helped the British to come to grips with the dynamics of Irish politics up to 1939. MI5 established an Irish section in September 1939, but until June 1940 it had only one officer, Cecil Liddell, and he was a fresh recruit and was only learning the ropes. At senior level, the organisation was virtually paralysed by the weight of war work and by its own organisational problems: in respect of Ireland as more generally during the phoney war period, 'it was difficult, if not impossible, to avoid the fatal and futile search for spies in the "in tray", instead of visualising the situation as a whole'. Effective action to dispel the chaos only began with the abrupt dismissal of its founding head Sir Vernon Kell after 31 years in office and his replacement by Sir David Petrie. These decisive developments came within a fortnight of the creation of the Security Executive under Lord Swinton to direct the activities of all the intelligence and security agencies in respect of the security of the United Kingdom.[34]

Both MI5 and the newly appointed British naval attaché Captain Greig were quickly convinced of G2's *bona fides*: all material passed to Archer was 'carefully dealt with. Almost without exception they were found to be without foundation', as were the many reports of submarine landings which reached Britain. In the absence of a coherent plan for coping with the security threat posed by Ireland, however, a number of amateurish efforts were made to establish information gathering and coastwatching organisations along the southern coastline by involving retired British officers and the like who lived in those areas. After Archer had pointed out to that G2 were well aware of much of this, Greig told the Admiralty that such clumsy intrigues 'tend to cloud the co-operation between us'. Nevertheless there were further such efforts, some of them initiatives of individuals and others organised from London, to establish covert networks – the Liddell history states that:

> In the autumn of 1939 very strong pressure was brought on SIS by the Admiralty to provide an organisation which could check the numerous reports of German submarines refuelling and landing personnel on the West coast of Ireland. SIS were unable to provide a coast watching service, but they increased their organisation so as to be able to provide some check on these reports.

As the military situation in Europe deteriorated in the spring of 1940, the British army in Northern Ireland (BTNI), which had to prepare for action either

---

34 Liddell history, p. 43; Hinsley and Simkin, *British intelligence*, p. 65.

to seize ports and facilities from the Irish or to eject any German forces which
might land on the island, also attempted to gather intelligence on routes and
strategic installations by sending down officers in civilian clothes on reconnais-
sance. This naturally provoked strong Irish complaints to Sir John Maffey,
although BTNI agreed to stop the practice if SIS 'provided the necessary information'. This stipulation was, however, at least partly overtaken by events following the establishment of liaison in June 1940 between BTNI and the Irish
army. That link wrought a transformation in the British military attitude
towards the Irish – in a discussion in Belfast in April 1941 of plans for the establishment by SOE of 'stay behind' sabotage and reporting parties in Ireland, a
brigadier emphasised that:

> No scheme could be agreed that entailed the taking into Éire of anything
> in the nature of explosives, arms, etc. unless the Éire Army Authorities,
> with whom he and his people were in close touch, were first informed. To
> introduce such stores without first informing the Éire Army leaders (or
> some of them) would wreck ... good relations ... and would lead to fur-
> ther concentration of Éire forces on the border, with the result that BTNI
> would be hampered, and the Germans left greater freedom of movement
> if they landed.[35]

By the spring of 1941, the Admiralty also took the view that the Irish could be
trusted on matters of concern to it such as coastwatching and counterespionage,
and by implication that more was to be gained from collaboration than from
clandestine activity (although some secret reporting continued, which G2 again
kept under observation without attempting to interfere with it as the communications were harmless and served to reinforce what the Irish were saying to
MI5).[36] Interestingly, 'C' was also a strong advocate of protecting the G2/MI5
link and the blossoming Anglo-Irish military liaison: in the course of a high level
battle to prevent SOE from mounting operations in Ireland, he warned against
clandestine 'action which if it leaked out, would be interpreted as clumsy interference', and added that 'MI5, whose valuable liaison with the Éire Defence
Ministry depends entirely upon mutual good will, have even stronger views than
are held here'.[37] After a long and complicated wrangle involving BTNI, MI5,
SIS, the chiefs of staff and, ultimately, the prime minister Winston Churchill,
SOE were forced to withdraw their only Dublin agent in June 1941, less than
three months after installing him, on the grounds that the Irish might be antag-
onised and liaison jeopardised.[38]

35 Note of a meeting between officers of BTNI and Sir Frank Nelson and Brigadier Colin
Gubbins of SOE, Belfast, 30 Apr. 1941, HW6/305. 36 O'Halpin, *Defending Ireland*, p. 226.
37 'C' to Nelson (head of SOE), 24 Apr. 1941, HW6/305. 38 Eunan O'Halpin, 'The real war

We have seen that, 'C's anxiety lest good Anglo-Irish security relations be jeopardised by 'clumsy' clandestine activities notwithstanding, an SIS network had been established in Dublin under Captain Collinson. This was 'increased and perfected throughout 1941, 1942 and 1943 until the invasion and liberation of France'. At one point in November 1941, the possibility of providing it with radios reached the cabinet before it was 'turned down on the grounds that the risk of discovery through indiscretion, with the consequent harm' to the MI5/G2 link, 'was too great compared to the value of the information likely to be supplied'.[39] It does not appear to have occurred to anyone in London that, if the Irish were so efficient at detecting and penetrating Axis and IRA covert activities, the chances were that they already knew a thing or two about what SIS was up to.

We have also already seen that MI5 regarded the Curry and Liddell histories as important elements in their fight against SIS efforts to gain complete control of post-war counterintelligence. It is clear from the Liddell history, furthermore, that Ireland itself became the subject of a dispute between the two agencies as the war neared its end. Collinson's SIS organisation in Ireland was cut back after the successful invasion of Normandy rendered its counterintelligence work largely redundant: in September 1944 SIS informed the Dominions Office that 'they proposed to reduce their organisation in Éire to the pre-1940 level, but to maintain a small nucleus which would be capable of expansion if necessary'. This plan was 'to some extent based on the assumption that the very good relations then existing' between MI5 and G2 would continue, although MI5 pointed out that these 'were entirely dependent on the political relations between the two countries and that therefore no assumption could be made that they would continue to be the valuable source of information they had been during the war'. SIS initially accepted this, but in March 1945 wrote to say that they now proposed to 'abolish the nucleus which they had maintained since September 1944', and it was 'closed down on the 31st March 1945'. 'C' did ask to be informed of any serious deterioration in political relations so that he could if necessary 'undertake the re-formation of his secret organisation'. In November 1945, however, a committee under Sir Findlater Stewart examined the problem of intelligence on Ireland. Contradicting 'C', he said that 'although Éire was in name a Dominion, it was in fact a foreign country'. There could be no question as to ' "C"'s responsibility towards the Service Departments' to provide operational intelligence which was beyond MI5's brief. Two weeks later he wrote that if the good MI5/G2 link was attenuated

> there would be no flow of intelligence from Éire until the Dominions Office again laid the task of getting it upon SIS. It must be recognised,

was in Whitehall', paper presented at seminar of the National Committee for the Study of International Affairs, Royal Irish Academy, 12 May 1999. **39** Liddell history, p. 50.

however, that until SIS had rebuilt their organisation in Éire (and this could take some time) little in the way of results could be expected.[40]

From these exchanges it is clear that the Irish intelligence requirements of both SIS and MI5 continued to centre on counterintelligence and security, with possible intrigue by the Soviet Union and its satellites becoming the main threat to be countered. There is nothing to indicate that either organisation saw intelligence on the IRA as a priority justifying the maintenance of a covert organisation in Ireland, or that anyone envisaged running any political or espionage operations against the Irish state.

There the documentary trail runs cold. From G2's point of view, the disbanding of the remains of Collinson's organisation in March 1945 must have come as a hammer blow, since they had penetrated it so effectively and presumably hoped to continue to monitor it. It is unlikely that the Irish had comparable success against whatever postwar nucleus SIS eventually set up. In any event, the MI5/G2 link continued to operate to mutual satisfaction for many years after 1945, with the United States' Central Intelligence Agency joining G2's liaison list from 1955. That such continuing liaison with MI5 did not guarantee immunity from British espionage was illustrated in 1972 with the arrest of a Garda occupying a highly sensitive security post who was working as a British agent. In intelligence, as in other aspects of human affairs, some things never change.[41]

MI5's Irish memories are, their flaws notwithstanding, an invaluable source on the history of Anglo-Irish relations during the Second World War. Both in what they say, and in their evident ignorance of the sophistication of Irish counterintelligence work against British clandestine activities, they are a testament to the competence and the subtlety with which the liaison was developed and maintained on the Irish side once the initial impetus had been provided by de Valera in 1938. The MI5 histories attribute the success of the liaison primarily to the helpful attitude of Irish officers; in reality it was due as much to the fact that it had been initiated and was mediated through the top officials in External Affairs, whose minister was de Valera. The liaison was, in short, founded on a clear direction from the key figure in Irish politics. The histories also have a wider interest, as they highlight some of the complexities which arise in interstate security relations, and the shifting and divergent calculations which may underlie such pragmatic partnerships. Above all, however, in tandem with other evidence they underline the strength which local knowledge, legitimacy and calm competence can bring in an otherwise grossly unequal security relationship.

40 Ibid., p. 97.   41 O'Halpin, *Defending Ireland*, pp 280-2.

Censorship as propaganda:
the neutralisation of Irish public opinion
during the Second World War

Donal Ó Drisceoil

For the duration of the Second World War the Irish government set out to neutralise Irish public opinion on the war by means of a wide-ranging and draconian censorship system. Reports of the Holocaust were suppressed, newsreels were
banned, children's games were seized and the expression of opinions on the war
and Ireland's neutrality was strictly controlled. One way of understanding the
wartime censorship and its role as 'neutrality's backbone' is to see it as a form of
propaganda.[1] Negative propaganda has been defined as 'the selective control of
information to favour a particular viewpoint',[2] which captures neatly a primary
objective of the Emergency censors. That objective was not the promotion of
one set of belligerents over the other – although Holocaust denial was official
policy, for example, it was not motivated by the crypto-Nazi agenda associated
with that phenomenon in more recent times. The aim was the promotion of that
image of the war and Irish neutrality that the government wished the Irish public to receive.

Irish wartime neutrality fulfilled both pragmatic and symbolic functions for
the state, and was operated on two partially corresponding levels. In practical
terms, the state was very poorly equipped defensively; it made sense to want to
avoid the horrors of war; Ireland had no imperialist interests under threat; and,
finally and crucially, neutrality was the policy that was least divisive in the
domestic political context. Domestic partisans consisted mainly of those republicans who still believed that 'England's difficulty was Ireland's opportunity' and
saw the old enemy's enemy as their friend, irrespective of the nature of Nazism,
and, on the other side, southern unionists who viewed Britain's war as their war
also. It was still only two decades since the war of independence and civil war

---

1 For a detailed account and analysis of wartime Irish censorship see D. Ó Drisceoil,
Censorship in Ireland 1939-1945: neutrality, politics and society (Cork, 1996); R. Fisk, *In time of
war: Ireland, Ulster and the price of neutrality* (London, 1985 ed.), p. 162. **2** J.A.C. Brown,
Techniques of persuasion: from propaganda to brainwashing (Middlesex, 1983), p. 16.

and anti-British feeling was still strong at a popular level; there was a real fear that if the Irish joined the war on the British side, it could provoke a German-backed IRA revolt, possibly leading to a second civil war. Symbolically, neutrality was an expression of the young state's sovereignty and independence of action from Britain. This was a vital element of the Fianna Fáil project and was central to the evolving ideology of southern Irish nationalism.

The two levels of policy referred to above were the public and the secret. At the public, formal level Irish neutrality was impeccably correct and impartial, as exemplified by de Valera's visit to the German representative Hempel to offer his condolences on the death of Hitler. At a secret level, however, Irish policy was extremely partial towards the Allies and there was extensive co-operation with the Allied war effort. This dual policy has been described as de Valera's 'double game',[3] a risky and ultimately successful strategy for preserving the state and its sovereignty at a time when it was potentially most under threat.

The Emergency censorship was a key instrument in this double game. It helped to hide the level of Irish involvement in the war (by, for example, banning references to the tens of thousands of Irish volunteers in the British forces) while simultaneously being central to the public presentation of impartiality. Frank Aiken and his team of eager civil servant censors, backed up by Military Intelligence, set out to 'avoid giving to any of the belligerents any due cause, and proper cause, of complaint', and to domestic partisans any excuse or encouragement to create trouble for the state or its policy – any opportunity or justification for questioning or violating Irish neutrality. The aim, in Aiken's own words, was to 'keep the temperature down', both internally and between Ireland and the belligerents. Maintaining the illusion of strict impartiality was perceived as vital to the state's survival as was the minimising of internal disagreement and dispute so as to prevent any of the belligerents from being tempted to fish in troubled political waters.[4]

The role of the censorship in papering over the gap between illusion and reality is well illustrated by reference to the subject of the first written direction to the press and one dear to Irish hearts: the weather. Because of the military value of meteorological information current weather reports and forecasts were banned for the duration of the Emergency. References to or photographs illustrating past weather conditions had to be held until ten days after the day to which they related. This led to the banning, for example, of a photograph of the Minister for Posts and Telegraphs skating on a frozen pond in Dublin; the stopping of an article in which the writer wondered whether he would be arrested for

3 J.J. Lee, *Ireland 1912-1985: politics and society* (Cambridge, 1989), p. 244. 4 Aiken, a close ally of de Valera, was the wartime Minister for the Co-ordination of Defensive Measures with responsibility for censorship; De Valera, *Dáil debates*, vol. 77, col. 3, 2 September 1939; Frank Aiken, *Seanad debates*, vol. 24, cols. 2614-5, 4 December 1940.

carrying an umbrella or saying 'it looks like rain'; and the withdrawal of an advertisement for tailored trousers for skating as late as January 1945.[5] While the Irish public and the Germans had to forego the benefit of Irish weather information, the Irish Meteorological Service was supplying the British with full meteorological data for the duration of the war.[6] The Irish, then, were being publicly impartial in ensuring that their media were not a source of militarily useful information for either side while simultaneously secretly pursuing the benevolent neutrality which sought to ensure that 'the British would not acquire by conquest much more than she gained through co-operation'.[7]

Aiken, in an important and revealing memorandum entitled 'Neutrality, censorship and democracy', presented to government in January 1940, defined propaganda as 'one of the most important weapons of war' and its expression in a neutral country, whether originating there or not, as effectively an act of war.[8] Such a framing not only justified the rigidity and extensiveness of the censorship (all war news was regarded as potentially propagandist) but also bolstered the government's claim to have been responsible for the 'success' of wartime neutrality. The failure to develop its defensive capabilities to the level necessary to defend its neutrality militarily meant that the state had to rely on good fortune and secret partiality for survival. The invasion and occupation of the state never became a strategic imperative for either side, Ireland was the most geostrategically fortunate of the European neutrals, while the existence of Northern Ireland satisfied Allied requirements on the island to a sufficient degree (along with the secret co-operation of the southern authorities) not to necessitate invasion or occupation. Irish neutrality suited German purposes so long as Britain held out and its strategic importance dwindled once the focus of war shifted east from 1941-2. Despite this, the need existed for symbolic, emotional and domestic political reasons for the government to claim full credit for its success. Aiken's memorandum characterised neutrality as 'a condition of limited warfare' against both sets of belligerents, in which propaganda was a central weapon. This war was in reality a phoney war, and the fruits of victory, as Joe Lee has pointed out, could only be enjoyed so long as the Allies won the real war.[9] Fortunately this was the outcome and censorship played its part in the victory of virtual Irish neutrality.

Other neutrals like Sweden and Switzerland had not abdicated their defensive responsibilities as the Irish had, nor did they develop the emotional dimension, self-righteousness and moral superiority which distinquished Irish neutrali-

5 *Irish Times*, 21 May 1945; *Dáil debates*, vol. 77, cols. 316-17, 27 September 1939; Department of Justice (D/J), No. 5A, 'Cork Examiner', proof deletion, 26 January 1945, National Archives, Dublin (NA).   **6** 'Help given by the Irish government in relation to the actual waging of war', 24 May 1941, D/FA (Secretary's files), A3, NA.   **7** Lee, *Ireland*, p. 244.   **8** Department of Taoiseach (D/T), S 11586A, NA.   **9** Lee, *Ireland*, p. 262.

ty.[10] Both the Swiss and the Swedes, despite their more precarious locations, allowed far more in the way of belligerent propaganda and freedom of expression on the war and the issues at stake than did the Irish.[11] Neither regarded the neutralisation of public opinion, the creation of 'a truly neutral outlook', or the establishment of 'moral neutrality' on the war as either necessary or desirable. Indeed, one Swiss newspaper was punished early in the war for advocating a policy of press reticence on the conflict with the object of making the Swiss 'neutral-minded'.[12] Such reticence was demanded of and forced upon the Irish press, cinema, books and journals, theatre and even private communications. The survival of the state, no less, was seen to depend on it.

The Press Censorship branch was given the task of ensuring that Irish newspapers gave as balanced and objective a picture of the war as possible. War reports were pared down as much as possible to official statements and communiqués issued by or on behalf of both sides. Blatant propaganda and propagandist terminology were disallowed and only official titles of states, leaders, armed forces, etc. were permitted. Thus, for example, the words 'Nazi' and 'Fascist' were prohibited as were 'Hitlerism', 'Reds' and 'Bolsheviks'. Hitler was always Herr Hitler and Goebbels was Dr Goebbels. War news generally goes beyond formal accounts of battles and is expected to offer 'hope, consolation or interpretation'.[13] The 'cold impartiality' demanded by the Irish censorship stripped the padding and colour from war reports in the Irish press and made the coverage anodyne and unengaging.[14] Reports of air raids were a particular target because of their strategic use by propagandists of both sides. Reports on the destruction of church property and hospitals and casualties to nuns, priests, doctors, nurses, women and children were stopped because of their inherent propagandist nature, 'whatever the facts may be'.[15] Stories detailing the impact of 'the blitz' on Irish people living and working in British cities were banned on the basis that it was 'not considered desirable nor in the interests of our neutrality to lay emphasis on any Irish connection with the war'.[16] Propagandist terminology included terms such as the Battle of Britain, which Frank Aiken personally rechristened 'the air battle over Southern England and the Channel in 1940' for the benefit of Irish readers.[17]

10 See Fisk, *In time of war*, pp 548-50 and Lee, *Ireland*, pp 262-70.   **11** See Ó Drisceoil, *Censorship*, pp 285-90.   **12** Letter to Joseph Walshe, Secretary of the Department of External Affairs, from the Irish legation in Geneva on censorship in Switzerland, 8 February 1943, Department of Foreign Afairs (D/FA) 214/66, NA.   **13** T. H. Qualter, *Opinion control in the democracies* (New York, 1985), p. 139.   **14** Joseph Connolly (controller of censorship 1939-41) in J.A. Gaughan (ed.), *Memoirs of senator Joseph Connolly (1885-1961): a founder of modern Ireland* (Dublin, 1996), p. 402.   **15** Thomas J. Coyne (controller of censorship 1941-5) to *Ricci mission news* editor, April 1945, D/J, no. 201, 'Irish Jesuit Publications', NA.   **16** Connolly to Frank Geary (editor), 24 December 1940, D/J, 'Press censorship reviews: Irish Independent', NA.   **17** D/J, R25 'Sunday Independent: stopped and deleted proofs', 16 March 1943, NA.

Atrocity stories were a particular concern of the authorities and it was policy to exclude reports of cruel and inhuman treatment. Thomas Coyne, controller of censorship from September 1941, stated that the 'publication of atrocity stories, whether true or false, can do this country no good and may do it much harm'.[18] The editor of the Fianna Fáil newspaper the *Irish Press* agreed with censorship policy on the issue, declaring that such stories had 'no other value than to inflame passions'.[19] The sense of moral superiority that became attached to Irish neutrality demanded that both sides be morally equated; if the belligerents 'turned out to have been unevenly matched in the savagery stakes' then both moral superiority and moral neutrality would have been more difficult to sustain.[20] Added to this was the insistence of many on viewing all atrocities through the lens of the British record in Ireland and the deep-seated anti-Communism which pervaded the culture: how could anyone, even the Nazis, be worse than perfidious Albion and Godless Russia? Censorship policy remained rigid as the details of the 'final solution' began filtering through and the nature and scale of the Nazi project of systematic mass murder was becoming clear to all but those most determined to ignore it and its implications. Buchenwald, Belsen, Lublin, Dachau, Auschwitz-Birkenau – none could be allowed disturb the neutral calm. The same applied to stories such as the Katyn massacre of Polish officers by the Soviets and atrocities perpetrated in the Pacific theatre of war, including the killing and ill treatment of many Irish Catholic missionaries in the area. A report detailing the burning to death by the Japanese of four Irish priests in Manila in March 1945, for example, was presented to the Irish public as an announcement of the deaths 'during recent fighting in Manila'.[21]

With France falling to the Germans in late May 1940, Coyne, then assistant controller of censorship, wrote a note to Aiken in relation to an editorial that had appeared in the *Leader*. 'In times so dangerous as the present', he wrote, '... the freedom of the press must go by the board and ... only one voice should be heard in respect of matters affecting our external and internal security, namely, the voice of the Government.'[22] Connolly, the then controller, agreed that the 'preservation of our neutrality and the determination to give no possible excuse for complaints by either of the belligerents far outweighs any temporary intellectual starvation that newspaper readers may suffer'.[23] Aiken was of the same mind and comment and opinion on the war and its progress was severely curtailed. When the press censors deleted a comment from an *Irish Times* editorial in late

18 D/J, Press Censorship Monthly Reports, May 1945, NA.   **19** William Sweetman to Frank Gallagher, 24 April 1945, Frank Gallagher Papers, MS 18,334, National Library of Ireland.   **20** Lee, *Ireland*, p. 267.   **21** *Irish Press* proof, 18 March 1945, 'Irish missionaries in the Far East', Office of the Controller of Censorship (OCC), 2/150, Military Archives, Dublin (MA).   **22** Coyne to Aiken, 26 May 1940, D/J, No. 30, 'The Leader', NA.   **23** Connolly to Aiken, 18 September 1940, D/J, No. 3, 'Irish Times', NA.

August 1941 which suggested that Japan was possibly bluffing with its threat to sink American ships carrying arms to Vladivostok, the assistant editor wrote to Coyne sarcastically commenting 'Evidently we are in danger of invasion by Japan.' Coyne's response summed up censorship policy regarding the expression of opinion: 'the war is indivisible ... the Battle of Britain is being fought at the moment by the Russians at Velikiye and elsewhere. So far as we can contrive, it is going to stay there. We are not going to have the newspapers transferring the fight to our doorstep. '[24] Even the all-powerful Irish Catholic hierarchy was not immune and the interference with published reports of Lenten pastorals from a variety of Irish bishops which made reference to the war (together with the censoring of Vatican statements) was one of the more controversial aspects of censorship policy.[25]

The single biggest obstacle to the achievement of 'newspaper neutrality'[26] was the fact that the Irish press was dependent for its war news on Allied sources. There was no Irish news agency and no Irish paper could afford a foreign correspondent. This was a significant difference between Ireland and other neutrals like Sweden and Switzerland, where newspapers had the benefit of their own agency and correspondents' war reports. In Ireland international news came almost entirely from the news agencies, principally British (predominantly Reuters and the Press Association) and, occasionally, American (Associated Press and United Press). This news was controlled and censored at source and was naturally slanted in favour of the Allies; the British news control system ensured that propaganda was disseminated under the guise of objective news.[27] The propagandist function of the agencies was clearly evident in their habit of issuing certain stories 'For Publication in Ireland Only'. These fed into British propaganda efforts to heighten anti-Axis feeling in Ireland, principally by reference to Nazi ill treatment of the Catholic church.[28] The temptation was ever present for Irish papers, for reasons of bias or convenience, to use the headings, captions and introductions provided by the agencies, thus reproducing the news with the slant provided. Also, of course, news unfavourable to the Allied cause was not supplied by the agencies at all. (German news agency reports were issued to the press via the German legation.) While the press censorship branch was consistently even-handed in its treatment of war news, the reliance on Allied news sources meant that overall coverage of the conflict in the Irish press reflected Allied priorities. Thus, while the war in Africa was 'never more than a side-show'

24 Alec Newman to Coyne, 28 August 1941 and Coyne to Newman, 29 August 1941, ibid. **25** See Ó Drisceoil, *Censorship in Ireland*, pp 220-33. **26** R.M. Syllie, 'Unneutral Neutral Eire', *Foreign affairs*, 24, 2, January 1946, p. 324. **27** P.M. Taylor, 'Censorship in Britain in the Second World War: An Overview', in A.C. Duke and C.A. Tamse (eds), *Too mighty to be free: censorship and the press in Britain and the Netherlands* (Zutphen, 1987), p. 174. **28** D/J, Unnumbered, 'Matter stopped – "For Ireland only"', NA.

for Hitler, for Churchill and the British media it was the greatest theatre of war, replete with heroic deeds, Desert Rats and Desert Foxes.[29] The Irish media reflected the disproportionate attention it received. The decisive Eastern Front, by contrast, was in the West, including Ireland, the most poorly and under-reported aspect of the conflict. This was partly because the British and Americans were not directly involved and partly due to the secrecy of the Soviet authorities and their suspicion of western war correspondents.[30] In July 1944 Aiken expressed his unhappiness to his censors about the imbalance in war reportage resulting from over reliance on British sources. He instructed that, where possible, announcements from Goebbels indicating 'what the German people are thinking' should be given publicity and to allow such material from German sources as had news value.[31]

German propaganda was disseminated through a weekly bulletin, *Weekly review of the German news agency* and via German Radio's Irish service known as Irland-Redaktion.[32] The bulletin, like the *Italian news review*, was tolerated by the authorities so long as it remained within the 'bounds of decency' demanded of the British press which circulated in Ireland. It had a circulation of about 3,000 and among its recipients were government ministers, TDs and senators, army officers, civil servants, priests, schoolteachers and others who the Germans hoped might be influenced by such material. An American intelligence report in November 1942 claimed that apart from 'a small group of fanatically anti-British individuals' the effect of printed Axis propaganda was 'practically nil'.[33] From 1941 the bi-lingual Irland-Redaktion service provided a nightly diet of news and talks focussing on Gaelic culture, anti-Catholic discrimination in the North and the evils of partition, British atrocities in Ireland, the history of nationalist resistance to British rule and, most forcefully, encouragement for Irish neutrality. Prior to that there had been a bi-weekly broadcast in Irish, targeted at Irish speakers who were assumed to have been the most receptive audience for anti-British propaganda. The influence of German radio propaganda appears to have been limited. There were fewer than 200,000 wireless sets in the country, accounting for about half the households in cities and towns and about 13 per cent in rural areas. Only about half of those sets, moreover, were suitable for reception of continental broadcasts.[34] The writer Francis Stuart, who broadcast on the service, on his return to Ireland 'hardly ever met anyone who heard me. I

29 P. Knightley, *The first casualty: the war correspondent as hero, propagandist and myth maker from Crimea to Vietnam* (London, 1975), p. 304.   **30** Ibid., pp 244-5.   **31** D/J, 'Instructions to press censors', 14 July 1944, NA.   **32** See D. O'Donoghue, *Hitler's Irish voices: the story of German radio's wartime Irish service* (Belfast, 1998).   **33** Report on Axis propaganda in Ireland, November 1942, Office of Strategic Services, 30131 (National Archives, Washington).   **34** D. Gageby, 'The media, 1945-70' in J.J. Lee (ed.), *Ireland 1945-70* (Dublin, 1967), pp 124-5; D. O'Donoghue, *Hitler's Irish voices*, Appendix 1, p. 184.

don't think anyone really listened'.[35] Some did, of course, primarily a small number of ultra-nationalists with fascist tendencies. Earlier in the war, when the Germans were in the ascendant, there was a more general audience willing to listen to promises of Irish unity and war reports from a winning side that were more likely to be accurate. Lord Haw Haw's jibes against the British were popular, but their impact beyond facilitating indulgence in armchair 'Brit-bashing' is questionable. The BBC, which also relayed American broadcasts, supplemented the neutral news of Radio Éireann for most listeners, pro-Allied or not, especially as the war progressed with the Allies in the ascendant, reflecting the cultural closeness with Britain and the desire to hear the latest from the (winning) horse's mouth.

Relatively widespread reception of the BBC, combined with the availability of English newspapers and the reliance on British news sources, provided a solid foundation for British propaganda efforts in Ireland. Despite the close ties between the two countries, however, the British chose to tread cautiously when it came to propaganda in Ireland. John Maffey, the UK representative in Éire, believed that anti-British feeling was the dynamic of Irish public opinion and early reports to the British Ministry of Information (MOI) from the likes of Elizabeth Bowen and Frank Pakenham indicated that British propaganda was likely to do more harm than good.[36] The British set out to put their case as strongly as possible within the limitations set by censorship, while attempting to avoid upsetting Irish sensibilities, particularly in relation to neutrality. The position of press attaché was the official one for British propagandists in neutral countries and from January 1941 until June 1943 the role was filled in Dublin by John Betjeman, the future poet laureate. The MOI believed that Betjeman was 'the sort of chap who could get on with the Irish' and using his legendary charm and humour he ingratiated himself in influential cultural, political and journalistic circles.[37] He began using Gaelic script in letters and used Irish phrases such as 'a chara' and 'is mise le meas'; he even began to sign his letters 'Sean Ó Betjeman, attasé na press'![38] Betjeman, who did not regard himself as a propagandist but more a public relations man, distributed MOI propaganda, Catholic papers such as the *Tablet* and the *Universe* and extracts from Radio Vatican and the European neutral press, which highlighted the anti-Christian nature of the Nazis. He also organised visits by literary, intellectual and other cultural figures and generally sought to promote a positive view of Britain and its war effort,

35 Fisk, *In time of war*, p. 407.   **36** Maffey memo on a conversation with de Valera, 24 December 1940, cited in T.R. Dwyer, *Strained relations: Ireland at peace and the USA at war, 1941-45* (Dublin, 1988), p. 56; R. Cole, "Good relations": Irish neutrality and the propaganda of John Betjeman, 1941-43', *Éire-Ireland*, 30, 4, Winter 1996, pp 34-5.   **37** Cole, 'Good relations', p. 37, quoting Harry Hodson, head of the Ministry of Information's Empire Division. **38** Betjeman to Department of External Affairs, August 1941, D/FA (Sec.), A 11, NA.

countering the anti-British reflex at a popular level and undermining sympathy for the Axis powers. Despite his efforts, however, secret British reports on public opinion in Ireland continued to note political hostility to Britain and a 'pose of isolationist virtue' which viewed Nazism and Anglo-American power as 'equally wicked'.[39]

English newspapers circulated relatively freely, though restrictions were placed on propagandist posters accompanying popular titles, while there were fifteen bannings and five seizures of cross-channel newspapers during the war. These actions, however, were all provoked by stories that cast doubt or aspersions on Ireland's neutrality. Other factors, principally transport difficulties and newsprint shortage, ensured a severe drop in circulation; in mid-1941 Betjeman estimated that as few as 20,000 copies of English daily and Sunday papers combined were available in the state.[40]

From October 1942 until April 1945 the US legation produced and distributed, without interference, *Letter from America* – a weekly newsletter that set out, in the words of the American representative David Gray, 'to tell the Irish people what their Censorship did not want them to know.'[41] This included articles on Nazi and Japanese atrocities, pro-war speeches from prominent Irish-Americans and accounts of the heroism of Irish people and Irish-Americans in the Allied forces. Its editor delighted in 'the pleasure of editing the only paper in Éire which can run cartoons poking fun at Hitler's whisker'![42] The *Letter* was not sold openly but mailed to a list that grew from 18,000 to 30,000 by the war's end.

The reports about Irish volunteers in the war in *Letter from America* were the only such published references allowed by the censorship. Irish newspapers were strictly controlled in this regard. There was a ban on all references to Irish people in the Allied, primarily British, forces, including, bizarrely, those from Northern Ireland. References in direct war reports, social columns and, most controversially, in death and obituary notices were prohibited. The censors claimed that:

> If matter of this kind was not strictly controlled there is a danger amounting to a moral certainty that some of our papers would be plastered day in day out with pictures and announcements about the British forces. This would have two results: it might mislead opinion abroad about the real position and feeling of this country and it would certainly provoke a counter blast at home which, in addition to making it difficult to maintain both the reality and appearance of neutrality, would be likely to give rise to internal disorder.[43]

39 Cole, 'Good relations', p. 42.   **40** Ibid., p. 41.   **41** Dwyer, *Strained relations*, p. 57.   **42** J. Carroll, 'US-Irish relations, 1939-45', *Irish Sword*, 19, 75 and 76, 1993-4, p. 103.   **43** OCC 'Note for Minister' on parliamentary censorship debate, March 1941, D/T, S 12381, NA.

Reference to the Irish connections of senior British army figures like Montgomery and Alexander was forbidden while attempts to 'play up' the Irishness of prominent individuals like Brendan Bracken, British Minister of Information, and William Joyce, Lord Haw Haw, were stopped. R.M. Smyllie, editor of the staunchly pro-British *Irish Times*, provocatively used a variety of ruses to get around the bans. In February 1941, for example, he listed the names of seven Irish generals and admirals in the British forces who had been mentioned in a broadcast by Churchill and identified them as Japanese! His favourite ploy was to use 'lead poisoning' when referring to bullet and shrapnel wounds while his report on the survival of former *Irish Times* staff member Johnny Robinson after the sinking of the 'Prince of Wales', when he described him as having survived a 'Boating Accident', became legendary and caused much embarrassment for the censors. Such resistance led to the *Times* being forced to submit each issue in full for censorship before publication from December 1942 until the war's end, a severe burden for the paper. The editor of the *Drogheda Independent* summed up the frustration with the ban on references to the Irish in the war when he complained that:

> So many people in my circulation area are either dying for foreign powers or marrying other people who are preparing to die for foreign powers or are having christened the children of people who are feared to have been lost in the service of foreign powers, I have to be continually on the look-out ...[44]

One of the most powerful media of propaganda and, for the Irish authorities one of the most dangerous because of its mass accessibility, popularity and inherent persuasiveness, was film. Features, documentaries and especially newsreels were utilised for propaganda purposes and the powers of the Irish film censor were extended to enable him to neutralise war films before they reached Irish screens. 'Mr de Valera' according to a report in the *Daily Mail* of 15 January 1942, 'insists that Irishmen shall be neutral in thought, word and deed – and also neutral at the pictures.' Such cinema neutrality was regarded as all the more important because of the collective dimension involved and the danger of disorder and disruption at screenings which favoured one side or the other. Thus, while war news was stripped of its propagandist colour in the press, film censorship sought to eliminate war coverage totally. Aiken pointed out that war reports in the press were 'in cold print, and if a man gets a newspaper in the morning he will not start either cheering or booing the paper.' In a cinema, however, 'somebody may start to "booh" and somebody may start to cheer and we do not want that sort of competition to start'.[45] Disruption of screenings by militant Republicans was common in the 1930s and this fact certainly influenced policy in this area.

---

44 Editor to Chief Press Censor, 7 June 1943, D/J, No. 24, NA. **45** *Seanad debates*, vol. 25, col. 369, 30 January 1941.

Ireland was part of the UK distribution market and Hollywood and British films dominated its screens. Well-known Hollywood features such as *Casablanca*, *Mrs Miniver* and *A Yank in the RAF* were all banned until after the war. Also prohibited was Charlie Chaplin's *The Great Dictator*, which satirised Hitler and Mussolini. Film censor Richard Hayes regarded it as 'vulgar propaganda from beginning to end … If that film had been shown in this country it would have meant riots and bloodshed'.[46] British films banned included *Desert Victory*, *In Which We Serve* and *Target for Tonight*. Newsreels were a vital source of war coverage and fulfilled a function analogous to television news in later years. They also 'bore the brunt of the propaganda war'[47] and for this reason were targeted by the Irish wartime censors. The strict demands of Irish censorship forced British newsreel companies to produce special neutralised editions for the Irish market. These presented to the Irish public a radically different world to that shown to their British counterparts, a world into which the reality of war did not impinge. At the height of the battle for France on 23 May 1940, for example, Gaumont's British edition was dominated by words and images of the war while its Irish edition featured such delights as the Kentucky Derby, a boat race in Australia, and the Pope receiving Italian royalty.[48] Despite prior neutralisation these newsreels still ran into trouble with the Irish censorship. In February 1942, for example, cuts included scenes of children feeding elephants in London Zoo and elderly women playing bowls – both groups carried gas masks, thus potentially evoking unneutral sympathy![49] These special newsreels were discontinued in May 1943 due to a raw film stock shortage in Britain. Subsequently, glimpses of the war flickered briefly on Irish screens, though these mainly featured innocuous shots of war planes, usually American and rarely British. In general, the war was kept from Irish screens and images of the war were not allowed to resonate with the Irish public – in the words of poet Seamus Heaney, 'The newsreel bomb-hits' remained 'as harmless as dust-puffs.'[50]

Theatrical presentations were not subject to official control but were kept neutral by unofficial and indirect methods, usually consisting of threats to withdraw licences or introduce legislation if producers did not co-operate. Theatres and music halls were warned that they would be closed down if they allowed entertainers, such as visiting British comedians, caricature statespeople and insult 'friendly foreign powers'. In November 1940 Lennox Robinson's *Roly Poly*, set in the Franco-Prussian war, was forced to close at the Gate following complaints from the German representative.[51] In April 1943 a play staged in Dublin's

46 *The Bell*, 3, 2, November 1941, p. 109.   47 N. Pronay, 'The news media at war', in N. Pronay and D.W. Spring (eds), *Propaganda, politics and film, 1918–1945* (London, 1982), p. 202. 48 Ibid., p. 207.   49 *Daily Telegraph* clipping, February 1942, D/J, 'Instructions to Press Censorship Staff', NA.   50 'Settings', quoted in D. Keogh, *Twentieth-century Ireland: nation and state* (Dublin, 1994), p. 108.   51 Coyne memo on censorship, September 1945, D/T S

Peacock Theatre entitled *The Refugee* had its contents radically altered to remove references to concentration camps while the eponymous hero was transformed from an Austrian Jew into a refugee from Hungary (religion unspecified).[52]

The open sale and exhibition of propagandist books was restricted, although propagandist works were supplied (appropriately, in the context of Irish neutrality, under the counter) to those who sought them out. The neutralisation drive extended to effigies, emblems and badges; even children's games were not immune. In November 1940 Woolworth's were forced to withdraw from sale a game called 'Plonk', the object of which was to get a dart into the mouth of Hitler, 'a Head of State with which we are in friendly relations'.[53] Jigsaw puzzles representing war scenes were seized and a board and dice game 'Target for Tonight' which featured an air raid on an 'enemy city' (Berlin) was withdrawn after censorship objections. In November 1942 a Garda at a funfair in Mitchelstown attempted to seize a gramophone record which featured the song 'Run, Adolf, Run' (to the tune of 'Run, Rabbit, Run'). The owner smashed it to pieces and it was decided that if the record were found to be on sale its importation would be prohibited.[54] Even unneutral statements and sentiments in private correspondence were removed as part of the postal and telegraph censorship, the main function of which was as a security mechanism.[55] The principal victims were the so-called 'West British', though others whose opinions were as unwelcome in private as in public included 'the violently pro-German' and those who 'let off steam on behalf of Stalin and the USSR.'.[56]

The Emergency censorship blanket was lifted on 11 May 1945, following the cessation of the war in Europe. (Three days earlier, on VE Day, Smyllie performed his final gesture of defiance when he rearranged the photographs of seven Allied leaders which had been passed for publication into a giant 'V' on the front page.) The ending of wartime censorship was greeted with relief by the press, the cinema trade and the public who packed the cinemas in the following months to see the many war films which had been banned. 'After so many years of lukewarm commentary and neutralised drama', wrote the *Irish Times* film correspondent, 'it is a great relief to see films that are publicly and shamelessly belligerent'.[57] That paper celebrated its new freedom with a series of photographs over the next two weeks under the heading: 'They can be published now: pictures that were stopped by the censor during the war'. Some of the excesses of

11445/8; D/J, No. 3, 'Sean Piondar', NA.   **52** Correspondence regarding *The Refugee*, D/FA, 216/303, April 1943, NA.   **53** OCC correspondence with the DEA, November 1940, OCC 2/55, MA.   **54** Directions authorising seizure of certain documents, 1 October 1942, OCC 5/41; Coyne to President of Drapers' Chamber of Trade, 9 December, 1943 OCC 5/37; OCC memo, 18 November 1943, OCC 7/24, MA.   **55** See Ó Drisceoil, *Censorship in Ireland*, pp 59-95.   **56** 'Organisation and administration – attitude of the public to postal censorship', D/J, Postal Censorship (NA); Gaughan, *Joseph Connolly*, p. 401.   **57** *Irish Times*, 21 May 1945.

the previous five-and-a-half years were now coming to light, but, for the most part, the true extent of censorship remained hidden and even that which was revealed provoked little discussion or debate. Relief that the war and its dangers had passed and the shortages and other impositions were at least at the beginning of an end, together with a sense of pride in the successful prosecution of neutrality, enhanced by de Valera's famous broadcast reply to Churchill's attack on the policy at the war's end, all contributed to a feeling that the ends justified the means. While there was horror, shock and anger at the revelations of the Holocaust, there was also disbelief and distrust, accusations that it was all British propaganda and a common feeling, expressed by one letter writer who asked: 'Why drag up all these unpleasant things ... life is sad enough without this beastliness'.[58]

Towards the end of the war, in the context of the horrifying reports from the liberated concentration camps, the censors claimed that the Irish people had been kept 'fully informed' of atrocities and other aspects of the war by means of belligerent broadcasts, the English press and the *Letter from America*. This is highly questionable. In general, as we have seen, belligerent propaganda was available to those who wished to seek it out, and propaganda that is sought out usually 'preaches' to the already 'converted' or those who wish to be converted. English newspapers, the American and Axis bulletins and belligerent broadcasts all reached a limited audience. They failed to shake the edifice of determined disengagement at a popular level or fill the information vacuum created by the censorship. Public opinion reports from Ireland by the British, Americans and Germans throughout the war support the conclusion that neutralisation was effective. Neutrality was supported by a large majority of the population, as was evident most clearly in the two wartime elections which were won by Fianna Fáil and the fact that the opposition parties all publicly supported that policy. James Dillon, deputy leader of Fine Gael, had to resign in 1942 following a speech advocating the abandonment of neutrality. Opposition did exist but it was small, divided and inconsistent, while the censorship was obviously a major hindrance to its development, both in terms of excluding information which would help to create, for example, anti-Nazi sentiment, and in blocking the efforts of partisans to promote one side or the other or build arguments in favour of abandoning neutrality. It is impossible to establish what difference a less rigid censorship would have made to the consensus about neutrality, especially in the second half of the war when the direct threat to Ireland had faded, the Americans were involved (important because of the close ties with the US and the fact that supporting the Allies would no longer be synonymous with supporting the British), and the Allies were headed for victory. The strength of localism in Irish political culture; the recent history of cultural protectionism and introspection; the con-

58 Quoted by Hubert Butler, *Irish Times*, 14 December 1978.

tinuing dominance of the British dimension in thinking about world affairs; the moral superiority which cast Ireland as not only outside of but above what was seen as 'a conflict of materialism, a struggle between two opposing but equally unspiritual sides';[59] the symbolic importance of sovereignty as expressed through neutrality – all of these factors and more must be considered. There may have been none so blind as those who would not see, but the government still felt the need to distort the image of the war to guarantee the desired response.

With regard to the role of the censorship in the actual survival of neutrality, it is probably true to say that had the invasion of Ireland become a strategic necessity or desirable option for any of the belligerents, they would not have needed the excuse of anti-neutral statements in the Irish press to justify such an action. Furthermore, the heroically neutral, unpolluted hearts and minds of a unified, resistant populace would not have counted for much in the absence of the requisite defensive firepower. The Swiss and the Swedes, by contrast, lay the stress on military rather than psychological defence. Ultimately, where the censorship was most effective (besides its security and various other domestic political functions)[60] was in influencing Irish public perceptions of the war in order to mould an illusory self-perception about neutrality: censorship as propaganda.

---

59 Fisk, *In time of war*, p. 549.   **60** See Ó Drisceoil, *Censorship in Ireland*, passim.

Three narratives of neutrality: historians and Ireland's war

Geoffrey Roberts

The conventional narrative of Irish neutrality during the Second World War goes something like this: The Irish Free State's declaration of neutrality in 1939 was undoubtedly the wisest and safest course of action. It protected the Irish people from the perils of war, asserted the country's sovereignty and independence from Britain, and, crucially, maintained the unity of the state at a time of great national danger. Neutrality was supported across the political spectrum and had the backing of the great majority of the population. Any other policy, such as joining the war on the allied side, would have split the country and precipitated another civil war. Ireland remained neutral throughout the war but it was a highly benevolent neutrality as far as the allies were concerned. Not so much neutrality as non-belligerence on the allied side – an ambivalence which reflected, in O'Faolain's famous phrase, the anti-British but pro-allied attitudes of most Irish people.

A frequent sub-text of this narrative is a sort of Irish version of the Churchillian wartime myth. Dev didn't just get away with it, as George Bernard Shaw said at the time,[1] he executed a brilliantly balanced policy which kept Ireland out of the war but on the right side of the conflict, thereby safeguarding the country's postwar future. As T. Ryle Dwyer put it, wartime neutrality 'was truly Eamon de Valera's finest hour.'[2] It is certainly a very compelling story, but is it true?

If the truth of history were a matter of consensus there could be no possible doubt about the answer to that question. The conventional narrative is not only the commonly accepted account of Irish neutrality, it dominates historical writings on the subject and pervades media, political and popular attitudes. It is given an airing – with scarcely a dissident voice – on the occasion of each and every anniversary of the war. Indeed, as the war recedes in time so the lauding of Ireland's role in it increases. The overwhelming impression conveyed by the media is that neutral Ireland didn't just have a good war, it had a great one! In

---

1 *Irish Times*, 31 March 1944. 2 T. Ryle Dwyer, *Irish neutrality and the USA, 1939-47* (Dublin 1977), p. 221.

June 1994 the *Irish Times* posed the question 'Were we right to stay neutral?' to nine respondents, including several prominent historians. Only one of those interviewed (Stanly Siev, vice-president of the Irish Jewish Museum) challenged the policy of wartime neutrality. All the others said it was either right, necessary or unavoidable in the circumstances of the time.[3]

There is much to be said in favour of this happy consensus but it is far from being incontrovertible. For most historians the truth about the past is not a matter of agreement but of reason, argument and evidence. Indeed, if anything historians define their role as one of questioning and challenging the accepted stories including, perhaps most of all, those put forward by their own colleagues. As Liam Kennedy aptly put it, historians have a 'tendency to spoil good stories'.[4] In this particular case, however, the aim is not so much to spoil the story as to suggest that the conventional narrative is far too uncritical of the neutrality policy and does not take sufficient account of the truth contained in alternative versions of Ireland's role in the war. There is more than one narrative of neutrality. Confronting these competing and contradictory versions of the past is a necessary part of the process of arriving at a more truthful account of Ireland's war.

The dominant, conventional narrative of Irish neutrality has a long and somewhat curious pedigree. It appears to have been born in editorial columns of the *Irish Times* in May 1945. With the end of wartime censorship the paper was able to publish a series of editorials putting forward its attitude on neutrality. The basic theme was that while the paper was not neutral in its attitude to the great struggle that had just concluded, it had acquiesced in the state's policy of neutrality, which had been supported by the majority of Irish citizens. There was some criticism of the conduct of neutrality (especially the workings of the censorship regime) but the editorials emphasised the benevolence of Irish policy towards the allied cause and, in particular, the contribution to the British war effort of the tens of thousands of Irish who served in Britain's armed forces or worked in its war factories.[5] This stance was elaborated by the paper's editor,

---

3 'Were we right to stay neutral?', *Irish Times*, 3/6/94. Following the publication of that article the present author wrote a letter to the paper criticising the pro-neutrality stance of the various contributors. There followed an extensive correspondence on the letters page concerning the merits and demerits of neutrality. 4 L. Kennedy, *Colonialism, religion and nationalism in Ireland* (Belfast 1996) p. 209. 5 'Out of the shadows', 12 May 1945; 'Aftermath', 15 May 1945; 'Turning away wrath', 18 May 1945. The 2nd and 3rd editorials were responses to the famous Churchill–De Valera exchange of May 1945. The first editorial may have inspired F.S.L. Lyons' famous metaphor concerning the psychological isolation of wartime Ireland. He writes: 'It was as if an entire people had been condemned to live in Plato's cave, with their backs to the fire of life and deriving their only knowledge of what went on outside from the flickering shadows thrown on the wall ... When after six years they emerged, dazzled, from the cave into the light of day, it was to a new and vastly different world.' (*Ireland since the Famine*, London 1973 pp 557-8). In 'Out of the shadows' the *Irish Times* editorialised: 'We feel as anybody must

R.M. Smyllie, in article on 'Unneutral neutral Éire' published in the influential American journal *Foreign Affairs* in January 1946. Writing for a sceptical Anglo-American audience, Smyllie defined Irish neutrality in the following terms: 'Éire was nonbelligerent – that is to say, she was not officially concerned in the war, although so many of her children served the allied cause; but she was never neutral in the generally accepted sense of the term.' Smyllie also introduced the argument that perhaps Irish neutrality suited the allies as well: 'It may be argued that Éire was of greater assistance to the Allies as an official neutral than she could have been as an active belligerent. For if Éire had been in the war, the Germans almost certainly would have tried to invade the island; indeed, in 1940 and thereabouts there was little to prevent them. If they had succeeded not only would Britain have had an enemy on her western flank, but the Americans never would have been able to send their vast forces to Europe.'[6]

The next major elaboration of what was to become the conventional account of Irish neutrality was that by T. Desmond Williams. In January 1953 Williams published an article entitled 'A Study in Neutrality' in *The Leader* magazine. Williams argued that 'foreign policy, like every other policy, is dictated not merely by the objectives of the state ... but also by the real possibilities of the situation'. Among the 'real possibilities' are the circumstances in which a particular policy is implemented. In this regard Williams highlighted the conjunction of favourable circumstances which made the maintenance of Irish neutrality possible at all. Such circumstances included the handing over by Britain of the treaty ports in 1938, the fact that control of Irish territory never became absolutely vital to any of the belligerents, the re-focusing of the war eastwards following the German attack on Russia in June 1941, and the importance in the Battle of the Atlantic of continuing British control of Northern Ireland which obviated the need to transgress Southern Irish neutrality. Like Smyllie, Williams emphasised as well the importance of 'unofficial' and informal Irish co-operation with the allies. Williams also introduced the theme of de Valera's great political and diplomatic skill in handling the competing pressures on neutral Ireland, a task which was aided by the presence of some sympathetic diplomats in Dublin, including both the British and German representatives.[7]

In the writings of Smyllie and Williams are outlined all the basic arguments of what might be called the 'pragmatic pro-neutrality' narrative of the Irish stance during World War II: a story of neutrality as a necessary policy which benefited Ireland and the allies alike.

---

feel who, having been confined in a dark cell for nearly six years, is released suddenly into the sunshine and blinded by the light.' **6** R.M. Smyllie, 'Unneutral neutral Éire', *Foreign affairs*, 2, 24 (1946). **7** 'A study in neutrality', *The Leader*, 53, 2, 31 May 1953. See also T. Desmond Williams, 'Ireland and the war' in K.B. Nowlan and T. Desmond Williams (eds), *Ireland in the war years and after, 1939-1951* (Dublin, 1969).

Smyllie and Williams, by and large, only had access to the public record of Irish neutrality. Subsequent generations of historians, particularly from the 1970s onwards, were able to utilise materials from Irish, British, American and German archives. As far as the developing narrative of Irish neutrality is concerned the main theme of this more recent historiography has been the detailing of Irish-allied co-operation during the war. Dermot Keogh provides the following summary of 'the extent to which Irish neutrality was prepared to be friendly towards the Allies':

> regular liaison between allied and Irish military authorities and the preparation of joint plans to defend the Irish state; intimate co-operation between G2 and Allied intelligence services; exchange of meteorological reports and the forwarding of all information to Britain concerning the movement of Axis planes, ships and submarines in the Irish sea; and permission given to Allied aircraft to overfly a corridor of Irish territory in northern Donegal for easier access to the Atlantic.[8]

Keogh is also one of the foremost contemporary advocates of the view that Ireland was neutral on the side of the allies. For example, in his *Ireland and Europe, 1919-1989* (a book dedicated to the memory of T. Desmond Williams) he argues:

> Ideologically, Ireland did not at any time tend towards emulating the authoritarian political systems of Catholic states in Europe. The struggle to preserve an independent foreign policy in the early years of the war emphasised the fact that the Irish state was led by politicians who shared a belief in the need to preserve Western democratic values. In the Second World War, Ireland took the side of the states that professed those political values ... Neutral status was not incompatible during the Second World War with active support for the Western democratic system. De Valera's 'constructive ambiguity' demonstrated how it was possible to reconcile national and global interests.[9]

The problem with this argument is that it is not at all clear that during the war Ireland took the pro-democracy side at all, let alone actively. It is, of course, pos-

8 D. Keogh, *Twentieth-century Ireland: nation and state* (Dublin, 1994), p. 120. See also: R. Fisk, *In time of war: Ireland, Ulster and the price of neutrality, 1939-1945* (Dublin, 1983), pp 327-32; R. Fanning, *Independent Ireland* (Dublin, 1983), pp 123-5; T. Ryle Dwyer, *Guests of the state: the story of Allied and Axis servicemen interned in Ireland during World War II* (Dingle, 1994); and various contributors to the the *Irish Sword*, 19, 75 and 76, 1993-4 (issue on 'The Emergency' 1939-45).   **9** D. Keogh, *Ireland and Europe, 1919-1989: a diplomatic and political history* (Dublin, 1989), pp 162-3.

sible to construe Ireland's pro-allied neutrality, such as it was, as having that meaning. But such benevolence can just as easily be interpreted as a pragmatic response to Ireland's position within the allied sphere of influence. Moreover, as Tim Pat Coogan notes, Irish-allied 'co-operative "measures developed over the years. During the war's early phase, when it looked as if Germany might win, Irish co-operation with Britain was curtailed.'[10]

In truth, de Valera's 'constructive ambiguity' was not only a matter of policy but of principle and of values as well. No doubt he, like most Irish leaders and officials, wanted to see a democratic victory in the war. But it is not so apparent that they all viewed the allied side in such an unambiguously clear way. This much seems evident from a reading de Valera's wartime speeches, including those collected in *Ireland's Stand*, published in 1946.[11] In this book there emerges an alternative narrative of Irish wartime neutrality to that being proposed by Smyllie and the *Irish Times* around the same time: a narrative of what could be called 'the neutrality of moral indifference'.

What was 'Ireland's Stand', as defined publicly by de Valera? It was certainly a stand of 'friendly neutrality' towards Britain and the United States, at least to the extent that de Valera would not allow Ireland to be used by the enemies of the allies. Neither was their any doubt that Ireland would defend itself to the hilt against any and all invaders (at least in principle; the practicalities of this were another matter at a time of a relatively declining defence budget).[12] Ireland also stood for the rights of small nations, not least its own right to sovereignty and national and territorial unity. As to the opponents of neutrality at home:

> Whoever would bring in a foreign power in here in defiance of the wishes of the vast majority of our people will have their name execrated by the Irish people ... To let in the stranger is easy; to get him out again may mean centuries of blood and sacrifice. The Irish people want neither an old master nor a new one.[13]

---

10 T.P. Coogan, *De Valera: long fellow, long shadow* (London, 1993) p. 568. Fisk (op. cit., p. 327) dates the transition in Irish policy from 'friendly neutrality' to 'benevolent neutrality' to 1942, i.e. after the US entry into the war, when it became obvious that the allied side was going to win. **11** *Ireland's stand: being a selection of the speeches of Eamon de Valera during the war (1939-1945)* (Dublin, 1946). Additional wartime speeches by de Valera may be found in M. Moynihan (ed.), *Speeches and statements by Eamon de Valera, 1917-73* (Dublin, 1980). **12** See J.J. Lee, *Ireland 1912-1985: politics and society* (Cambridge 1989), pp 234-6. One should also point out that, at least in the early war years, the Irish defence posture was directed against Britain as well as Germany, including plans based on support from the latter in the event of a British invasion from Northern Ireland. See T. Farrell, ' "When theory ruins practice": military professionalism and suicidal defence planning by the Irish Army during World War II', paper prepared from the British International Studies annual conference, Leeds, December 1997. **13** Speech at Review of Defence Forces, Mullingar, 5 October 1941. *Ireland's stand*, p. 51.

Completely absent from de Valera's speeches is any sense of the great moral and political issues of the Second World War. The war was neither just nor unjust, simply bad, and potentially very dangerous for small nations like Ireland. But, to be fair, de Valera was speaking on behalf of the state, in the context of an inflexible and rigidly defined policy of neutrality. In a statement to the Dáil in June 1944 he drew an interesting distinction between the policy of the state and the attitudes of individuals:

> As far as the individual citizen is concerned, there is no question of indifference implied in the neutrality of this State. The neutrality of the State was adopted in the interests of the community as a whole as a definite national policy under the present circumstances. As I say, it connotes nothing as to the feelings of individual citizens with regard to the States at war ... I have my own view on that matter, but it is not for me to give expression to those views, because my official duty is to say and to maintain that as a State we have adopted and are pursuing a policy of neutrality.[14]

But even when the war was over de Valera persisted with the expression of neutral attitudes. In his famous radio broadcast of 16 May 1945 – the one in which he locked horns with Churchill – the war that had just ended in Europe was defined as a tragedy and as an ordeal which neutral Ireland had survived. There was no welcome for the allied victory nor even any recognition of the nature of the allied cause, save for some recognition of British forbearance in not invading Ireland during the war. What mattered to de Valera was that Churchill and the world should recognise 'that there is a small nation that stood alone, not for one year or two, but for several hundred years against aggression; that endured spoilations, famines, massacres in endless succession; that was clubbed many times into insensibility, but that each time, on returning consciousness, took up the fight anew; a small nation that could never be got to accept defeat and has never surrendered her soul'.[15] Such rhetoric was worthy of Churchill himself.

De Valera's radio broadcast came hot on the heels of his infamous visit to the German ambassador in Dublin to present his condolences on the death of Hitler.[16] One can discuss the specific reasons and circumstances of this political gaffe, but perhaps more important was its symbolic meaning. As Robert Fisk comments: 'Morally, it was both senseless and deeply wounding to the millions who had suffered in the war; politically, it could have been disastrous. But symbolically, it could not be misunderstood: Éire had not accepted the values of the warring nations and did not intend to do so in the future.'[17] At the time the

---

14 *Dáil Eireann: official report*, 94, p. 1355.   15 Moynihan op. cit., p. 476.   16 See D. Keogh, 'Eamon de Valera and Hitler: an analysis of international reaction to the visit to the German minister, May 1945', *Irish studies in international affairs*, 3, 1, 1989.   17 Fisk op. cit., p. 537.

Washington Post speculated on the importance to the incident of the 'moral myopia' which Ireland and other neutral states had imposed upon themselves during the war as an aspect of the rationalisation of their neutrality.[18] Such had been the basic stance of the Irish censorship regime which forbade the publication of pro-Allied and pro-Nazi propaganda in equal measure.[19] It would a gross exaggeration to say that in relation to the war Ireland's domestic regime was one of moral indifference, but there was more than a modicum of moral distancing from the great global struggle. And it was not only de Valera, Frank Aitken and his censorship bureau, Fianna Fáil, and extremist republicans who thought England's danger was Ireland's opportunity. Scepticism and cynicism about the moral and political righteousness of the allied crusade was much more widespread.[20] Even the leaders of Fine Gael felt moved to defend neutrality on the grounds that the choice of which side to support was not at all clearcut. General Mulcahy found 'it hard to say that the United States, France and Great Britain can completely wash their hands of responsibility for the situation in Europe today.' According to W.T. Cosgrave:

> If we in this country take the line that the difference between the belligerents is democracy on the one hand and autocracy on the other, the sinlessness of one and the guilt of the other, then I want to say that neither appeals to me. Democracy may have as many sins to its credit and may be as faulty a form of government as an autocracy.[21]

This moral distancing from and questioning of the allied cause continued to reverberate throughout the postwar period. Although usually confined to the letter columns of newspapers, it sometime found reflection in the historiography. For example, Joseph Carroll in his widely-read 1975 text *Ireland in the war years* makes the following (retrospective) reply to contemporary (that is, wartime) critics of Irish neutrality:

> The fate of Poland, the *casus belli*, and other eastern European countries in the post-war settlement made a mockery of the attempt to indict the neutrals on moral grounds for not joining the war on the side of the alliance which included the totalitarian state which had ruthlessly absorbed the Baltic states, half of Poland and had started the war as a tacit ally of Hitler. Fervent Catholic though he was, de Valera had never any time for the

---

18 Cited by Keogh (article), op. cit., p. 81.   **19** On the censorship policy: D. Ó Drisceoil, *Censorship in Ireland, 1939-1945: neutrality, politics and society* (Cork, 1996).   **20** In this connection see Fisk, op. cit., pp 548-51.   **21** *Dáil Eireann: Official Report*, 84, p. 1874, 1881. Mulcahy and Cosgrave's comments were in response to James Dillon's speech to the Dáil in July 1941 urging, on moral grounds, that Ireland join the allied side of the war (on which more below).

'Christian crusade' argument in favour of abandoning neutrality, and the entry of the USSR into the war show the absurdity of such an argument.

Carroll comments further that 'no country jumped into World War II out of high moral motives'.[22]

Carroll's argument overlaps with those of ultra-revisionist British historians who have questioned even British participation in a war against Hitler on the grounds that it had many undesirable outcomes, such as the undermining of British imperial power and the establishment of Soviet domination of Eastern Europe. So: better Hitler than Stalin? No, but why not attempt peaceful coexistence with Germany and strive for an internal reform of the Nazi regime (as happened in Gorbachev's Russia in the late 1980s)?[23]

The defenders of Irish neutrality, like the post-hoc advocates of British neutralism, are entitled to their moral and political judgements, but to question the validity of the allied cause on the grounds that in practice the results of the war did not live up to the high ideals of the allied crusade[24] is to evade the central issue of the desirability (or not) of the destruction of Nazism. For Ireland the allied defeat of the Axis powers was a victory, albeit a tarnished one, for the democratic values it as state stood for and a guarantee of its continuing independence and sovereignty. The allies in winning the war protected the freedom independent Ireland had won 20 years before. During the war many thousands of Irish people took this kind of view of the allied cause and enlisted in the British armed forces.[25] Of course, by no means all enlisted for explicitly political reasons but it would be patronising to suppose that most did not know and approve of the cause they were

---

22 J.T. Carroll, *Ireland in the war years* (New York, 1975), pp 168-9. Carroll's point about jumping into the war for high moral motives is doubtful. A number of Commonwealth countries did declare war on Germany voluntarily – for reasons of morality as well as obligation and self-interest. See R. Ovendale, 'Why the British Dominions declared war' in R. Boyce and E.M. Robertson (eds), *Paths to war: new essays on the origins of the Second World War* (London, 1989). **23** See for example J. Charmley, *Churchill: the end of glory* (London, 1993). **24** In relation to the oft-repeated point about Soviet subjugation of Eastern Europe I and others have argued that this was not a result of the war but a function of the outbreak of the cold war. Before about 1947 the Soviets pursued a relatively benign policy in Eastern Europe. Their postwar aims in the region did not exactly measure up to western democratic standards but were far from the brutal authoritarianism that they were to impose in the late 1940s. See G. Roberts, *The Soviet Union in world politics: coexistence, revolution and cold war, 1945-1991* (London, 1998), chapter 2. **25** See A.J. McElwaine, 'The forgotten volunteers: Irish service in the British armed forces during World War II', M.Phil. thesis, University College Cork, 1998; and R. Doherty, *Irish men and women in the Second World War* (Dublin, 1999). Also: M. Dungan, *Distant drums: Irish soldiers in foreign armies* (Dublin, 1993) chapter 3; R. Doherty, *Irish generals* (Dublin, 1993); R. Doherty, *Clear the way! A history of the 38th (Irish) brigade, 1941-47* (Dublin 1995); B. Girvin and G. Roberts, 'The forgotten volunteers of World War II', *History Ireland* (Spring 1998); and T. Neylon, 'Brave hearts, long memories of warriors in exile', *The Examiner*, 12 March 1998.

fighting for. In any event, their contribution to the allied cause, together with that of tens of thousands of Irish war workers in Britain, far outweighed the secret and unofficial contributions of the Irish state. But Dublin did at least turn a blind eye to the Irish military volunteers leaving the country and actively facilitated the mass migration of Irish labour to Britain during the war years.

In his broadcast on 13 May 1945 Churchill had lauded 'the temper and instinct of thousands of Southern Irishmen who hastened to the battle-front to prove their ancient valour'. He spoke also of 'Lieutenant-Commander Esmonde, VC, of Lance-Corporal Kenneally, VC. and Captain Fegen, VC and other Irish heroes that I could easily recite' and confessed that when he thought of them 'bitterness by Britain against the Irish race dies in my heart.'[26] But de Valera chose not to comment on this part of Churchill's speech. Yet it was an obvious retort to complaints about Irish neutrality to point up the role of the Irish vol- unteers – as Smyllie and the *Irish Times* were eagerly doing. But De Valera remained silent, as did successive Irish leaders, until 1995 when at the Island- bridge national war memorial Taoiseach John Bruton paid tribute to Irish people who had 'volunteered to fight against Nazi tyranny in Europe'.[27]

The length of this long official silence is difficult to explain. It inception in 1945 was almost certainly connected to deeply hostile attitudes to the volunteers at the end of the war. These surfaced in a debate in the Dáil in October 1945 on Order 362, a decree under the Emergency Powers Act which sentenced more than 4000 Irish soldiers who had deserted to join the British army during the war to seven years 'civil disability' should they return to Ireland i.e. the withdrawal of all rights to welfare support for themselves and their families. Dr O'Higgins of Fine Gael objected that these men were being singled out for special treatment [other categories of deserters were being treated differently] 'for the crime of going to assist other nations'. In response Deputy Walsh of Fianna Fáil argued: 'Desertion from an army is desertion ... and doubly dangerous to the army from which desertion takes place if the deserter joins another army which might conceivably be fighting the army from which he deserted ... We hear this song and dance about Belsen camps and so forth and about the glorious place the Irishmen who were in the British army won for themselves ... Freeing deserters to a possible enemy ... is simply putting a premium on desertion and a premium on treason.' Deputy Colley (FF): 'people who think that the policy of neutrality adopted by the huge majority of our people was not sufficient for them ... it is necessary to show them that their duty was first to their own country.' And Deputy MacCarthaigh (FF): 'not only did they desert their own army but they broke the declared policy of this country by fighting with another army while they were bound, as citizens of this State, to a neutral policy.'[28]

---

26 W.S. Churchill, *War speeches, 1940-1945* (London, 1946), p. 250.   **27** *Irish Times*, 29 April 1995.   **28** Citations from M. Connolly, 'The untouchables: order 362, 1945', BA history dis-

Ireland and Irish neutrality first and last was, it seems, a prevalent attitude in 1945. Even before the Dáil debate *The Leader* was editorialising against the 'roll of honour' of Irish allied service personnel being published in some newspapers. Such rolls, it argued, should consist only of those who had died fighting for Ireland.[29] As to the volunteers:

> Every citizen of this neutral state who joined a foreign army did an actual or potential wrong to his own country. The only place of honour and duty for an Irish soldier during the war was in the Irish army.[30]

Such attitudes to the volunteers were in line with the moral ambiguity of the state in relation to the allied cause. Such moral ambiguity did not long outlast the war. By 1948 de Valera was hinting that except for partition Ireland might have participated in the war on the allied side.[31] 'In spite of its – politically unavoidable – neutrality during the war, this State had no ambiguity towards the issues involved', an *Irish Times* editorial reassured its readers in June 1994, 'and there can have been few people in positions of power who did not believe that a victory for Nazi Germany would have been an unmitigated disaster.'[32] In relation to the volunteers the position is still not so clear. Where do they stand in the pantheon of Irish heroes?[33] Unlike the Irish volunteers of the First World War they cannot be classified, as they were in the media on 80th anniversary of that war's end, as either heroic victims of British imperialism or as brave fighters in the Redmondite campaign for an independent Ireland. The most obvious categorisation is that of anti-fascist crusaders fighting for Irish interests as well as those of the allies – a characterisation commensurate with the self-image of the volunteers themselves, most of whom supported Irish neutrality and saw themselves as fighting for their country as well as for a cause. But that raises an awkward question: could their neutral country have done more?

sertation, University College Cork, 1999.   **29** The *Leader*, 16 June 1945.   **30** Ibid. 26 June 1945, p. 6. The *Leader* was equally blunt about the policy of neutrality, which 'Ramrod' defined as a policy of 'national self-preservation' and 'national selfishness' (2 August 1945, pp 8–9).   **31** Speech in New York, 3 April 1948 in Moynihan op. cit., pp 497–505. In this speech de Valera returned to one of his favourite wartime themes when addressing American audiences: that the decision of a small nation to involve itself in war was far graver than that of a big one. Not only is the very existence of a small state threatened by participation in war, it has very little power to influence the conduct of the war or shape the peace that follows.   **32** 'Remembering D-Day', *Irish Times*, 6 June 1994. A year later, however, the paper's editorial column struck a different note: 'It is not fashionable now to regard De Valera's decision to stay out of the war as entirely pragmatic, and justifiable solely on those grounds; but as he stated it, it was a contingent policy'. 'Fifty years of peace in Europe', *Irish Times*, 6 May 1995.   **33** This question was prompted by Kevin Myers 'An Irishman's diary; column in *Irish Times*, 26 June 1999. Myers, it should be noted, has waged a long campaign, in the *Irish Times* and elsewhere, for public recognition of the Irish veterans of World War II.

There are certainly those of us who have argued so in retrospect.[34] But, more importantly, there were those in Ireland who thought so at the time. In the arguments of people like James Dillon it is possible to discern the contours of a third narrative of Irish neutrality: the *anti-neutrality* story. To be sure, this is mainly a counter-factual rather than actual narrative, in the sense that it speculates on a course of action that could and should have happened rather than one that did. Nevertheless, such counterfactual reasoning and speculation does play a central role in the formation of historical understanding. The understanding of 'what was' is enhanced by explorations of 'what might have been', of alternative possibilities and choices.[35] In the case of wartime Ireland it can help expose both missed opportunities and the limits of the state's pro-allied neutrality.

James Dillon was the main political opponent of neutrality in Ireland during the war.[36] In 1942 he was forced to resign as Deputy Leader of Fine Gael because of his opposition to neutrality. But when neutrality was declared in September 1939 he had supported it. Responding to de Valera's statement in the Dáil on 2 September 1939 Dillon said:

> Circumstances, I agree, require that this country shall be neutral in this war, if it is humanly possible to keep it neutral. But does that imply or is it to be taken as meaning that the people of this country are indifferent to the issue of the conflict now proceeding? I think it is right to say now that I do not believe they are indifferent. I believe the vast majority of our people place their sympathy on the side of Poland, France and Great Britain against Berlin and Moscow.[37]

It was not until July 1941 that Dillon made a decisive break with the policy of neutrality. In an unexpected intervention in a Dáil debate[38] on the financing of

---

34 See B. Girvin and G. Roberts, 'Dev's phoney war', *Cork Examiner*, 1 June 1995. For another critical view of Irish neutrality see H. Shearman, *Anglo-Irish relations* (London, 1948), chapter XX. **35** In this connection see G. Hawthorn, *Plausible worlds: possibility and understanding in history and the social sciences* (Cambridge, 1991). **36** I should make it clear at the outset that Dillon later changed his mind about Irish neutrality during the Second World War, although why and in what specific way, remains unclear. The source on Dillon's oft-noted change of heart appears to be an interview conducted by Fisk in 1979. **37** *Dáil Eireann: official report*, 77, pp 13-14. Senator Frank MacDermot, another wartime critic of neutrality, took a similar position to that of Dillon. On 4 October 1939 he told the Senate: 'We must not for the sake of neutrality throw morality to the winds, and by degrees debase our own minds and our own outlook. One other thing I have to say about this policy of neutrality, this policy in which we all acquiesce. Some people like it more than others, but in the circumstances it was the only practical policy for this country. I do urge that we ought not to take a tone of moral superiority on the strength of it', *Seanad Eireann: official report*, 23, p. 1163. **38** *Dáil Eireann: official report*, 84, pp 1862-71. The *Irish Times* front page splash on 18 July was headlined: 'MR DILLON CREATES DÁIL SURPRISE; PARTICUPATION IN WAR ADVOCATED, BASE FOR BRITAIN AND U.S.A.'

Foreign Affairs, Dillon criticised the government's 'policy of indifferent neutrality': 'I say that it is not a correct course of conduct. I say it is not in the true interest, moral or material, of the Irish people.'

Dillon urged that the country exercise its sovereign rights and ascertain what 'co-operation Great Britain and the United States of America may require to ensure success against the Nazi attempt at world conquest.' This co-operation should include air and naval bases in Ireland in order to secure the Atlantic lifeline between Britain and the United States. Dillon advocated this course of action because 'on the side of the Anglo-American alliance is right and justice and on the side of the Axis is evil and injustice'. But more than that, Dillon believed that a moment of Providence had arrived for Ireland. The fate of Christianity in the world hung in the balance and Ireland had a glorious opportunity to play a critical role in the defence of Christian values.

> I should like to see this small, weak country of Ireland demonstrate, as it has never been demonstrated in the history of the world before, that it is not by bread alone that man must live and that, whatever may have been the material squabbles that precipitated war in the world, to us the only issue of significance is whether Christianity shall survive ... I am convinced that, were we to accept that charge and face that duty, posterity would have it to tell that in the darkest hour of crisis, when danger seemed heaviest and perils greatest, Ireland, recognising her destiny, faced it without counting the material cost and that, whatever her losses were, the undying glory of having stood as a nation for great principles and in defence of the higher freedom had secured for her and her people immortality in human history.

When Dillon spoke (on 17 July) the Soviet Union had just entered the war following the launch of Operation Barbarossa on 22 June 1941 – an event which Dillon considered a stroke of luck for Christian civilisation, which had been given time and opportunity to further prepare its defences against the Nazi menace. But, perhaps more important, although the United States had yet to enter the war the Anglo-American alliance had already taken definite shape by July 1941. The argument that Ireland had a duty to support the United States in the war was to become a major theme of Dillon's critique of neutrality.

Because of censorship and the stifling of debate on neutrality Dillon found it difficult to make his voice heard, but there were some opportunities. In February 1942 he made a speech to the Fine Gael Árd Fhéis in which he called for an Irish-American alliance. The United States (which had entered the war in December 1941) was under attack and in danger, he told the delegates, and required Ireland's help – support which was necessary to protect Irish independence and sovereignty.[39] This speech cost him not just his place in the party leadership, but his membership of the party as well. Dillon was not deterred. He kept up his sniping in the Dáil on neutrality[40] and in the June 1943 general election stood (successfully) as an independent candidate. In a series of speeches during the campaign he again urged support for the allies, especially the United States. Dillon also raised the issue of partition, arguing that it could only be ended with the goodwill of the Northern Protestants which could in turn be secured with the help and goodwill of the allies.[41]

In November 1943[42], and again in June 1944,[43] Dillon had exchanges in the Dáil with de Valera about neutrality. On the latter occasion Dillon highlighted the pro-allied shifts in policy of neutral states like Portugal, Spain and Sweden and demanded to know why Dublin had earlier that year refused an American demand to remove Axis diplomats from the Irish capital. Once again Dillon reaffirmed his principled position on neutrality:

> I am not and have never been neutral as between the [Allies] and the Axis and it is a constant source of shame to me that our people who have so long been the champions of liberty in the world should now be represented before the world as knowing no difference, being quite unprepared to take sides in a conflict between Germany ... and the Commonwealth of Nations and the United States of America ... I have constantly repudiated the doctrine of neutrality and have constantly kept before our people their obligation in honour at least to make their attitude clearly known between Germany ... and the United States of America and the Commonwealth ...[44]

Dillon's interventions had no impact on the policy of neutrality, but they do provide the gist of an alternative course of action that could have been followed by Ireland.

First there is the question of the moral and political issue of the war. Dillon argued consistently that the country should make clear which side it was on. Taking such a stand was not necessarily incompatible with a formal policy of neutrality – although it would undoubtedly have posed problems for that policy. Moreover, as the war progressed circumstances became more and more propitious for taking such a stand. These circumstances included the re-focusing of the war on the Eastern Front, the entry of the United States into the war and an end to the threat of a German invasion of Ireland or of massive enemy bombing

---

39 *Irish Times*, 11 Februrary 1942.   **40** *Dáil Eireann: official report*, 89, pp 506, 716, 718, 764-86 [February 1943].   **41** Reports of speeches in *Irish Times*, 8, 14, 19 June 1943.   **42** *Dáil Eireann: official report*, 91, pp 2102-30. This exchange is reprinted in *Ireland's stand* op. cit.   **43** Ibid., 94, pp 1132-355.   **44** Ibid., pp 1340-1.

attacks. Of course, taking a stand on the allied side was not the same as fighting on the allied side. Dillon himself never advocated an Irish declaration of war, only that Ireland lend what support it could to the allies and be prepared to suffer the consequences. Such a stand would probably have led to formal participation in the war, but perhaps not until quite late in the day.

This first point has bearing on the second issue. It is frequently argued that the fundamental obstacle to the ending of Irish neutrality was internal political opposition to supporting Britain in the war.[45] Dillon always claimed that there was considerable public sympathy for the allied cause, particularly after the American entry into the war. Other evidence suggests that in summer 1940 the country would have been split two-thirds to one third in favour of participation on Britain's side.[46] Without doubt a break with policy of neutrality would have provoked considerable internal dissension, political conflict and, quite probably, an IRA campaign of violence. But how big a split and how violent its manifestations would have depended on political preparations for ending neutrality and on the timing, form and circumstances of any change in policy. In this respect a range of options were available to de Valera and other political leaders. Dillon's own strategy was to argue the pro-allied case, to make the most of American involvement and to attempt to rally the Irish people to fulfil their historic and god-given destiny. Dillon's religious fervour may not be to everyone's taste but there were plenty of secular versions of a call to destiny – witness Churchill's rallying of the British people during the war. An entirely different script of the domestic politics of neutral Ireland could have been written had de Valera and others had the political will to pursue a pro-allied policy (and not just on the quiet).

A third issue concerns the historic opportunity the war offered to overcome North-South divisions on the island of Ireland. Dillon for one recognised the importance of the inter-allied context in overcoming Protestant opposition to ending partition. In the context of being on the same side, and perhaps engaged in a common war effort, there would, at the very least, have been opportunities to secure some forms of North-South co-operation and unity. As it was, neutral Ireland and Northern Ireland drifted further apart as a result of the war and Unionists were able to use their support for the British war effort as a means to safeguard both partition and Protestant supremacism. It might have been other-

45 Garret Fitzgerald is a particularly vocal advocate of this point of view. See his 'Neutrality came from fear of ourselves, not Germany', *Irish Times*, 6 May 1995. FitzGerald is quite wrong to suggest in that article that on the question of Irish entry into the war James Dillon 'raised his voice only after the United States involuntarily became a belligerent'. See also G. FitzGerald, 'The origins, development and present status of Irish "Neutrality" ', *Irish studies in international affairs*, 9 (1998), pp 11-19. **46** B. Girvin, 'National interest, Irish neutrality and the limits of ideology', unpublished paper, p. 10.

wise. In June 1940 the British offered to work for a united Ireland in exchange for Eire's entry into the war.[47] This was a desparate and somewhat extravagant offer. (Around the same time Churchill was trying to stave off a French surrender by proposing the unification of Britain and France.) But the offer to Dublin was serious and well-intentioned and despite the opposition of Unionists, it did, arguably, present the possibility of the beginning, in the midst of war, of a sort of peace process. Blocking the way was the policy of neutrality and de Valera's unwillingness to contemplate even a partial revision of that policy. Ironically, de Valera's counter-offer – a British withdrawal from the North and a united, neutral Ireland guaranteed by the US – was the one most likely to have turned the country into a battlefield and dragged it into the war. A civil war in the North followed by German intervention and British counter-attack was the most likely scenario to unfold in that eventuality.

No single narrative of Irish wartime neutrality has a monopoly of the truth. The pragmatic pro-neutrality version of events has the merit of emphasising the difficult realities of the time and of detailing the real, if limited, aid Ireland lent to the allied cause. The narrative of moral indifference exposes the limits and parochialism of the State's vision of the great unfolding drama of the Second World War. The anti-neutrality alternative highlights what might have been had different political choices been explored. What is needed is a new narrative of Irish neutrality which better encompasses the complexities, contradictions and ambivalences of Ireland's war.[48]

---

47 On this episode: J. Bowman, *De Valera and the Ulster Question, 1917-1973* (Oxford, 1982), pp 218-39; P. Canning, *British policy towards Ireland 1921-1941*, pp 272-81; G.R. Sloan, *The geopolitics of Anglo-Irish relations in the twentieth century* (Leicester, 1997), pp 203-5; Keogh, *Ireland and Europe*, op. cit., p. 131ff; Lee, op. cit., pp 248-50; and C. Oleary, 'Professor Lee's Ireland', unpublished paper. **48** The book which comes closest to achieving that goal is undoubtedly Fisk's outstanding *In time of war*.

Notes on contributors

BRIAN BARTON is the author of *The blitz: Belfast in the war years* (1989) and *Northern Ireland during the Second World War* (1996).

TRACEY CONNOLLY is a graduate of University College Cork. In 1999 she completed doctoral research on Irish emigration in the twentieth century.

RICHARD DOHERTY is a military historian. Among his publications are *Irish generals: Irish generals in the British Army in the Second World War* (1993) and *Irish men and women in the Second World War* (1999).

BRIAN GIRVIN is Senior Lecturer in Politics at Glasgow University. He is the author of *Between two worlds: politics and economy in independent Ireland* (1989) and *The right in the twentieth century: conservatism and democracy* (1994).

CORMAC KAVANAGH is a graduate of the University of North London and is currently doing postgraduate research with the Open University on the wartime Irish volunteers.

AIDAN McELWAINE is a graduate of University College Cork. He recently completed an M.Phil. thesis on 'The forgotten volunteers: Irish service in the British armed forces during World War II' (UCC, 1998).

JOHN A. MURPHY was Professor of Irish History at University College Cork. He is a former member of Seanad Éireann and the author of *Ireland in the twentieth century* (1975, 1989) and *The college: a history of Queen's/University College Cork, 1845-1995* (1995).

DONAL Ó DRISCEOIL lectures in the Department of History at University College Cork. He is the author of *Censorship in Ireland 1939-1945: neutrality, politics and society* (1996).

EUNAN O'HALPIN is Professor of Contemporary Irish History at Trinity College Dublin. He is the author of *The decline of the Union: British government in Ireland 1891-1920* (1987) and *Defending Ireland: the Irish state and its enemies since 1922* (1999).

GEOFFREY ROBERTS is Statutory Lecturer in History at University College Cork. He is the author of *The unholy alliance: Stalin's pact with Hitler* (1989), *The Soviet Union and the origins of the Second World War* (1995) and *The Soviet Union in world politics: coexistence, revolution and Cold War, 1945-1991* (1998).

Index